CHANGING TIDES

Jo Hamlin

I would like to dedicate my book to;
(mum) Sandra Shaw 1944 - 2004
(Dad) Ray Dawson
my family Nigel and Lily for giving me the confidence to write
and all the wonderful staff & crew on the ships.
Thank you

CONTENTS

Title Page   1

Copyright   2

Dedication   3

Introduction   9

Changing Tides   11

CHAPTER 1 - AT THE START   12

CHAPTER 2 - THE INTERVIEW (2 weeks before)   20

CHAPTER 3 - NEWS   28

CHAPTER 4 - THE HOUSE   35

CHAPTER 5 - THE SHIP   42

CHAPTER 6 -THE SALON   52

CHAPTER 7 - FIRST TIMERS   57

CHAPTER 8 - REALITY HITS   64

CHAPTER 9 – NINE DAYS AT SEA   68

CHAPTER 10 - NO ROMANCE   72

CHAPTER 11 - WHAT A DAY!   84

CHAPTER 12 – STORMY NIGHTS   91

CHAPTER 13 - CHRISTMAS DAY   97

CHAPTER 14 - HAPPY NEW YEAR   107

CHAPTER 15 - THE HEN PARTY   114

CHAPTER 16 - TWO-WEEK CRUISING   117

CHAPTER 17 - CROSSING THE EQUATOR   124

CHAPTER 18 - A FAR CRY FROM PARADISE   129

CHAPTER 19 – VOYAGE OF TERROR!   134

CHAPTER 20 - THE PILGRIMAGE   143

CHAPTER 21 - THE LAST LEG   146

CHAPTER 22 - END OF AN ERA!   155

CHAPTER 23 -THE COSTA DAPHNE   157

CHAPTER 24 – IT'S A HARD LIFE!   163

CHAPTER 25 – IT'S COLD OUTSIDE   170

CHAPTER 26- MIDNIGHT SUN   174

Chapter 27 – Home   179

CHAPTER 28- MIAMI HERE I COME!   185

CHAPTER 29 - FUN & GAMES   192

CHAPTER 30 – HERE I GO AGAIN   197

CHAPTER 31 - REUNITED   209

CHAPTER 32 - NEW YORK , NEW YORK   213

CHAPTER 33 – DID THE EARTH MOVE?   222

CHAPTER 34 – FANTASY OR ECSTASY?   227

CHAPTER 35- 'THIRD TIMES A CHARM?'   234

CHAPTER 36 - THE SUN   239

CHAPTER 37 – HEAD OVER HEELS.   247

CHAPTER 38 - GRENADA   252

CHAPTER 39 - HEAVY HEART   256

CHAPTER 40 – HEART BREAKING.   260

CHAPTER 41- MY SHINING STAR!   269

CHAPTER 42- LIFE GOES ON.   275

CHAPTER 43- MISDIRECTION   279

CHAPTER 44- DETERMINE   284

CHAPTER 44 - CATASTROPHIC DEMISE 289

CHAPTER 45 – NEW BEGININGS 296

INTRODUCTION

As I sit looking out of my bedroom window looking towards the hills of Somerset on a grey, rainy day in October. I think back to how my life once was. Working as a hairdresser on the cruise liners, it was all I ever wanted to do.

This is a memoir of my time working onboard various cruise ships sailing all over the world. The highs and lows of relationships, places and situations, the good, the bad, and the downright ugly. The disasters that happened to my fellow crew members. The places we visited, the scrapes we found ourselves in and a story of life back home which never stopped influencing my decisions, some of which were totally out of charactor.

All the names have been changed to protect those wonderful people I met, without them this book would not be possible.

The situations and stories are solely based on how I personally remember them. Time frameworks are a matter of interpretation.

CHANGING TIDES

By Jo Hamlin

<u>12/10/2020</u>

<u>R.I.P</u>
<u>Mrs Sandra Shaw (1944-2004)</u>
<u>Captain Geraldo</u>

<u>Disclaimer</u>
This is a personal account taken from my own memories and point of view during my time on the cruise liners. All names have been changed and event altered to make this a marketable and compelling read. At no time have I based my characters on any one person, the personalities have been a combination of many people that I have met over the years.

CHAPTER 1 - AT THE START

Approaching a house which I rented in Surbiton. I could feel the anticipation growing inside my stomach, as though someone was tugging on a rope, pulling it tighter and twisting it forcefully in circles.

Would it be there or was it just another wasted journey? I thought, trying to convince myself half-heartedly that it would be different this time. It happened to be the fifth visit that week.

The rain was pouring down hard, the sky looked like a charcoal blanket being stretched out over my head, suppressing any positive thoughts that may have innocuously attempted to engage themselves. However, not even the smallest glimmer of sun was coming through, no silver linings or streams of sunlight whatsoever, just the heavy and pervasive feeling of seemingly never-ending dullness.

As I got closer to the house, my eyes were fixed on the letter box and the glass door that encased it. The house was down a suburban street, complete with red brick houses, uneven pavements and a slight run-down feeling to it. In all fairness it was nothing special, just a three-bedroom house.

I knew that I would have failed catastrophically, had I seen a small white envelope, and my dream would be over forever. But if by some miracle it was a nice A4 size white envelope, the job was mine and my life was about to change for the better. Even though it had only been a couple of weeks since my interview with the hair, beauty, and fitness spa of Santuaries, on board the cruise ships, it surely felt like it had been an eternity.

At 21, I had completed five years of hairdressing, three

of which comprised of my apprenticeship. The hard slog that I had undertaken from 16 years old was quite the endeavour. From what I have heard over the last 35 years people seem to have the impression that hairdressing is a simple job to do. I can assure anyone thinking of going into the industry that it is and has never been an easy job. The first year alone was spent, sweeping floors, making tea and coffee, shampooing and neutralising clients hair, leaving my hands so sore and split that I thought they would bleed forever, when I tried to put my socks on. My feet hurt so much that I could have sworn I had razor blades sticking in the soles of my shoes, stabbing me every time I put weight on them. The boredom of watching for the hundredth time a roller being placed strategically in the white hair of an 80-year-old lady from the council estate in Letchworth who had, had the same style for the last 20 years and repeated the same story of her daughters daily routine of making sandwiches for her children's packed lunch was extremely frustrating. Not to mention the weekly hikes up to Tottenham court Road in London for my college classes. Trying to contemplate the anatomy and physiology of the hair structure and Ammonium Thioglycolate compound that can break disulphide bonds within the hair during a perming process. I had not even thought that I would be stepping into a court room to establish the law and what would happen if I were to make a mistake. That was just the start. The constant late nights of staying behind after the salon had closed for the practical training, the long days and with one day off a week, would takes its toll. I was exhausted, but I had to persevere to achieve my ultimate goal of becoming a qualified hairdresser. The pay was diabolical of £27.30 a week. It was toped up by the odd 10 to 50 pence that a grateful client would give me for giving them an extra special scalp massage at the back wash. That was a generous tip back in 1985 and did make a massive difference to me.

I had moved many times to different salons up and

down the south of the UK, spending time improving my skills, course after course, doing photo shoots and fashion shows to build my portfolio, waiting until I was qualified and old enough to finally be in with a chance to do a job I loved, and travel the world onboard the cruise liners.

As I reminisce about the time when I was 10 years old and living in Stevenage, a new town at the time, which was created from the overspill of London. I remember looking out of my bedroom window, dreaming of what was out there, beyond the trees, and the slate roof tops of the houses that ensconced us. They always seemed so stifling almost claustrophobic to me that I sometimes felt that I couldn't breathe. I just couldn't shake off the feeling that there was a bigger world out there waiting to be discovered by me. Of course, the images were only in my imagination back then, but there was no such thing as the internet, smart phones or emails.

My life had been quite uneventful during that time, in the sense that we were a family of four living a life in a three-bedroom house in Stevenage where Dad went to work in London as a plumber and central heating engineer, whereas Mum stayed at home to look after us kids. My Dad would leave early in the morning, before it got light, and returning after dark.

My brother David who was 2 years older than me would come home from school and watch *Blue Peter* and *Grange Hill* on the T.V. together. I would argue with him at any given opportunity as most siblings do to try and get my own way and watch the programmes that I liked better, *Scooby Do* and *Inspector Gadget*. He used to drive me crackers, no matter how calm I thought I was being, even if I was happy, he always had the uncanny ability to wind me up. I was convinced that he derived immense satisfaction from that.

I remember one day looking through some old black and white photographs of my Dad when he was a teenager. There were lots of lovely ones of him and my Mum as Mods, riding on their Vespa and posing in a rather photogenic manner. There was one picture in particular which stood out to me and remains firmly entrenched in my memory. It was a black and white picture taken when Dad was 16, back in the early Sixties. It had folded corners and tatty edges, some browning in some areas which clearly suggested that the picture quality had degraded over the years.

He was standing at the base of a large mountain in Switzerland. The top was covered in snow. He had a truly genuine smile that made his whole face light up. He wore a backpack and hiking boots with long socks that his trousers were tucked into, looking like *Indiana Jones* going off to his next crusade. It was probably nothing like that but that's the one that's stuck in my head that invigorated me. Apparently, when they were there, because the war had not long been over, they had felt that they were not welcome in some of the places they had travelled to. Yet in others they were welcomed with open arms. It must have been awful to feel so unwelcome.

That photo was responsible for my need to travel plus I used to watch *Hill Street Blues* and *The Streets of San Francisco* back in the Seventies, which gave me a fascination with America. Maybe, you could arguably say that I had it in my blood from early in my life.

My parents had separated when I was 16, just as I was embarking on my exams at school, not great timing of course, but Mum felt the need to finish her 20 year marriage with my father to embark on a new life with her boss at work Al. Grass and greener springs to mind!

It left my Dad heart broken and my brother with the need to do great harm to this person, (never did) and my life was left in tatters, beyond belief. The loss I felt was inconceivable. A tear springs to my eyes, seeping down to the computer and disappearing into the keyboard as I am writing and remembering that horrid day when my whole world changed.

It was a Sunday morning not unlike any other. Mid-April when David and I were in the living room watching T.V. Mum and Dad were in the Dining room which was separated by two glass internal doors enabling us to see their silhouette. I remember Dad sitting to the right and Mum facing him. The whispered murmurs of their voices droned in the back ground which didn't alert us that anything was wrong, until I heard Mum running up the stairs and Dad crying with his head bent over the table.

"What's going on" I looked at David concerned.

"I'm not sure, you go and find Mum and I will see to Dad."

I opened the door that lead to the hallway and looked up the stairs to find my Mum on the stairs curled up with her head in her hands sobbing. I couldn't understand what was going on but ran to comfort her. Putting my arms around her as she had done to me numerous times over the years.

"Mum, what's going on, why are you crying" I wiped a tear from my own eyes. I couldn't bare seeing Mum cry.

"I can't do it anymore, I can't be with your Dad, I just don't love him"

The words stung like a bee. Word I never dreamt I would ever hear coming out of Mum's mouth. I always thought Mum and Dad were so happy. In 1985 it wasn't very common for parents to divorce. I think I only knew of one person's parents in the whole of my year at school.

" Why? What do you mean you don't love him?" I could hardly believe it the   impact of what Mum was saying was inconceivable. I was frightened, my body was shacking uncontrollably, I could feel the blood draining from my face, the tears rolling down my cheek. Mum just cried not giving me the answers I so desperately needed. What to do? What to do?

"I'll be back in a minute" I said to Mum squeezing her shoulder as I left her perched on the top step, still weeping.

I run back to the living room nearly smashing into

David who was towards me.

"What's Mum saying?" His voice was highly charged

"That she doesn't love Dad anymore"

"What does she mean she doesn't love him? All Dad is saying is that he loves her and that he can't live without her. They are not making any sense. We need to do something!" The panic was starting to rise in his voice as the situation descended into emotional chaos.

We heard the front door slam. *Mum was leaving.* We watched her figure walk up the path with her bag in one hand and her car keys in the other. I could feel the bile rise in my throat at the enormity of our situation. Dad was sobbing heart wrenching sobs of distress. I ran after Mum pulling at her arm, pleading with her not to go. Dad had run to the door shouting at her.

"Chris. Chris, come back"

She turned expressionless, red eyed and black eye liner smudge down her face.

"It's for the best" She got in her car and drove off.

My head spun and my mind could not grasp the concept that she had gone.

Dad collapsed in a heap on the floor. Like a rag doll. Limp and lifeless. His world, the love of his life, his soul mate and reason for living had disappeared. Forever.

"Get Fred and Betty" David said pulling me towards the door. A fleeting idea to get our neighbours from across the road.

"You stay with Dad, I will go" I said taking off as quick as I could.

Fred and Betty had been friends of Mum and Dad's for over a decade. We spent a lot of time in each other's houses mainly on a Saturday or Sunday night, listening to *Barbra Streisand* and *Fleetwood Mac* whilst they polished off the latest bottle of Ouzo they had brought back from their recent holiday to Cyprus.

I sprinted out of the front door, not bothering to close it

due to Dad blocking the entrance. I ran across our small green outside our house, across the road and up a path that wound around the tree lined expanse of grass adjacent to their house. I bolted through their gate and knocked hard and fast until both Fred and Betty came to the door, wondering what all the commotion was about.

"Please you need to come quick, it's Dad" I was breathless, stumbling over my words. "Mum's left, she's saying that she doesn't love him anymore"

Fred came straight away with Betty following in hot pursuit after she had locked up. We found Dad still on the floor with David crouched beside him, trying to stand him up and move him out of sight of the street.

"Victor, Victor" Fred repeated until he caught Dad's attention. "You need to move from the doorway mate, everyone can see you."

" I don't care, I don't care about anything Fred, she's gone"

"I know mate" he lifted Dad from the floor which wasn't easy. Dad was six foot whilst Fred was a couple of foot shorter. Between David and Fred, they managed to move dad into the living room, just as Betty was coming through the front door.

"Oh! my darlings, what has happened" Betty said hugging both of us kids in unison. Betty was lovely, a motherly person in her early fifties, a large lady, cuddly and calming. Just like her husband Fred. I burst into tears, sitting next to Dad, looking at him to reassure me that everything would be ok. Unfortunately, that never happened.

David and I were left pretty much to our own devises for the rest of the day, as Betty and Fred tried to get Dad back to some sort of normality in light of the situation. It was extremely difficult.

Over the next few months, I stayed away from school to look after my Dad. He would not get out of bed for days on end and my brother went out of his way to wait outside of

Mum's place of work contemplating what he would do to Al, Mum's boss. He was the reason that Mum had left.

After I had turned 14, she had decided to go back to work full time. She managed to get a job at a sunblind company in Stevenage, where she was a Secretary / P.A to the M.D. She was over the moon when she got it. Unfortunately, that had led to a several nights when she had gone out with her colleagues for dinner. These nights out must have been with Al not with her colleagues.

When Mum had walked out on us, she had gone directly to Al's house to be with him. She married him 2 years later. She couldn't take us kids with her because Al didn't want kids in his house. When I found that out I was crushed to think Mum had chosen him over us. She found that decision one that she would never be able to shake. Ever.

CHAPTER 2 - THE INTERVIEW
(2 WEEKS BEFORE)

At the Hotel in London we were all dressed up in our smartest suits, shiny shoes, hair immaculate, make up done, looking as nervous as hell waiting for our names to be called. We were asked to go into a large conference room where there were chairs set out for us in rows. At the front of the room were five larger chairs facing towards us, with the management team waiting, checking us out as we sheepishly walked in.

The room was dark, and shadows lurked around every corner with heavy curtains at the windows. The old musky smell that wafted into my nostrils sent the hairs on the back of my neck into disarray. It reminded me of my old nursery school, which sat in the middle of a dark wood. Very Victorian and eerie to say the least. I could have heard a pin drop in the room from the anticipation. The quietness was deafening, not one person spoke, just smiles of acknowledgment passed around the room.

The introductions from the management team was short and sweet. We were told what to expect, the interviews were in three stages. The first would be an   introduction of ourselves and information about the job (just to get us hooked in even more), followed by an individual interview with each of us, and lastly, we would have to do a practical demonstration of our skills and a written exam. We would have to qualify each section to go onto the next.

My stomach was doing somersaults and my palms were sweating, I had always suffered with anxiety, but it was not going to stop me. I needed this and desperately wanted to succeed. We each took it in turns to introduce ourselves and tell everyone in the room a little about our history. One by one each took it in turns to spill the beans, about why they were there and their back stories. Some of them were really good, having us all in stiches and divulging certain events which brought them to that point. I couldn't help but feel completely out of my comfort zone and very inferior.

Finally, it was my turn. I stood up and dug deep. To my surprise the voice which came out of my mouth was one that sounded as if I had been doing it for years, confident, clear, not at all portraying how I actually felt. I looked around, and the people in the room, seemed really interested in what I was saying.

"My name is Jo Dawson and I'm 21. I never intended to become a hairdresser, I was originally going to college to do Art and Design, but when I found out that my best friend was going to earn money, I found myself being pulled more and more towards the hairdressing industry as an easier option, not realising how hard it would be to get qualified" I looked around finding a few people giggling and some nodding in agreement.

"To my delight I found my knish. My creative side excelled during my time in London where I was chosen for creative director doing photo shoots for an organic colouring company. I've since followed my passion to develop my talents for hair-up after finishing a course with *Nicky Clark,* where we copied the *Jessica Rabbit* format for the *Marseille Wave.* I was half expecting to see *Roger Rabbit* make an appearance." The response of laughter felt great. I loved it.

I rounded up my short synopsis of my career so far with my dream of working onboard the cruise liners and travelling the world. Not forgetting to mention the   fabulous characters I hoped to meet along the way.

Thank goodness that was over. I thought. I could breathe again albeit for a short time.

After the job description was explained to us about the Hairdressing, Beauty and Fitness roles that were available, (these were basically the same as you can find in a normal land-based salon) we then went through a short summary of ship life and what to expect. This blew me away. The head of Hairdressing Sally explained

" Your time on board is never your own. In one way or another there will always be someone with you. A cabin mate, a staff member, an officer, a passenger or a client. One way or another you are part of a team and this team will become your family. You must look after each other and look out for each other at all times. If you are a gossip? Leave it at home. There isn't any room for squabbles. If there are any, they need to be dispelled straight away and get on with the job at hand. We will teach you everything you need to know during your in-house training sessions before you go out onto a ship. This will include knowledge about your products and knowledge about the other services which are not your own. Your training will include sales techniques and how to conduct a demonstration. You will be taught lifeboat training onboard and you will have to comply with ship rules. These vary from ship to ship. For hairdressers you will learn basic beauty techniques and beauty you will learn to shampoo and remove colours. You will be provided with flights, meals and hotel accommodation. Most of you will be travelling to pick up your ship alone. This means finding your way around the globe. There is no room for shyness or   homesickness, even though most of you will experience both of these during your first contract. You will get over it. We are your guardians, we will look after you, but you must keep us informed at all times, either directly or via your managers. If any of you have any doubts please feel free to leave or do not return if you are lucky enough to be called back." Sally finished with a large intake of breath. So did the rest of us. If there was anyone left without their mouth open, I would have been surprised. That was it in a nutshell and I felt like I was joining the navy.

We left the room and took our places back out in the hall for coffee. No-one uttered a word. It was another very dark room inside a very old part of the building, it felt damp and had that musky smell again, like mildew and very old clothes that had been shut in a suitcase for many years. I stood alone as did everyone else checking out the competition. Why do we do that? why can't we just pleasantly pass the time of day?

We were taken in one at a time for a personal interviews. Imagine the management team on the large chairs and I was sat on a small chair looking up at them. I felt very intimidated, and extremely insignificant. I guess that is how I remember it probably not how it actually was.

I answered the questions as well as I could trying to make my voice sound professional and as matter of fact as possible.

" So, Jo, tell us why you want to join us? and what you think you could do to enhance our teams?" Sally was quite scary under her glamourous exterior. Sally Jones was the head of recruitment for Sanctuaries. She has been there for 15 years and saw the company through different changes over the years. She started as a team member on the ships and worked her way through the ranks. She must have been in her late 30's but looked a lot younger.

They seemed happy with my answers, some of which I had repeated from my earlier explanation of my career during the introductions. I was nervous.

"I think I can bring my energy and my desire to achieve the best I can on everything I do. I love my job and I think I am good at it. I know my work inside out. I'm not shy and none of what you said scares me. I am willing to do what it takes, to hit my targets and help out wherever I can. I'm a great team player and love the fact that we can help each other" I finished hoping that I didn't come across over confident. They seemed happy but you never really know do you.

I went for yet another coffee. By that point the coffee buzz was really kicking in, playing havoc with my bladder. I found a corridor where the toilets were, hoping to kill some time as the wait was agonising. I heard a couple of girls talking, telling each other that they were working at the land-based salons of the Sanctuaries and thought that they had it in the bag.

"It's just a formality Trish, I tell you. We are in there kid no question."

The peroxide blonde, in a bright pink suit late 20's and the life backcombed out of her hair, whilst chewing gum strutted off slamming the door behind her. That certainly didn't help my nerves.

Waiting! Waiting. Finally, we were all called back into the dark conference room looking at each other, not knowing which way it would go. We sat down in silence, you could hear that old pin drop again, this time it was bouncing along the floor like a heartbeat, or perhaps that was just mine thudding in my ears?

"If your name is called, please make your way back outside". Sally announced talking through her nose like one of those announcers in a train station that no-one can actually understand. I saw the two girls walk out who had been talking in the toilets earlier. *Well that's it then.* I thought. *Curtains for me.*

I waited but my name did not arise. My stomach sank. I thought that was it, home time. There were about 10 of us left out of 45. I was not hopeful. What had gone wrong? I was so sure I had made a good impression!

Then I heard Sally speak.

"You have got through to the practical session. This afternoon you will go out to Oxford Street and find a long-haired model, you will be demonstrating a long-layered cut, a set, and finally a hair up for a formal occasion. You will be assessed on this then you will take a written exam. Once this is finished you can go, and we will notify you by post if you have been successful or not. Any questions anyone?" she waited, but no one spoke.

"ok break for lunch" she added.

Looking around the room we all looked petrified, but nobody spoke.

We had half an hour to grab something to eat and find a model to demonstrate our wonderous creations on.

The streets were busy, which made it difficult to concentrate. It was just a swarm of heads bobbing up and down, everyone was on a mission. I found the lady I was looking for after asking a few, who just didn't have time.

"Hi, my name is Jo and I'm doing an interview to work on the cruise ships." I explained holding my hand out to shake hers.

"Would you help me by being a model for me. I just need to trim your hair and put it up into a French Pleat." I gave her my sweetest smile. Really what could the poor women say?

"Sure, that sounds exciting" I was flabbergasted.

And so, the games began.

The assessors were not giving anything away, their faces were contorted into a stare which would make the Sahara Desert freeze over I'm sure. So far so good. Mandy my model, was under the dryer with large rollers in her hair and a hair net encompassing them. She looked like *Hilda Ogdon* minus the wrinkles.

Now the hard bit getting this mass of hair into a pleat. Where was my old Italian boss Marco, when I needed him? He trained with Vidal Sassoon apparently. He was so picky about this style. Also, if you got it wrong, he would hurl rollers across the salon and told you to take it out and start again, with hands waving in the air. He was of Italian descent and an old school hairdresser. But I have him to thank for a lot of my skills today.

I took a deep breath, I had finally finished, and I must say I was pleased with the result. But who could tell if this was enough? Mary my model looked like a film star. It helped that she was very beautiful and tall. It made my job a lot easier.

Back in the large dark room, desks were set out individually and girls were sat spaced out working hard. It was so quiet; the cogs were turning inside their heads. I sat down and took another deep breath and nothing, I knew nothing, not a bean. Blank. It was all I needed. In tests my head just swam in circle, with answers dashing in and out and screams from inside saying *here you go again, you'll never be able to do this.* With the blackness of time and infinity stretching into the distance I went into panic mode. My breathing quickened, the beads of sweat appeared on my forehead and I couldn't catch my breath. I looked around wondering what I should do. I panicked more. I had to get out of there. I looked straight ahead trying to focus on something else, when I caught Sally's eyes smiling at me mouthing if I was ok. I nodded. She could tell I'm sure she could. I focused on the window and calmed my breath by breathing in and out. Saying it over and over in my mind until my breathing emulated the word. I stabled out and calmed myself. Always the minute anyone fired a question at me, or I sat an exam, I just got a mental block and went into panic mode.

The words were not flying around off the paper like something out of a Disney film anymore they settled onto the page and I understood the questions, and I knew what I had to do.

The in-depth essay of colour correction came easily to me. I had to explain the method and products I would use on a client with fine hair, black roots and peroxide blonde ends with brassy mid-lengths who wanted to turn to an ash base nine.

All done. That was it, all over, I had done my best, the relief was exhausting, and so the waiting game began. I walked outside the door into the dark, busy, rainy night of London and took a deep breath. The smelly air never smelt so sweet! The traffic was back to back and the hum of the engines was a very familiar sound. It was October and the cold really started to take a hold on the season. Christmas was coming.

CHAPTER 3 - NEWS

So, there I was approaching the front door. I could not keep my eyes off of it. Maybe I should have been looking at the road, but I couldn't help it. There was something white in the letter box, half in half out. I could not make out how big it was. I got out of the car and walked to the front door narrowly missing a car as it honked its horn breaking the daze I was in . The butterflies were doing those old familiar summersaults again, tickling every inch of my rib cage. I could tell no one had moved in as everything looked just as I had left it three days ago. Typical of me deciding to move during an important time of my life, but the other two girls who I was sharing the house with needed to move on. I had no choice, but the timing could have been better.

I had moved to London from Plymouth when the store that housed my salon was burned to the ground allegedly by some arsonists trying to prove a point. We were the floor above the furniture department. The company were great, paying us over the Christmas period and replacing all our equipment which had been lost in the fire. Plus helping us find alternative employment.

My best mate Lorraine and I decided to except an offer of a transfer to Kingston - Upon - Themes in Surrey still working for Glemby International. After many a move of homes and jobs, we found ourselves sharing a house along with another girl called Pat also from Plymouth, who had decided to transfer a few months after us. The girls had boy-friends who they were moving in with, I decided I was going to travel the world. I just didn't believe that the humdrum life of a nine to five job was the best I could do and just wasn't for me. I always knew that there was more to life and a big world out there that I need to explore. I had also been let down drastically, by Pat and my then boyfriend.

A year before my interview, I had gone out with a colleague from work to a club. Josie wanted some moral support and was feeling so depressed about a recent break up, that I thought it would be nice to take her out and get a fresh look on life. We had a blast, dancing the night away into the early hours. I was feeling great. Things were coming together, job, friendships, social life, and I was finally in a trusting relationship where I could go out, have some fun and Toby would be waiting for me when I got in. We didn't live together, but he spent most of his time at mine. Lorraine lived upstairs in a bedsit which was part of an old Victorian house situated on a leafy avenue in Surbiton. Toby had a twin brother called Liam who was Lorraine's boyfriend. Convenient.

When I got home that night, Toby was not in my bedsit. *He had probably fallen asleep at Lorraine's* I thought. I went to bed exhausted from all the dancing. The next morning, I ascended the stairs to Lorraine's flat. I had a gut-wrenching feeling of dread that I just couldn't seem to shake. Perhaps just the hangover from the previous night's drinking. I tapped on the door and waited. Lorraine's happy voice didn't seem quite as joyful as usual.

"Hold on" She said hesitating before opening the door.

" Lorraine, it's me" I said "Can I come in"

"Just a minute" I could hear the muffled whispers of hushed voices coming from behind the door.

"Everything ok in there Lorraine" I added.

She opened the door at ajar and peered outside into the corridor. Something was up I just knew it. She seemed very sheepish and despondent. Jumpy even, as if she was hiding something. I was so unprepared for what she told me.

"Everything ok Lorraine, you seem a little out of sorts" I

said, looking at her concerned. That expression soon turned to disbelief and astonishment when the truth about Pat and Toby came to light.

Toby and Pat had slept together whilst I was out. I couldn't comprehend anything else. Lorraine had told me she was sworn to secrecy, but she couldn't lie to me. She was running after me trying to keep up, as I descended the stairs, two by two, determined to get back to my flat quickly before the enormity of the betrayal really hit home. Lorraine only watched as I disappeared inside my door.

I fell back against my door as it slammed behind me. Glad to be back to familiar ground. The ache in my heart was hurting and the nausea was overwhelming. We had been together so long, and I thought we were ok. I only just made it to the sink before I threw up. I wiped my face and stood dead in my tracks when the knock on the door echoed around the small room.

"Jo, it's me Toby," he said with a stammer. "Can we talk."

At that moment I knew exactly what to do, I grabbed a bag and slung some clothes in it for a couple of days away. I needed to get out of there. As far away as possible before I said or did something unforgivable. I pulled open the door and came face to face with Toby.

"Jo, can we talk," he repeated.

"I have nothing to say to you," my voice was filled with hatred. "You and Pat of all people," I spat the words at him. Trying not to gag with the thoughts of the two of them together. I couldn't even allow myself to think about the consequences and turmoil their actions would pose on all our friendships. It was an end of an era. I sped pass him and straight out to where my car was parked, only to find Pat sitting on the wall directly outside my window. I don't know what possessed me but the overwhelming feeling to create harm was all encompassing. I dropped my bags, ran behind her and kicked her straight in the back with my foot. Winding her, she collapsed to the ground. There was no emotion in my face as I stared at her wincing on the ground below my feet.

I didn't say a word, my face spoke many of them. I left her there on the floor. How could they. The last thing I saw from my rear-view mirror was Toby helping her up and Pat shaking him off abruptly. Suddenly the pent-up tears flowed, and the sobs wracked my body, robbing it of the ability to drive, barely allowing a breath to be drawn. I pulled over out of sight and just let the sobs take over. The four-hour drive to Mum's house in Cornwall seemed to take double the time. I couldn't shake the images I had conjured up on my head of the two of them together. It wasn't just what they had done, it had brought back the anxieties I felt when my Mum walked out on us. The realisation that I couldn't trust anyone was very overpowering. As time went on, we did eventually overcome that awful time, but it wasn't easy and never the same.

I didn't have a key to the house anymore, so I was hopeful that I could get to the post without calling the landlord, not lawful maybe I know, but I needed to get to my letter. Fortunately, the letter had fallen from the letter box and laid on the path. Result! Great for my situation as the other would have delayed me even longer. I am so impatient which didn't help.

I walked up the path closer and closer, to my surprise, bingo. My name was on the envelope with the logo of the hair and beauty company Sanctuaries.

Don't get too excited. I thought. It may not be, or could it be? I grabbed it, ran back to the car and tore open the envelope. I don't think I took a single breath in that whole time. My excitement was unbearable.

There I read.......

Dear Miss Dawson,

Thank you for attending the interview and trade test at Sanctuaries. We are delighted to offer you the position of Hair-

stylist at our Maritime Division

Your employment with us will commence on the 2nd November 1992 at the Sanctuaries salon, London W1 at 10 am with Sally Bloomfield.

During your time with us you will undergo intensive specialist training necessary for you to satisfactorily carry out your duties as and when you are allocated a ship.

When training your wages will be £35 per week plus commission. Accommodation is provided during your training. Your uniform will be charged at £25 plus vat. You must order a minimum of three. This charge will be deducted from your wages. White tights and white shoes must be worn during your training.

Please let me have your bank details, a 10-year passport number and P45. You will also need a U.S Visa. A Sea Farers medical must be obtained from your doctor. Give me one copy and take one with you.

You will need to provide all hairdressing tool and whilst training a pen, folder and A4 paper. It is essential that you have access to £100 to cover additional cost of traveling expenses (not flights) when joining a ship.

Finally, please sign the attached contract and return these with your acceptance letter as soon as possible.

Yours Sincerely

Heather Chasten

Operations manager.

I sat there for at least another half an hour letting the information sink in.

I read it over and over again. The rain still beating down hard on the windscreen, but I was now in a bubble, I could not believe it. Finally.

The enthusiasm was rising in my throat I just wanted to scream, I had to tell someone before I exploded.

Mum, I thought, *I would go home and call Mum.* I knew she would be happy for me, but at the same time disappointed that I was going to be away for eight months without seeing me. My mind cast back to the moment Mum walked away. I was starting to understand how hard that must have been for her yet dismissing it almost immediately. How do you walk away and leave your kids?

The minute I got in I picked up the phone dialled her number. The phone felt like it was ringing for ages. Mum was still living in Cornwall with Al and her Labrador Emma.

I was grinning from ear to ear when Mum answered.

"Hello," I could barely contain myself and just blurted it out.

"I got it Mum; I got the job on the ships."

"Wow, slow down, you got the job with Sanctuaries?"

"Yes, I can't believe it, I have just got the letter now, I'm so excited."

"Calm down Jo, now breathe, that's great news."

I didn't stop talking for the next hour or so, (not unusual for me) I took a breath.   She was so happy for me I knew I had made the right choice. After I had phoned Mum, I spent the rest of the day phoning everyone Dad, David, my friends, landlord and anyone else willing to listen.

I only had three weeks to arrange so much. The first was the doctors for my medical. I was going to have to find somewhere to store my stuff, I had to write my resignation letter for the salon I worked in. I needed to post my acceptance letter, check my passport, get a visa, go shopping for dresses (great) and I needed to buy a suitcase. I also had to sell my car, update my equipment and have a party to say good bye to my friends. That was going to be hard. So much to do. I could barely breathe.

I realised that amongst all of my excitement I had forgotten one but very important thing, I will need to say goodbye to my Mum and Dad. My stomach churned. I hadn't thought about the goodbyes and what it would actually mean at all.

Mum lived four hours away from me in Cargreen, Cornwall, I saw her at least twice a month. Dad wasn't so far away. Eight months apart, was going to be tough, especially as I knew my Mum's relationship with Al wasn't great. Mum never complained to me, she just said he was away working hard. She had moved down there a few years previously. I found myself moving to be close to her. I was 18 and didn't really know where I wanted to be. All I knew was I wanted to be near her. It was going to be so hard putting thousands of miles between us. What was I thinking?

CHAPTER 4 - THE HOUSE

My Dad took my suitcases out of the car, turned to me and said

"What have you got in 'ear luv, the bloody kitchen sink." Laughing he picked them up and carried them inside. He was brought up in Tottenham, in fact a couple of streets along to where the house was situated, in Beaconsfield Road. He lived there until he was 21. My Mum had lived in South Tottenham, at College Road. They met at a Tottenham Royal dance back in 1961 and married in 1965 at St Ann's Church. They had lived there together for a year until they moved to the new town of Stevenage. Very up and coming in 1966.

I walked in and was surprised that I was one of the first. The house was massive. An old house not at all modern. The aroma was a lovely vanilla smell that wafted up my nostrils sending the hairs dancing around inside. The décor was very bare of home comforts, just the essentials, sofa, T.V. armchairs, and a sideboard. The walls were white and the carpet an old grey colour that was well worn. There was a chap already there called Steve. He was a massage therapist, British and a very strong northern accent. His smile was warm and friendly, and his eyes lit up when he spoke. Dad took my case to my room where apparently, I was sharing with another girl. Awkwardly Dad said his goodbye's and left. I did see him again before I went to the ships, so I was not too worried at that point. I had brought tea and milk with me, so I could make myself a drink, after living alone since I was 17 you became self-sufficient and think of little home comforts. People started to turn up very quickly after my first encounter with Steve, bringing with it the deafening sound of chatter. Funny but most did not bring much with them at all as far as food and drinks were concerned.

The others seemed nice and we were all so excited to start in the morning. We chatted for a several hours that night finding out more about each other. Things soon sank to the gutter as the lads wanted to play truth or dare.

Carol (Hairdresser), Steve (Massage Therapist) and Laura (Beauty) were sitting on one armchair. Cassie (Hairdresser), Arthur (Fitness Instructor), Michael (Hairdresser,) Ted (hairdresser) and Fran (Beauty) were sat on the floor with a bottle, spinning it to see who the next victim would be to answer the truth or dare question. Whoever wouldn't answer had to do a forfeit of drinking a shot of vodka down in one.

The bottle landed pointing at Ted a 22-year-old from Hackney.

"Oh, typical that I have to be the first." He said rolling his eyes in the air.

"So, how many girls have you slept with?" Cassie giggled.

"Blimey, why not just jump right in there, come on don't be shy" The sarcasm in his voice was funny.

"Ok about thirty, not many"

"Not many" I said with my mouth open. "You are joking, aren't you?" my naivety was shining as bright as a star.

"Come on Jo, surely you must be up there somewhere?" Ted said laughing, trying to extract info out of me before my turn.

"No way" I laughed as I poured myself another drink.

Next up was Fran who was my new roomy. She spun the bottle and hilariously it landed right back at her. We were in hysterics.

"Ok Fran," said Michael wiping his eyes, trying to control himself. "What is your most embarrassing moment ever?

"I couldn't possibly say," she said voluntarily downing her drink and wiping her mouth whilst blushing profusely.

The games carried on well into the night, but I really wanted to keep a fresh head for our first day. I made my exit then, not yet ready to share my inner secrets with a bunch of strangers.

Fran was a beauty therapist, the same age as me and from London. Not everyone was from London! They had come from all over the UK. Laura was from the U.S. Our room had literally 2 single beds with pillows sheets and a blanket. That was it, no wardrobes no draws nothing. It was very minimalistic and bland, with cream aertex walls and a light bulb, no shade just a plain bulb. *How the other half live?* I thought. It was starting to get very cold so wearing socks jogging bottoms and a long sleeve t- shirt I snuggled down to get some well-earned rest.

The next morning was all a bit strange, sharing the house and bathroom with eight strangers that I barely knew, took a little getting used to. It was nothing compared with the amount of crew onboard a ship. I dressed in my interview suit as we hadn't been given our uniform and nervously made my way to have some breakfast. I meet the others running around ironing shirts and putting make up on in the dimly lit mirrors scattered about the house. Finally, we were all ready and headed off to the tube station.

It was raining again, as always, gloomy and dark. The streets were empty, quiet and a bit unearthly if I'm honest. We managed to work out what tube we needed and where to get off.

How exciting I thought until we got on the tube. *Oh, my goodness what a squash.* The smell it was like a wet dog with a mixture of god-awful aftershave. I had forgotten what it was like as I drove most places. For the first time since I was 17, I had no car. In the previous years I had come to rely on it so much.

I tried to hold my breath until the next station, but I think I would have passed out. So, I wrapped my scarf around my nose and hoped for the best. Good job we were in good spirits and I personally couldn't wait to find out what was in store that day.

The first thing on the agenda was a briefing from Julie our head of department. She explained about the company and the format of the next few weeks. Similar to our letter we had received. We started off with the training in the different areas, i.e. the hairstylists would have beauty treatments and learn about the beauty products, and vice versa. We had sales technique training, where we would show our clients what we had used on their hair by putting the products in front of them. It allowed to clients to pick them up, smell them, test them out. The phycology of sales with Sanctuaries was if the person held the product, it would feel like it was theirs and they would buy it. It did work after a little practice. The products of Elemis and Rene Guinot were lovely and sold themselves most of the time. The demonstrations proved a little harder to master, especially talking on the microphone. 'That was all new to me.' I hadn't realised that I would have to do Demos. She also explained that once the training was completed then we would be allocated our ships dependent on our achievements. The ultimate was a world cruise, which hardly anyone got straight away considering you usually had to prove yourself in sales beforehand.

First up was getting our uniforms, these were so frumpy, a pink uniform with a baby blue lapel and a flap over to one side. It had no shape to it at all and a matching baby blue belt to accompany it. They were awful. A far cry from my Wimbledon Village salon, which was high fashion, black and white of anything.

Yuk was all that came to mind. The beauty therapist had white uniforms with baby pink lapels and belts and the managers had black of the same, which was by far the better choice. The lads had black trousers, white shirts and a tie. Why did they get to wear the most normal stuff?

The other must was our hair and make-up had to be immaculate every day. Long hair was to be put up which I didn't have, and short hair blow dried every day. Full make up and a wonderful product which we all came to know, and love was Brazilian Glow. I still remember to this day the sales patter.

A powder made from a blend of rare, finely formulated minerals, oils and crushed shells. It could be used as a bronzer to the face and body mixed with moisturiser, a blusher, eye shadow, lipstick and nail varnish

I sold shed loads of these over my contracts at $45 a pot it certainly made up the commission. We were allocated one of these per cabin. Needless to say,   during our training periods we had a wonderful time trying out all the products and treatments. Even the fitness instructors had to have them. I remember one of the lads trying the eyelash tinting as we were short of models. His name was Craig, very attractive, muscle bound fitness instructor, with blonde hair and blue eyes. A strong jaw line and about six foot tall. He had turned up around midnight at the house, so I never met him until he was assigned to be our model. It was so funny, he had lovely long eyelashes. When we were finished, well he looked fantastic, (if he were a girl). I will never forget his reaction when we showed him in the mirror, he went ballistic, jumping all over the place, shouting.

"Get this crap off of me." I'm laughing now just thinking about it. It did make me giggle. Somehow, we managed to calm the lashes down, but it took several weeks to come off completely. His macho image did take a slaughtering, and the ribbing from the other guys was hysterical.

I was in the training academy for three weeks watching most of the others go off to the ships, with only a few of us left in the house, I was beginning to wonder if I had made it through?

It was   Friday. If we did have a ship to go to, we would find out about it on that day, so we could travel on a weekend, not that this made much difference in ship life, as everyday was a weekend. Differentiated by the ports of calls rather than of days of the week.

The weather was horrid, cold, damp, raining and windy well it was the end of November. Everyone was starting to get ready for Christmas. All the shops had the decorations in central London looked wonderful with the lights up. That afternoon I had a call from Julie a 45-year-old ex-hairdresser, to go to her office.

"Here you go" said Cassie excitedly "It's your turn." she continued smiling like a Cheshire cat.

I was given a letter to whom it may concern (customs and security) for the   Festival. One of the smaller ships in the Caribbean. I was so excited and couldn't wait to tell the others. But within an hour I was called back again with a change of plan, someone had dropped out of a transfer to the M/N Achille Lauro and requested a hairdresser straight away. My heart sank as I saw my dream of the Caribbean fall from my hands, especially when she announced that I was to pick the ship up in Genoa in Italy. I was slightly despondent as most of the others had flown out to exotic places like Miami and L.A. The cruising wasn't confirmed but they assured me I was capable of doing the job.

We were a small team of three. Rachelle was the manager and Tamsin the beauty therapist. I was to meet Tamsin at Heathrow airport in the morning and we would fly out to Italy and meet Rachelle on the ship. She was already getting the salon up and running. The ship had been in dry/wet dock (refurbishment) and was due to sail on the Sunday. There wasn't any time to waste.

It was one o'clock in the afternoon and I was allowed to go and get myself sorted ready for the off in the morning. I was given the information of where to get my ticket from at the airport and all the flight details. I hurried back to the house in Tottenham to pack my bags and pick up any last things I needed I was starting to shake with anticipation. My heart was racing, and my head felt dizzy. The time had arrived, D-day had come. Could I cope, oh I did hope so. I had waited so long for that moment to arrive. My emotions were starting to get the better of me, when I found myself wiping a stray tear from the corner of my eye, when I thought about Mum.

I called her and Dad to let them know about my imminent departure. My Dad said he would take me to the airport and Mum would meet me there to say good bye. Oh god I felt sick what had I done? what had possessed me to take on the challenge? The realisation of what I was about to do hit me like a rocket blasting off into space with me on the tip. I would be away for eight months.

I would have to let my family know the contact addresses when I got to the ship as I still wasn't even sure of the cruising. It wasn't like today with e-mails and mobile phones, so readily available. It was 1992 the dark ages, well the start of us all walking into the communication era with mobile phones for each of us at any rate. As a mere mortal and broke hairdresser, I didn't have the funds for all of that and they were a little like bricks to carry around. All I had was £100 in my purse, a case of clothes in one hand, and my hairdressing equipment in the other. I was so excited.

CHAPTER 5 - THE SHIP

My flight was early so Dad came to pick me up at 4am, to get to the airport in time for check in. The rest of the gang were up as usual to wave me off, it had become a ritual for us, which I thought was sweet. It was pitch black outside, cold as ice and so quiet you could hear the birds in the trees doing their morning chorus. For London that was incredible, the traffic noise normally starts early, but not today, maybe it was a little too early. I had woken up with the jitters that morning with anticipation of what was to come. I felt that the adventure was about to start.

"Have fun, make sure you've got your passport," they said laughing. I said my goodbyes. Quite sad to make such good friends and then to say goodbye so soon. That did however become the normal, living such a transient lifestyle onboard ship. I still cannot bare to part from people and say goodbye, I find it so hard. We got half way to Heathrow when Dad looked back at me in the car.

"You 'Have got your passport haven't you love?"

"Yeah, of course I have it's in my bag" I said confidently.

"Could you just check for your old man," he said starting to look a bit worried.

"I've got it don't worry," I was a little peeved that he didn't trust me.

"Just check will you." he said firmly. Dad could be quite scary at times, especially at 4am.

"Ok, ok I will check, stop the car, it's too far to reach,"

Huffing and puffing like a wolf out of the three little pigs, I got out of the car. It was so dark, and cold, I fumbled around in the boot trying to find for my bag. I put my hand inside the pocket where it should have been, my stomach jumped into my mouth as I realised that it was missing.

"Oh No! My passport, shit Dad it's not here, double shit," I suddenly had an image of it laying on the kitchen table back at the house. *Shit, shit, shit.* I thought.

"Oh bloody 'ell Jo, Dad shouted. "I told you to check everything, now get in the bloody car, and stop saying shit," I hadn't seen my Dad that mad in since I was 16 years old, coming in at 2am when I should have been back at 11pm.

With that he swung the car around and headed back to the house, trying not to break the speed limits. We approached the dimly lit street, and I could see my house mates were in the street already, laughing and waving what looked like my passport in the air. Dad was not amused. His face was deep set and stuck in a stern frown.

"Have you forgotten something you nutter," Steve mocked.

"Ok you got me I didn't check," I said laughing and relived all at the same time. I got back in the car; Dad just smiled

"God help you if you're like this now," I mutter under my breath something about being fine but thought it best to keep my head down and stay quiet for the rest of the journey.

We arrived at the airport with plenty of time. I saw Mum and rushed over to give her a big hug. Mum and Dad were friends after the divorce. It had taken some time, but I sure was glad it was all ok. It helped in these situations when they had to be somewhere at the same time. Al Mums husband always looked awkward and never had much to say. He dressed in slacks and an old blue jumper. He wasn't a good-looking man in my opinion, but Mum liked him. His character was of a typical salesman, who believed his own pitch. Even to people he was closest too. We exchanged pleasantries but I always had the impression he had his own agenda. I never did like him. He was shifty, his eyes were too close together and beady. Later in the years to come it became quite apparent just how shifty he could be.

I set off to find my soon to be cabin mate, whom I now fondly refer to as my little big sis (she was slightly younger than me but taller) and my partner in crime. We found her standing with her Mum, she turned around and with the biggest grin on her face she ran towards me. She knew straight away that I was a Sanctuaries girl, that was never made clear to me why, I just imagine that it was because of the hair and makeup being done to an inch of its life and a certain glowing powder that we all used.

"Ello lovely you must be Jo," she said in a wonderful Northern accent. I was so relieved. She was from North Yorkshire, with long dark, curly hair, very slim and completely gorgeous, not to mention that everything she was wearing colour   co-ordinated. Even though I was relieved that she was lovely my heart sunk a little. I knew my wardrobe had a lot to be desired. I had not taken the time to shop well for the trip, not to mention the fact I was very short of funds. I just couldn't afford that type of clothing. She skipped over and gave me a massive cuddle and a cheery smile. We just clicked.

"You'll be alright with me kid, let's go get a drink,". Tamsin had been on the ships before for one contract, so she knew all about what to expect and started to fill me in on what to expect that day. I wasn't really paying that much attention, as I was too busy looking at Mums face. We said goodbye to our families, which was horrendous I couldn't stop crying. I had been dreading that moment, ever since the realisation a few week back. I clung to my Mum and the tears just cascaded down my face. I just didn't want to go. She whispered that things will be fine and to   enjoy myself. She stroked my hair like she did when I was young, and I believed everything would be ok. Dad nearly squeezed the life out of me. Hugging me so tight that I couldn't breathe and

I'm sure I turned a nice shade of purple. I think if Tamsin had not pulled me away, I would never had left. We headed towards departures. I watched my Mum and Dad fade into the distance, knowing things would never be the same again, I wouldn't even be able to pick up the phone when I wanted to and speak to them. Even though my heart felt like it was breaking, I would not miss all the arguments between myself and Dad. Somehow, we could never see eye to eye. Every time I went to visit him, we ended in arguments. Looking back, I now know it's because we are so much alike. Wearing our hearts on our sleeves, trying to get our own points of view across without really listening. That's how I felt all the time since the divorce, never being listened to, or taken seriously. Unfortunately, both of my parents were trying to make their lives better, by moving on with different partners and somehow, I got left behind. My Dad was going to the post office club in the old Town Stevenage most Fridays and Saturdays with his mates. Which I can understand now, but back then I couldn't understand why he was asking me to be in at a certain time, yet the house would be empty when I returned. He also met Trish, who has turned out to be an amazing woman but at 16 years old all I could see was another woman coming into my home telling me what to do. The arguments it caused were horrific. The constant shouting at each other. I knew exactly what buttons to press with my Dad and he me. I felt I was losing him, and I never knew how to communicate that to him. I had lost my Mum and he was next. He did come to a point once when I thought he was going to knock ten bells out of me but refrained thankfully. That scared me. I knew I had gone too far. My Dads mother Edith didn't help. She must have been in her 60's at the time, with brown tightly permed hair and thick foundation that you could draw a line in. Just after Mum had left, she was around our house with my Dad and David. She was asking me questions about my Mums relationship with Al and when it had started. Like I knew! It soon descended into an argument.

"Your mother is just a no-good Slut," the word hit me like a steam train.

"Well your one of the reason's she left Dad," I hit back as hard as I could for someone of 16 years old.

"She is a nasty slag, leaving my son like that, and you're no better arguing with him all the time," She spat the words spraying droplets onto the carpet.

How I didn't hit her out of frustration and hurt I will never know. I walked off and left the house. We never spoke again. I tried to explain to Dad how I was feeling about what had happened, but it always ended the same way. I felt no-one understood me, I was so alone. The final event that brought everything to ahead was when I was 17. Dad and Trish were going on holiday abroad. I wasn't invited but Trish's two boys who were 8 and 10 were. I felt left out.

"I don't want you in any later that 11pm" Dad said walking off out the door.

" Dad, come on, you won't be here anyway."

"I don't care, you treat this house like a bloody hotel, coming and going at all time. Clothes all over the floor. You never listen to a word I say," he shouted from the landing.

"But Dad..."

"Don't but Dad me. I'm sick of it. I tell you what, if you don't buck your ideas when we get back, you may as well find somewhere else to live," with that he left, leaving me standing there, mouth wide open and tears streaming down my face.

I was so mad and upset at what he had said, that whilst he was away, Mum helped me find a small bedsit in Stevenage Town centre. On their return he found my room empty and me gone. He didn't know where I went until David dobbed me in and let it slip where I was.

Tamsin took hold of my arm and off we went, through the departure doors, with one last look at my family and tears streaming down my face they were gone, I was so distraught that we headed straight to the nearest bar.

"Two wines please," said Tamsin. "Start as we mean to go on!" She had a massive grin on her face. It was 6am. I didn't want to upset her or be a kill joy, so I went along with it.

We talked all the way to Genoa. Tam filled me in on ship life and the fun she has had, and the places she had seen. I couldn't wait.

We flew into to Genoa airport and got a cab straight to the ship. Tam   negotiated with her pigeon Italian and manage to get a good price. A lira was the currency of Italy before the euro took over in 1999. It was about 2200 Italian lira to the pound then. So that   meant   that a cab from Genova airport to the port was thousands of Italian Lira.

"Oh my," I said as we approached our ship. Looking up at the enormous blue vessel that was before us.

I had never seen anything so big. The enormity and the sheer size of it seemed to feel my entire peripheral vision as it towered above us. The Achille Lauro was big, blue and old. The MS Achille Lauro was a cruise ship based in Naples, Italy. Built between 1939 and 1947 as a passenger liner for the Rotterdamsche Lloyd, the ship was named after the grandson of the founder of the Rotterdamsche Lloyd who was taken hostage and shot during the war. The history of that ship was immense. In 1965, she was sold to Star Lauro, (now MSC Cruises) and renamed Achille Lauro (after the company owner). Achille Lauro entered its service in 1966 carrying passengers to Sydney, Australia. That must have been quite a journey in those days.

It was extensively rebuilt and modernized after an on-board explosion and was converted to a cruise ship in early 1972, during which time she suffered a disastrous fire. The ship had nothing but disaster after disaster. A 1975 collision with a cargo ship, and another onboard fire in 1981 took her out of service for a long time, probably best. Lauro Lines went bankrupt in 1982. The Chandris Line took possession of her under a charter arrangement in 1985, shortly before the hijacking. Yes, that's right hijacking again. The ship was hijacked by a members of the Palestine Liberation Front in 1985, I found this information out later I might add when they played the voyage of terror during our cruise to Egypt and Israel in the cinema. What a shock it was to find out what had happened during the exact same cruising albeit 7 years on. I had no idea of the traumas and back ground on the ship when I was 21. Its only now that the historical aspects intrigue me as I reminisce.

The cab took us directly to the passenger gang way, the only time we would actually use this entrance. The cabby over charged us, of course, us being British and young girls.

I walked up the gang way with my suitcase dragging behind me, a large bag and hairdressing equipment, balancing in both hands and my hair totally dishevelled. No make-up left after the teary farewell from my parents back in the UK. I must have looked a right sight, I felt totally out of my comfort zone and not glamorous at all. Honestly what a first impression?

When we walked into the foyer, our manager Rachelle was waiting for us with our area manager Frank. He was a tall thin man, English, approximately 34, well turned out and dressed in the latest Italian fashions. Or what I presumed was the latest fashions, as I was not really that versed on styles of different countries.

"I take it you had a good journey," he said with a devil-ish glint in his eyes.

" Yes, great thanks" I beamed a smile trying to cover the fatigue that was setting in.

Rachelle our manager was 22, very pretty, petite and blonde with a beautiful sandy completion, quite Scandinavian looking. Tam was in straight away, very   confident and bubbly. Chatting to them both like she had known them for years. I followed her lead.

We sat and waited for what seemed like an eternity as

our crew cabins were blocked with equipment still being loaded. It was mayhem. Italians shouting really fast at each other trying to move furniture, equipment and such like. I was starting to wonder whether we would ever depart in one piece let alone on time. Crew were running all over the place, staff were arriving, officer were walking about like they owned the place, well they did I suppose. Dark tanned skin and slicked back hair in their white uniforms, very handsome. I just sat there totally amazed at how anything got done.

The decoration was old and very much like a hotel, with the pursers office to one side and lifts to the other. Plastic was still on the carpets throughout the main foyer area. Some crew were cleaning and polishing everything. What a nightmare it was, so noisy I couldn't hear myself think. It was like a clip off a Benny Hill show. I had the music playing in my head, which made me smile.

I was feeling tired, I had been on the go for 12 hours already and it was only 3pm. Finally, Rachelle gave us an all clear to go to our cabin and change, just scruffs, as we were going to clean and stock the salon with products and equipment. Tomorrow was the dreaded embarkation day, and everything had to be ship shape. (Sorry I couldn't resist that one) we would sail at 5pm.

Rach gave us a plan of the ship, and tried to explain where we had to go to get to our cabin, but I don't think either of us were listening, as there was some sort of altercation going on between two delivery men by the gangway. Both were trying to get onto it with equally large loads. Neither were going anywhere at that rate. Not surprising map reading was not my forte and we were lost. We went on a magical mystery tour trying to find our cabin. Up and down what seemed like an endless amount of staircases and corridors that all looked the same. We found ourselves on the lower Decks which didn't have any carpets and smelt like fuel. It was also below sea level, a dead give-a-way that we were in the crew area. We found some stairs, well a rusty old ladder, which lead down to an even lower Deck. Could there be any more Decks? We looked at each other and laughed, knowing that over the next few months, the ladder could be problematic when intoxicated with alcohol. We threw our bags down, straddled either side with our legs and attempted to descend them like they do in the films, it was hilarious. Needless to say, it didn't work quite like that and we ended in a heap on the floor.

Our cabin was in the corner opposition the casino staff accommodation. We opened the metal door to find that we couldn't even swing a cat in it, it was literally so small I could just reach from one side to the other with arms opened wide. It had bunk beds with curtains around for privacy. This is an important thing to note as privacy just didn't enter our vocabulary, or should I say Tams. There was a small metal wardrobe the size of a kids wardrobe installed at the end of the beds and which had four draws underneath it. Through another metal door was a shower and toilet. At least we didn't have to share that with anyone else just the two of us. I had heard some very strange stories about fifteen people to one shower. A slight exaggeration I'm sure. I found out later that there were 10 people in one corridor which doubled as a cabin. The waiters and cabin stewards shared those.

I somehow ended up with the top bunk Tam was very slick, she knew that the bottom was always the best place. There were straps like seat belts to stop us falling out if it got rough. That hadn't even occurred to me that the sea may get rough. My stomach started churning again, in anticipation of the ships movement, I rubbed the back of my neck nervously with the thought.

Once we looked around our cabin which took all of five seconds, we unpacked our stuff and got settled. We were so excited but looking at Tams stuff, my shoulders started to hunch over, and my chin dropped, I had seriously under packed my clothes. I just thought that we would be in our uniforms most of the time. Tam informed me about the evenings and going ashore. I didn't really think that we would be doing a lot of that. I just had to make the best of it and use what I had, vowing to shop at the earliest opportunity.

Once we had got settled, we headed off to try and locate the salon. That was fun. I thought that I would never find my way around the ship it seemed massive (not as big as some of the ships I encountered later in my career). This one could cater for approximately 1200 passengers. We stuck to the passenger areas for the time being, as these were sign posted on each Deck with labelled maps of where we were. There was however a whole new world below Decks, which we were to find out about later. Up on Promenade Deck was the Hairdressing salon. On the left-hand side of the ship, called the port. My Mum helped me to remember, with a little saying, *there's no port left in the bottle.* But aft, stern etc always got me confused and still does to some degree. I had to learn them as difficult as it seemed as everyone (except passengers) talked using the correct terminology. Front and back, right and left would have been fine by me.

Then there was the language barrier, everything was in Italian. Apparently, head office had told the ship that we were fluent speakers of Italian. What a joke! Not knowing, that I was about to embrace a crash course in the language from Tam, learning all the swear words first of course, then the salon words, then the everyday stuff. What an earth was I letting myself in for?

CHAPTER 6 -THE SALON

The salon was small but perfectly formed. We entered from a door which took us straight into where the back washes and a reception desk were. I stopped still, whilst moving my eyes to look at my surroundings, my head slowly swivelled to catch up with them. The Ritz it was not. With a heaviness in my body I walked through a small arch to the right where three hairdressing stations with draws either side stood against the wall. As I looked up my eyes started to widen, and the joy came flooding back. I saw the most amazing views out of two panoramic windows that were set each side of the arches. My heart started jumping around as the excitement my imagination pictured the scenes that would float into view from that very spot. Most of the time we could only see the deepest blue of the sea with the tops glistening white and foam lick creations would form on the crests. Rach was already in there trying to decide where we were going to put everything. I perked up a little when I realised that we could make the salon into whatever we wanted. With a little imagination and lots of creativity it did look great. She gave a key to Tam for her beauty room and showed us where the Beauty and Fitness rooms were. They were on the starboard side (right side) just across the passageway to us. The Beauty Salon was a small room with nothing in it at all, and the so-called fitness room had a few weight, a bike and a rowing machine and that was it. Not very enticing or motivating for the budding fitness fanatic.

"I guess I will have to make the beauty room look more professional" said Tamsin glumly. Her face reflected how I felt when looking at the salon for the first time.

"Yep, we are going to have to find us some porters and trolleys to bring up all of our equipment and stock from the crew Decks below.' Rachelle smiled as she headed back into the salon, whilst pointing us in the direction of the lifts.

There was one that we could use until the passengers embarked so not too much hard work. We jumped in and made our way down to the crew gangway. There was a large pallet of products and furniture for us waiting dockside. We grabbed a large trolley to export our goods back to the Promenade Deck. It didn't take us too long, but it was a struggle trying to drive the trolley through the torrent of people seemingly coming in the opposite direction.

Once we had done that, we thirstily made our way for a coffee and a meeting with Rach on Lido Deck to discuss how things would work during our time onboard.

The view from up in the upper Deck were fantastic. We could see for miles. The Lido Deck had a bar and a kidney shape swimming pool, but unfortunately, we were unable to use it, as it was for passengers only. We sat down for coffee and Rach started to explain about the protocol on the ship.

"You have to sign for all of our drink, which will be paid for at the end of each cruise via a bill," she said smiling. Later I realised how easy it was to let this get out of control. "All of your meals would be provided for in the crew staff mess. As for the rest of the ships facilities were concerned, you will be able to join in after work."

Being staff we could use anywhere, but we were not allowed to sit on stools if there were a lot of passengers around. This seemed obvious to me as they had paid a lot of money to be on there after all. It did not stop us gathering in the disco and sitting where we wanted. No-one said anything.

There were no phones onboard, except in the radio room, it was expensive to call home, so we would have to wait until we got to shore and use the crew telephone kiosk.

It was a little cheaper for us with our crew passes

"The ship takes all currencies, so it is up to you to use the daily conversion rates to convert all into U.S dollars. We have to wear our uniforms during opening times but any other times we could wear the dress code for that day on the ship, that was printed in the daily news magazine," She continued on "We do not open in port but may be asked to volunteer for other duties to help with passengers. Salon times at sea were 8-8 pm and in Port we could go ashore, but we have to be back ready to work an hour before the ship was due to sail," Rach expelled a large breath.

"I think that's everything," she added.

I finally got my hands on the itinerary. My mouth gradually dropped when it dawned on me where we were off too. My eyes started to blink quickly; I couldn't believe what I was reading. It started off with Genoa, where we were, then Palma Majorca, Lisbon, Casablanca, a tingling sensation was increasing with intensity, the destinations were getting better. Tenerife, then an amazing nine days at sea. I hope my stomach will hold out I thought holding my hand on it. Walvis Bay South Africa was the next port, Cape Town, Durban, and Bazaruto back to Durban. Port Lois Mauritius, back to Durban. Then Christmas Day was in Mauritius. (Mum who would be very jealous about that one.) There was a few sea day in between these Ports.

The New year cruise was Mauritius overnight, back to Durban I carried on I couldn't take it in, I was amazed, all my dreams were coming true. I read on, this time my voice was quivering a little at the thought of all the exotic places that we were going to see. All my dreams were within touching distance. Cape Town and Durban were two main Ports on our itinerary, which were classed as our home Ports.

The cruising to Durban and Cape Town carried on for a couple of weeks then it went to another major change. Durban, Nose- be Madagascar, Comoros Mozambique, Zanzibar, Mombasa overnight, I had struck gold, and on my first contract too. Several weeks of that then off to Port Lois and on to the Reunion Islands. On the 11th March, a few days before my birthday, it all changed back to Europe and Tenerife, to Madeira, Casablanca then Southampton. I thought that I was going to explode at any minute with excitement. My hands were shaking, and the palms were sweaty.

I felt so overwhelmed by everything, that I was glad of the quiet time to   concentrate on sorting out the salon. The waves of excitement were flowing over me as all the different places that I had dreamed about from my bedroom window, all those years ago were now becoming a reality.

I went to check on Tam once I had finished my jobs in the salon to see how she was getting on, and that that Frank (the area manager) was going to take us out to dinner. Rach asked me to jivy Tam up.

I walked into the Beauty Room and the aroma from the aromatherapy burners smelt divine, like freshly cut Lavender with a touch of Jasmine, I could have floated off on that alone. I remember even now, 27 years on that we used Elemis Products, they are now my favourite product range today.

The place did look professional, a large couch, shelving had been made out of old cardboard boxes covered with material that Tam found lying around, and some   products which had been strategically placed to show them off nicely. There were flowers placed sporadically around the room, and oils burning on the opposite sides to give full effect.

In the corner stood a Cathiodermie machine from Guniot that lifts the facial features by stimulating the facial muscles, there were posters on the walls advertising these luscious treatments, and gentle lighting glowing from the candles which seemed to soften the edges.

"Blimmy," I gasped, she was good at her job, from the empty shell it was a few hours ago to the tranquillity of a Spa. A totally different place. It certainly set the scene for relaxation.

We had changed for dinner and met the other two on the gangway. A cabby took us to a lovely restaurant overlooking the sea. This time we didn't get over charged as Frank could speak fluent Italian. We ate well and drank some wine, not too much mind, we had embarkation the next day, and plenty of time to get to know alcohol. It felt like we were miles away from the hustle and bustle of the ship. The crew and staff were still trying to get her ready for the big day.

We could hear the waves just trickling into shore and the hushed voices coming from inside the restaurant behind us, whilst people enjoyed their dinner. Reluctantly we headed back to the ship and called it a night. I sighed as I pulled the covers over my head in my bunk and sank down, exhausted from the day, but somehow unable to sleep. I kept thinking of Mum and Dad and that lasting impression of them standing at the airport, it was imprinted on my memory. The smiles fixed on their faces but sadness in their eyes, as they watched their youngest child, fade into the distance of departures at Heathrow. What had I done?

CHAPTER 7 - FIRST TIMERS

The alarm went off and I opened my eyes trying to figure out where the hell I was. It was so dark; I couldn't even see my hand in front of my face. Surely, I had been asleep. I had no idea of the time or day for that matter. Then I remembered, I was on board the ship. I was on the top bunk in my cabin which was going to be my home for the next six to eight months, I felt sick and excited all at the same time. Tam was still asleep beneath me. So, to get out of the bed without waking her was tricky. *I've got to try and get down without breaking my neck.* I thought. I couldn't see a bloody thing.

Gently I lowered myself to the floor missed the last step and ended up in a heap next to Tams head. Laughing under my breath, trying not to make too much noise, I got up and felt my way to the bathroom, not quiet knowing where the bed ended and the door to the bathroom started. I stubbed my toe on the corner of the bed, and collided head first into the metal door, as if I had been fired from a cannon.

I was laughing uncontrollably, embarrassed and ego dented, I tried not to wake Tam but failed catastrophically. She woke up, turned on the light and laugh at the site of me crumpled up on the floor by the bathroom.

"Oh Jo, don't worry about turning on the light, I really don't mind," she said trying to stifle her giggles.

My pride was hurt but no other injuries were sustained fortunately. Once I had pulled myself together, I managed to get ready and find our way to the crew dining room, which was really buzzing now that most of the staff were on board.

We smiled at several friendly faces and made our way over to the table that Rach was occupying.

"Go and help yourself," she said pointing to an area full of food on hot plates in the far corner. "The food is ok, your standard stuff, toast, eggs, bacon, rolls, hams, meats of all descriptions, a continental breakfast." She said licking some egg from her bottom lip.

It was well known that the food was quite good on most of the ships. Just not the Achille Lauro. I sighed, looking around to see what I could eat, nothing really appealed. I decided to just grab some coffee instead. I wasn't really that hungry anyway. Once breakfast was out of the way, we went to the salon and started to plan for the upcoming cruise.

Embarkation was starting at 1pm. We had to be at the passenger gangway in our uniforms ready to meet and greet the passengers. Once the ship had set sail, we would do a sail away promotion on Deck, then, Boat Drill. *Boat drill!* I thought, the situation presented itself to the fore front of my mind, I had not even considered a Boat Drill. Let alone taking part in one.

Rach ran through the procedure, and where we would be stood to direct the passengers, after which we would go to the muster stations for a run through of emergency evacuation of the ship.

It was becoming apparent that we would have to take part in the Boat Drill and that we could be called upon at any point to demonstrate putting on our life jackets. I felt very nervous. *What if I got it wrong? What if I made a mistake?* I though. From now on I would be in the middle of everything not just standing on the side lines.

Embarkation was hysterical to say the least, the passengers were every nationality except for British, or that's how it seemed. By the time we had finished I could say Welcome on Board in five different languages French, Italian, Spanish, German, and of course English or what I thought was the correct pronunciation in all of the above mentioned. Tam was my onboard tutor for all fraises, I'm not sure what I might have actually been saying, especially as I got a very stern look from one Italian lady. Tamsin had complete hysterics at my expense, and I still don't know to this day what I said, but I can guess that it was very rude.

We stood there handing out leaflets, trying to explain in different languages where the salon was located, and which treatments were on offer. My head was spinning, my feet were aching, and my throat was raw. We were only half way through the process. Passengers were making appointments like it was going out of fashion, and the formal night, 24 blow-dries and hair-ups were booked in a row, pre-straighteners I might add and that was just in one afternoon. How my feet hurt, pulsating and stinging, like I was standing on pins.

Once we had finished embarkation, it was time for a quick coffee then up to the salon with our life jackets to get ready for Lifeboat Drill. The ship had left Port by then. Not that I had any idea of that until we went up to the salon and noticed the far-reaching views of the ocean from the windows. It was really calm. My first sail away and I had missed it.

The lifeboat drill made us laughed at how funny some of the passengers were. One gentleman was trying to put his feet in the round hole which was obviously for his head.

"Excuse me sir" I said in my sweetest voice. "Let me help you with that" I helped him out of the small hole that he had put his feet in and popped it over his head.

"Goodness, that's incredibly stupid of me, he said with a very posh British accent.

"Don't worry sir, it happens all the time," I lied.

"Well executed." Tam said laughing behind her hand.

"Does that happen a lot Tam?"

"Yeah," she added still laughing.

I couldn't believe it. Even me as a novice I knew that round hole was meant for your head. Tam explained how to recognise the traits for each nationality. Obviously, it wasn't the same for each person but on a generalised observation of people, it pretty much hit the nail on the head. The Italians were usually so intent on talking that they never paid any attention to the drill at all. The Germans did every step to the letter, making sure they knew exactly where to go and what to do. The English just looked scared, but with a stiff upper lip and keep calm carry on essence about them. The Spanish were similar to the Italians and the French just did their own thing. The Americans took every think literally and left their very intelligent brains by the dock side because they were on holiday. I don't want to offend as it is just my opinion. The emergency drill was announced over the loudspeaker.

"Todo el personal a sus puestos de reunion," " Todo el personal a sus puestos de reunion"

Translated was all personnel to report to their muster stations. We had to stand by the lifts with our life jacket on and directing all the passengers to their muster stations. During this time, I answered all the normal questions of where everything was, as well at the oddities, such as what time is midnight buffet, how long is a half an hour massage, do these stairs go to the front and back of the ship, that was just the tip of the ice burg compared to the American ships I eventually sailed on. Surely it was more important to find out what happens during an emergency drill?

We followed the passengers through, where I eagerly waited to find out what to do myself, in the event, unlikely as it seemed, a ship was to go down, sink, catch fire, etc, etc, at that point I was just as clueless as the passengers.

I was informed that I would be having a Boat Drill myself the next morning at 10am with all of the other rooky crew. That's one I paid attention to; you never knew when it would come in handy!

The rest of the day progressed, and we took it in turns to go to dinner in the staff dining room. It was very nice, surprisingly, very Italian, with Mozzarella, tomato and basil, spaghetti, meat dishes which looked familiar, but unfortunately, I couldn't really tell you what it was, but all looked very tasty and the smell wafted tantalisingly under my nostrils waiting to explode onto my taste buds.

I felt a little anxious as I was the only one in a baby pink uniform, I sort of stuck out a bit. How embarrassing, however, I did feel a little better later when I saw the uniforms the casino staff had to wear. They were in bright red stripy waist coats, stripy green shirts and bow ties. A little giggle escaped from my mouth, quickly looking to see if anyone had heard me.

Once we had finished work, at 8pm, we went back down to our cabin. I tried not to fall down the ladder again. Now I know why sailors glide down with their feet either side of the steps. Quicker and faster, the ship was starting to move a bit by then. I didn't try it mind you, just in case it didn't work. I sat on my bunk thinking that's it, I'm done in, I can't move. My shoulders hurt when I climbed up to my bunk, feeling every inch of the muscles screaming at me to stop. *Nice shower and to bed,* I had thought with great relief, oh no, Tam had other ideas, when she flung open the cabin door behind me, making me jump out of my skin.

"Come on love' get your glad rags on it's time to party." Boy was I in for a treat.

Normally the protocol was up at 7am, breakfast at 7.30am, in salon at 7.45am ready for clients at 8am. Then a coffee break in morning, lunch staggered for two hours, (that was when I went back to bed or sunbathed, the longer I was on the ships the more sleeping, outweighed the sunbathing). Then back to salon, afternoon break if time, then finish at 8pm, down for dinner, back to bed for a couple of hours, then out again about 10 or 11 o'clock to have fun and party until the early hours, usually 5 or 6 in the morning. That was then repeated over and over every night for the eight months. Phew, I'm tired even thinking about those days now, snuggled up in bed at ten most nights.

So off to the shows it was. I actually was quite excited about seeing them. The dancers were amazing in their feathers and sparkling costumes, that just about covered their essentials, and not leaving anything up to the imagination.

A few drink in the Lido Bar then off to the disco. It was great very tame and manageable. I could stand more of that treatment.

The next morning, we were in Palma, Majorca, which was our first stop then we had a sea day, onto Lisbon, Casablanca then Tenerife, that was the last stop before our mammoth nine-day sea crossing to Walvis Bay South Africa.

Palma was beautiful with Palm trees and a definite holiday feel to it. The heat of the sun burning down, causing me to sweat terribly in my white jeans and T- shirt. The three of us got off in each of the Ports, but the one that I remember the most was Casablanca, it was so different to anywhere I had ever been. We didn't go too far but we had a little walk around, not too far from the docks. I was a little nervous because it was the first time I was in a foreign country without Mum or Dad.

The smells were different, spices, the air was very warm, and I could imagine that Rick's Cafe was just around the corner, from the film Casablanca. It's the very essence of Morocco and my first taste of the culture. The sights didn't disappoint either very authentic with the archways and wonderful architecture, nothing I had ever seen before, even though I had been to several countries when I was younger. Greece and Spain mainly. Nothing compared to the feeling of authenticity and how humbled I felt standing there. I watched with ore, looking at the people and watching their daily routines evolve. We didn't have much time and was back on board and in the salon before I knew it.

I was ready for the evenings appointments to start the gazillion blow-dries I had booked in for captain cocktails.

What glamour, the ladies didn't disappoint, with their out-landish bouffant hairstyles and false eyelashes. Dallas had nothing on them.

The chatter in the salon was one of excitement. Dorothy an American lady in her 60's, from New York wanted the works. She wanted her hair to put into a bun at the nape of her neck, with a diamante beret to finish, followed by a make-up from Tam.

"So, girls, will I see you all in the disco tonight" She said

"I'm sure you will, dancing the night away" I said smiling.

"What do you girls usually do in the evenings? Secret rendezvous I imagine, with some tasty waiters?"

"Oh, Dorothy, you have been watching to many films. We don't do that on here"

"Ok Jo, if you say so" She winked at me whilst touching her nose. "I'm sure by the end of my cruise, my dear, you will be spilling the beans of life below decks?" she added laughing and nodding.

I left it at that for the time being. I had no idea myself what to expect. I'm sure it wouldn't be too long before I found out.

We left our final Port of Tenerife to embark on our nine-day sea crossing to Walvis Bay. We watched as the dock side slide into the distance and the tranquil blue waters of Tenerife turned a deep blue and became part of the gigantic ocean that we had to cross.

CHAPTER 8 - REALITY HITS

We ventured into the disco and the ship was really starting to move. The passengers had disappeared from the main areas. Apparently, it happened quite often when the ship was moving a lot. There were sick bags lined along the handrails in case someone got caught out. I started to turn an ashen colour and felt a little sea sick, but Tam assured me she would help take my mind off it. Yeah! she sure did that alright!

The disco was where I had my initiation into crew life true ship style. My manager Rach and my wonderful cabin mate Tam thought that it would be great fun to introduce me to yellow birds and Tequila slammers. (The Yellow Bird is a cocktail of Bacardi Light Rum, Galliano, Crème de Banana, Orange Juice, and Pineapple Juice.)

I asked Tam why they were called Yellow birds? and her answer was simply

"Yellow birds they make you fly "laughing as she started to wave her arms up and down in a flapping motion like a bird.

I knew I was in trouble then, we all stood at the bar counting down to drink the yellow birds down in one. Yuk! My tongue was pushed up against the roof of my mouth as I flinched and recoiled, trying not to gag. Next up was a Tequila slammer. This became mine and Tam's signature drink. God only knows why as it was also disgusting. However, at twenty-one it all seemed like a good idea. (people wonder why I don't drink now!

Our ritual was sitting on the bar stools, whilst Tam

would shout

"E, Arturo, due Tequila boom, boom por favor" (translates roughly into, hey Arturo, two taquila slammers please) In her pigeon spanish. Not sure how much he understood, more than what he was letting on I'm sure. Arturo was small, very dark and a little over weight, black hair and a large smile with fantastic white teeth. He must have been in his mid to late forties, but of course I could be very wrong, he may have been alot younger. Everyone seems old to someone who is a twenty one.

With that Arturo stacked us two taquila shots with salt and lime. I looked and thought, *what am I supposed to do with this*? very nieve. Tam all knowing guru of ship life, enlightened me on the process of drinking this horrific drink.

"First you put the salt on the back of your hand, take the taquila in a small shot glass, bang it on the table three times with your other hand covering the top until it fizzes, drink it down in one, then take the salt that has been on the back of your hand and lick it off, shove the lime in your mouth. That's it, it's supposed to relieve the horror that was happening to your taste buds" she said trying to convience me that it would be lovely. In my opinion it only added to the drama of the drink.

The next bit was the best (or should I say worst) part. We hooked our feet under the bar footrest lent backwards, so we were upside down, let the taquila rush to our heads and sat up very quickly. How on earth I didn't throw up, or fall off, was beyond me. So without putting a finer point on it , the yellow birds plus taquila really finished me off for the night. You can imagine, Tam and Rach were in hysterics watching me run around like a lunatic flapping my arms, pretending to be a bird. It was fun at the time.

Suddenly, I got very hot and started to sweat, I could feel my cheeks burning, my eyes trying to focus on something, anything, that wasn't moving. Impossible task, when the ship was going ten to the dozen, up and down, side to side. We used to call it around the world, when the ship spun on it's bow like a spinning top without actually spining. Front in the sea, port side, starboard , aft all taking it in turns to dip its part in the ocean. Waves were crashing over the top of the ship, and I lost my footing and crashed to the floor with the next bump. I asked Tam if she could go with me back to the cabin. With the ships movement I didn't trust myself to get back safely and quite frankly I was scared

When we walked, the floor would come up to meet your foot rather than the other way around, and then dissappearing as if we had just stepped off a curb. Walking in a straight line was almost impossible. We got down to Foyer Deck ok, then the stairs started to get a little steeper the further down we went, it was tricky at the best of times, let alone with a body full of alcohol. Tam must have had a stomache of steel thats all I could say. I think I was now turning a tasty shade of green rather than the ashen grey. Down to Deck A then Deck B then it was time to tackle the ladder. I stood frozen to the spot. I felt as though I would plunge to my death into the abyse below, Ok, it looked and seemed steeper than normal. Tam however thought that it would be fine and charged passed me singing,

"This is how you do it baby"
She, slipped, grabbed me, mid flight, causing the both of us to come crashing down ontop of each other at the bottom of the ladder.

At that exact moment the casino lads came out to see what all the noise was, after all it was 4am. Being Italians they were highly amuzed at the stupid, drunk, English girls. We had got an awlful reputation, the girls from England that was, about drinking too much on the ships, and we had just added insult to injury confirming the reputation that pre-ceeded us. However, they did help us up, and carried us back to the cabin. We had not even been introduced properly. We said our good nights, Tam was giggling and I thanked them, whilst trying to hide my embarrestment, and sheepishly dived into our cabin, my face was flushed and I was wincing from the humiliation. I could have died on the spot.

The alarm was ringing, I had only just gone to bed and boy did I feel bad. It was seven am, and I had officially had two hours sleep and felt as sick as a dog. The ship was still rollling around and so was my head. I could't believe I had to work. Tam's head popped up from the bunk below and smiled a wery smile.

"Come on" she said "brecky and you will be fine"
I really don't know how I made it up to the salon. My first client was waiting, thankfully it was one of the dancers. I had to keep excusing myself to run to the toilets and throw up. Well what could Rach have said, she had gotten me into that mess.

After I had finished my client, she sent me into the beauty room for a lay down. I did feel better even though the ship was certainly giving it some jip still. Tam's stomach of steel was fine. I had to get her secret if I was going to survive another eight months.

CHAPTER 9 – NINE DAYS AT SEA

I got through the following nine days at sea, without too much hardship. I Learnt where to take our towels, to get them washed in the laundry, it was right down at the bottom of the ships lowest Deck. Everyday seemed the same, dragging the towels along the Lido Deck to the crew door. The wooden Deck made it alot easier to slide the plastic bag along. Looking out to the ocean, I could see the suns rays hitting the creast of the waves, causing the light to jump back off them like sparkles dancing to a tango and then float off into the sky. The sun seemed to melt back into the sea, ready to start over on each crest of the waves. I had to squeeze into a very small lift, but It would go no further than rope Deck. So tugging the towels along to the ladders I flung them down closly followed by me doing my sailors impursination. I reached the chinese laundry at the lowest Deck. I hated doing it, as it was like being on a battle ship. Everything was grey and dimly lit. The chaps in the laundry were always happy to see us. Proberly because they didn't see many people or the light of day very often, visits were to a minimum. It was just how you would imagine it to be. Floor to ceiling sheets and towels all rolled up and disheveled on one side then on the other were large commercial shelving units in battleship grey holding the most neatly folded bedding, towels, uniforms and sheets that you could possibly imagine. Spotlessly white. The heat was intolerable, sweat was poring from me. *How do these people stay here all day?* I couldn't wait to get back to the fresh air above, it was stifling.

The sea was quite rough all the way to Walvis Bay, South Africa, but by the time I stepped off in the heat of the sun in the port, I had got my sealegs. Unfortunatly nobody had told me you gain land sickness. That was when your whole being feels like it was still going up and down, and you felt very queezy, yet you are on land. My legs were wobbly, almost jelly like, it was the strangest sensation.

Walvis Bay was great. We had joined one of the excusions to see the pink Flamingos. What a sight that would have been. Unfortunatly it was not the season for the area to be covered with the pink sea of birds, there were however a few sprinkled about who must have missed the memo. Still it was wonderful to see them in their natural habitat. We stayed only a few hours before it was time to head back to the ship again. After the nine days at sea it was a nice relief to be off the ship, albeit for such a short time.

We were due into Cape Town early the following day. The experienced staff had told me what a wonderful sight it was to see us coming into port. Tabletop Mountain was a glorious sight. So, there I was at 5 am standing at the front of the ship, up above Lido Deck near the funnels, watching us come into port. I must say it was amazing. Table Mountain was and still is a flat-topped mountain overlooking the city of Cape town in South Africa. It also forms a part of the table mountains national park. The flat top of the mountain was covered by fluffy white clouds. We were going to try and get to the top once the ship had docked. Apparently, we had to take the cableway which takes people from the lower cable station on Tafelberg Road, to approximately three hundred metres above sea level, to the plateau at the top of the mountain.

The sight of us docking didn't disappoint. Unfortunately, Tam and Rach didn't make it up, but we were all meeting with Stan the puppeteer and Charles the shop manager at the gangway at seven to go up the mountain.

There they were sure enough already to go. I couldn't quite believe what was happening and frequently had to pinch myself to know that I was actually doing it all. My Dad would have loved the trip. Not so my Mum. Especially since when we went to Tenerife when I was about ten or so, we headed up Mount Tidy. It involved a cable car. My Mum was so afraid, she came down early before us, only to have one of the passengers pull the emergency stop lever, which made the cable car come to a grinding halt midway to the bottom, leaving them dangling for half an hour whilst engineers try to fix the problem. My Mum was in tears by the time she got off the other end, she vowed never to go on another as long as she lived, and she never did.

Stan was a funny guy, he was in his twenties, English, and stood about five foot two tall (the same as me,) black hair, sharp features, and bright blue eyes. He was a small framed man, which was ideal for his puppeteering. He was amazing when he performed. The puppets were slightly smaller than life size and so realistic. He wore black, so no one could see him. They would dance around to music, and Stan would tell stories, quite fascinating to watch. He was a gay man and loved making jokes about all the talent on board. He didn't mean performing either.

Charles on the other hand was a very well turned out man. He was from Italy, and stood about five foot eight, slim, glasses and dark hair. He was a very serious character in comparison to Stan. He was also a gay man and proud. For me it was not surprising. The majority of the men in my industry were gay and usually good looking, which was always the case. Even though Charles and Stan were like chalk and cheese personality wise, they were the best of friends. Not sure if they were a couple or not, they were both fabulous human beings, and we all got on great.

We finally reach the top of Table Mountain and the cable car was great fun. At the top the view was incredible, fluffy white cotton wool clouds, tiny little houses and trees in the distance. We could even see the ship in dock. There were some friendly little furry creatures which looked like large brown guinea pigs. In fact, they are called Dassie. They are the nearest animal relative to the elephant. It's highly amusing as they were all so small.

There were very few people at the top, but I did spot some familiar faces from the crew on the ships. A very talk, striking guy with dark features, and an amazing sun tan, walked past with a beautiful smile on his face. I turned around to see who he was looking at, but there was no one there. Surely, he would not be looking at me. Dismissing the idea straight away, I continued on with our tour putting all thought of a ship board romance out of my head. Tam had already warned me that they don't last, once off the ship, and knowing how attached I could get I took her advice.

The clouds rolled in at the top of Table Mountain, making it hard to see anything. It was very mysterious, something out of a movie. The temperature took a sudden dive, it went so cold very quickly as the sun sunk behind the clouds and without any warning, we couldn't see a thing below. It had taken a complete turn for the worst. It took on an uncanny feeling which made us uneasy. We headed back down before it got any worse and left us stranded.

CHAPTER 10 - NO ROMANCE

It was Captains cocktails night, and the hair salon was busy, busy, busy, for me and Rach, even Tam helped out on our side because the call for makeup was as popular as the hair ups. Everyone wanted to look their best in their tuxedos for the chaps and formal dresses for the ladies. All very glam and in 1992 we had the left over from the eighties fashion. Shoulder pads, big hair, and sequins. Not sure that was a good thing, but Dynasty and Dallas sprang to mind.

For me this was the best ever night, I loved putting hair up. I must say I was getting very good at it back home, in London before I joined the ships, I worked for a company that sold organic hair colour, called Herby, and I used to do many photo shoots with them to help build my portfolio, it was great. But on the ships, after the fifteenth hair up, the novelty soon wore off. The diamante studded hair slides were selling quite well at $55 (US) a piece. It was the boost I needed, and the extra money came in handy, as the lovely bar bills were getting a little out of control. I found it so hard to sell anything, but it was how we made our commission, it was paramount that I meet my targets. Unfortunately, I didn't quite grasp the concept of sales until I hit the American cruise liners the following year.

Mrs Chapman of cabin 251 State room was an extrovert who was done up to the nines and that was just to get her hair done. I couldn't wait to see what she looked like at the formal night. She was in her late 60's and full of life, calling everyone darling and ducky. Quite the quaint essential hight profile English women. She entered the salon with all the air of a countess and the bank account to match.

" My darling girls, how wonderful it is to make your acquaintance. My name is Mrs Chapman, but you can call me Penelope. Now which delectable soul has the honour of doing my voluptuous locks tonight." She said smiling and winking at me.

She was a fascinating character. She was like one of the suspects in an Agatha Christie murder mystery. She wore a flowery, flowing purple and pink dress,   embroidered with lace and sequins around the edging. Her collars were lace, and a feather was tucked into the corner of the right side. She wore a floppy hat made of suede which also intertwined with feathers of pink and purple. Her dress hung at mid-calf and the skin coloured tights were a little too dark for her natural complexion. Her make-up was full on with pencilled in eyebrows in a brown and matching hair colour again too dark for her. Her lipstick was a dark pink and the foundation was so thick, you would leave a line if running your fingers through it. She was larger than life in personality and in stature. Yet she was harmless and her show like performance was definitely covering up some hidden agendas or secrets.

" Hi, Mrs Chapman, my name is Jo, and I will be doing your hair today" I said holding out my hand ready to shake hers. She looked and smiles, tapping my hand gently, without actually shaking it.

"Charmed I'm sure" she replied sinking into the inviting chair I had made ready for her at the back wash.

"What would you like me to do for you today" I ran my fingers through her hair, which had had the life back combed out of it.

"I would like it refreshed in the same style if you would be so kind, I have heard such wonderful things about you girls, I'm sure you can work your magic."

Her hair was in a simple pleat, so I went about shampooing and conditioning the hair before I could even get a comb through it. The colour which she had on her hair had left it in a terrible state, so with the magic of a treatment and some fabulous products I set her hair with rollers and put her under a dryer for thirty minutes to set, whilst I carried on with Mrs Burns from cabin 614 lower inside cabin. So different from Mrs Chapman, a sweet 75year old from London. She was naturally grey with rosy cheeks and a Motherly way about her. I just wanted to cuddle her and give her everything I could for free. So, I set about giving her the works, conditioning treatment, blow dry, makeover. All done to a quality standard before Mrs Chapman was dry.

Mrs Burns loved her new look, even though it was very natural and hi lighted her high cheek bones and outlined her wonderful full lips, she felt a million dollars. I loved watching then go out with a smile and a swagger about them.

I took Mrs Chapman out from the dryer and chatted about where she was from and she was very happy to tell me about her previous four husbands had all died of heart trouble.

"Can you believe it darling, all four of them dying of heart problems, I think the coroner thought there was a conspiracy going on, so I have decided no more husbands for me. I will settle for a boyfriend, and my dear he is thirty years younger than me. He won't be dying of a heart attack I'm sure." She winked again at me as I giggled and looked at Rach. He sniggered as she turned to hide her surprise on her face.

"So are you lovelies courting someone on here, or do you have a beau in every port."

"Goodness no way." I said " I want to visit too many places; I've got no time for that" I said determine to get my point across.

"I see" she said touching her nose with her finger, as if to say your secret is safe with me. We laughed.

"Well let me tell you a tale about cruising. No -one is what they seem, be careful and cautious who you let in and don't trust anyone, except your immediate family" she pointed to Rach and Tam who had just walked in the room catching the end of the conversation.

"All I will say is the men on here are very happy to accommodate" She laughed a high pitched squill. I just stood with my mouth open for once lost for words.

"Mrs Chapman, I shall be waiting eagerly for your next appointment to find out what you may like to divulge to us." I couldn't wait. I showed her my finished masterpiece finished off with a beautiful diamante comb place in the crevasse of her pleat. She loved it.

"well my beautiful soul, you have outdone yourself, what lustre you have given me. I shall be back soon" She paid and disappeared in a waft of expensive perfume.

We were all left standing staring after the intriguing women, not wanting to wait to find out some gossip, but not being able to help ourselves to surmise what she had meant by her comments.

We finished our clients gone 8pm. By the time we cleaned up it was almost 9pm. Down we went to dinner hoping there was something left for us, we sat and had a lovely bowl of gnocchi. The potato pasta was wonderful, and the sauce was to die for. *That was worth all the hard work.* I thought casting my mind back to Mrs Chapman's comments. Looking around I started to wonder who she could have been talking about. *That would have to wait* I thought. We decided to try and make midnight buffet after changing into our evening dresses. I was so excited, my eyes sparkled with the anticipation for the night that was to come. I had never been to anything like it before. At home my Saturday night consisted of picking up my friends and driving to the Fridge in Brixton, that was a night club. We would dance all night. No drinks, I had no money, only for the entrance. Plus, the usual attire was jeans with boots and some sort of grungy top. I was in a small dance group at the time and it was at the start of the hip-hop era. Loved it, but things suddenly got very grown up onboard, and I suddenly felt a little paranoid.

My dress was just black. No frills, no sequins, just plain black and sleeveless to the knees. Tam on the other hand, had obviously done it all before. Her dress was black but to her ankles, backless, sleeveless and with small diamante's around the front neck line, figure hugging and absolutely stunning. It looked as if it had been made for her. Wow she looked stunning. Mind you she had the best figure all in proportion. You know the type of girl that would look good in a dustbin liner. She didn't think so herself mind. She thought like most of us girls that she was fat. She could not have been further from the truth. I couldn't help feeling very drab in comparison. I had never liked the shape of my body and I was small which didn't help.

Looking at her with envious eyes, wishing I had more money and time before to go shopping with Mum. Oh well too late now. Looking back at the pictures I wish I saw me then as I do now. Being in my fifties I would love my figure to be like that again.

We went into the Lido bar where we usually met all the other crew staff. The shop assistance (i.e. shoppies as they were fondly known), dancers, and casino staff etc. I felt very conscious, like their eyes were bearing into the back of my head. Was my skirt tucked into my dress showing my knickers? Did I have toilet paper attached to some part of my anatomy? As I turned around, I was greeted by the same striking eyes and smile that I had seen earlier at the top of Table Mountain, those eyes, they just jumped right out at me. My body was melting to the spot. I was unable to move. My hands were clammy, my legs were tingling, and the room felt like it was spinning out of control. That man was in an officer's uniform. He was extremely handsome in his white dress jacket and formal black trousers; very dapper. At that moment I realised I had been staring for a little too long, turning away rather quickly, but finding it difficult to drag my eyes away. I blushed and carried on behind Tam hoping I could cover up any embarrassment. Tamsin stopped and turned around to see where I was, as she did, I walked straight into her, banging my head on her chin.

"Oh my god , sorry Tam" I said trying to disguise my embarrassment.

"Not to worry, are you ok" she smiled a bit confused as to why I was so close. I laughter and fobbed her off with a dizzy smile.

As time went on the man got under my skin and my clumsiness got worse. Tam looked at me, still confused. She didn't have any idea what was going on with me . I looked back over my shoulder to see if he had noticed, but to my relief, or was it my disappointment he was gone.

The glamorous midnight buffet was so elegant, with an array of lavish dishes such as escargot, lobster, delectable desserts with lashings of cream piles high, and of course a magnificently carved ice sculpture. Amazing, the lights twinkled between the displays and the flowers were so beautiful, red, golds, and purples all structural flowers arranged to dazzle, what a fantastic sight. The whole essence of the night was somewhat magical and as long as we let the passengers go first, we could taste some of the delicious food ourselves. Just as I filled my plate with delights, I heard a soft whisper in my ear.

"Are you enjoying your dessert" He said as the hairs on the back of my neck stood to attention. The smooth Italian accent sent shivers down my spine. I turned around; I was face to face with the officer from earlier. I could feel the redness flow up through my neck, into my checks, burning like the sun. I stuttered, as I tried to answer, but yet had nothing to say, I could feel his eyes burning through to my very sole. Just as I thought we were finally going to get somewhere, he left, that was it, that was all I was going to get. On reflection he was a guy who knew exactly what he was doing. Just doing enough to reel me in.

Tam was straight onto it, asking me what was going on. Just as I thought she would drop it; she was back on my case. She told me that things could get messy if you play at the top of the tree. (Officers level) I assured her that I had no intention of dabbling there or anywhere for that matter. I don't know who I was trying to convince me or her.

I never was very lucky in love, always meeting the wrong person or the right person at the wrong time. Or maybe they were just excuses, used to get as far away from me as possible. My insecurities came back with a vengeance as I remembered the incident with Pat my friend and ex - boyfriend and the hurt it caused. Very awkward to say the least.

I had convinced myself that no man would find me very interesting. I went to the bar for a round of tequila's with Tam, putting the whole idea of an onboard romance completely out of my head.

It was getting on for 3am sitting in the casino lads cabin, having several bevvies when Marco decided he was starving and needed some food. He was one of the casinos croupiers. At 29, he had completed six contracts all over the world, so he knew what he was doing. He spoke perfect English, much to our shame and after our first encounter, seemed a really nice guy.

"Where are we going to get food from at this time in the morning, everywhere is closed, even the crew bar," I asked.

"Just follow me, I have an idea!"

The five of us(three other casino guys) followed Marco to the door, up our ladder, out onto rope Deck. We passed through another door on the opposite side and descended down into the kitchens where the men were baking focaccia bread. It smelt delicious and tasted that way to. Hot and gorgeous with rosemary on the top. The cooks didn't mind us taking some and never asked for anything in return, it was great and very kind, however I did extent the curtesy and would give them a free hair cut in the salon every now and again. If I had carried on eating like that I would never have gotten into my uniform by the end of contract, let alone anything else.

It was heading towards five am, yet another early morning getting into bed. I   seriously needed to get some sleep as the next day we were heading into Durban . I didn't want to miss it. I needed to get off and call home. I hadn't had much time to stop to think about anyone back at home, but I had an emptiness in the pit of my stomach, and the longing to talk to Mum and Dad. It was so hard because I was unable to pick up the phone when I wanted. I really missed everyone. Especially Mum, I was not sure what was going on there, but I knew all was not well. Her letters had become more and more distracted. She had stopped telling me about anything that was going on at home. Not like before when I would get song and verse on everything. She had stopped mentioning Al completely. I needed to get to the bottom of it.

I succeeded in getting up early and went on my own to the crew phones which were dockside. It was 8am in Durban, so it meant that it was 10am in the UK. That was the best bit, not having such a huge time difference. I called Mum at work.

I was so pleased to speak to her. I told her where I was and that I would send her my itinerary in my next letter home. Of course, I couldn't wait to tell her where I would be on Christmas day. Mauritius, I blurted it out like a jet engine and   proceeded to tell her about all the places that we were to visit during the time on the ship.

"You're a lucky girl, I can't believe that, all these years I have said to you that one day I will spend Christmas day on a beach in Mauritius and now my little girl is going to do it for real." She gushed down the phone, feeling a little envious no doubt.

We told each other about the weather and what we had each been up to. I tried to steer the conversation towards her and Al, to see if anything was wrong, but my mother was fantastic at putting on a brave face and covering up. I know where I get it from now. I missed her so much, my heart felt as if it would leap out and crawl down the phone line.

Time was running out and the little voice of the operator told me my minutes were about to expire. I just managed to say goodbye when the line went dead. I stood there for a while thinking it was just like at the airport all over again. It was such an expensive call. The Rand was very good to the pound, I believe it was five Rand to each pound then, but it still racked up and after calling Dad as well, my money got eaten up very quickly. I decided to keep the calls to a minimum and write more. So much for finding out what was going on with Mum. It did eventually come to light later, during my last contract on board the Oceanic.

I headed back to the ship, the sun was out but I couldn't help thinking of everyone back home, that weighed really heavy on my heart. I felt so low and such sadness, I wondered aimlessly through the ship in a complete daze. Just as I entered the hall to where my cabin was, I noticed something on the door. It was tied to the handle, a small red rose with a note. *Blimey she's done it already* I thought. Tam had managed to have the lads after her already. I looked at the note and to my disbelief it was addressed to me, but who would do that, and why? I couldn't think straight; my emotions were in turmoil from the conversations I'd had with my family. I opened it up and read

"*To my English Rose. X*"

Oh no this is lovely, but why would they not say who it is? Then suddenly it occurred to me that it must be Tam and Rachelle, pulling a fast one on me again. Well it wouldn't be the first time. A couple of days ago I was in the salon by myself and the phone had rung.

"It is the commandant here" (the captain) the voice had said.

"I need you to come and do fog duty adesso (now), per favour (please), all of the crew and crew staff must attend, and now it is your turn" he said in a very husky Italian accent.

"I'm sorry but I cannot leave the salon at the moment I am the only one here" extremely confused, why no one had told me about it before.

"Ok but as soon as your manager returns, please can you come to the bridge with your life jacket and some binoculars, which you can get from me" he added

"Ok." I put the phone down then realised that it surely couldn't be true, and how I had never heard of it up until then, seemed a little suspect! I didn't feel comfortable with what was being asked of me at all. *I really didn't want to it, and what if it's a wind up, I would look such an idiot.* On that note Tam and Rachelle walked into the salon, they had a suspicious look about then. I sat for a while not saying anything until Tam asked if I had heard from anyone. *Hang on she has never asked that before,* I thought.

"No '' I said sheepishly

"Are you sure? No one?" she looked from me to Rachelle and back to me again.

"No. Why?" I said trying not to laugh I knew that it had to be those two.

"Oh no reason, just wondered" said Tam, but she could not hold out any longer and burst into hysterics. I knew it was the both of them. The fog duty had been a classic for new crew members. Come up to the bridge and do fog duty, giving them binoculars and a life jacket to wear. Standing there whilst the officers all laugh at them. It reminded me of when I did my work experience at B.A.E (British aerospace) in Stevenage. My brother had an apprenticeship there, he and his mates took great delight in sending me off for 'long stands', 'buckets full of sparks' and 'sky hooks.' They thought it was funny. I did Not!

The rose I had got on the door was not mentioned to the girls, I wanted to see if they cracked. I put it away in my draw and waited, nothing was said, and two days had passed since I received it, but they hadn't said a word. Wow, they were good.

It was demonstration time in the main lounge where passengers would come along to see what we offered in the salon. It was my first real demo. I was so nervous I could feel my legs shaking, my palms were sweating, and I seemed to have   developed a stutter. I had been on stage before doing hair at fashion shows in London, but I had never had to talk before. *What if I stumble or kept saying the same word over and over? Keep calm,* was all I kept saying to myself, *what's the worst that could happen?*

Tam was busy setting up her couch, and I was getting my chair and trolley ready. It was so typical that whenever I needed to concentrate on something, the ship would start to move. The trolleys were rolling and so were the displays. *Who puts wheels on things when it's going on board a ship? Honestly!* We packed some bed roll from the beauty room under the wheels which seemed to do the trick. By that time, I was turning into a jabbering wreck.

The first lot of passengers started to turn up, then, some more, and before we knew it, we must have had over 50 people in the room. I could see Mrs burns and Mrs Chapman smiling from the previous formal night. Tam smiled. She told me on her last ship she had over five hundred people in for the demos. I was glad of just the small amount that turned up to start me off, I don't think I could have coped with many more. On my future ships I had two and a half thousand into the main theatre during our demo's.

To my relief it went without a hitch, apart from a several naughty words (double–entendre) that Tam had decided to make up along the way. She would say you need to dip your wick into the aromatherapy oil's and massage the flange and palming off massage treatment. We had a saying about looking at someone's hair, 'Vardar the Ria' (look at her hair what a mess) the passengers didn't understand what she was talking about, thankfully, but we were trying not to laugh especially when the passengers would come and ask for a treatment using these connotations, they didn't realise what they had asked for. Even Mrs Chapman the experience cruiser didn't pick up on the terms. It was very unprofessional, but it kept us amused and did not harm anyone, as far as we know!

CHAPTER 11 - WHAT A DAY!

I will never forget how it felt when we had dropped anchor off the coast of Bazaruto Island (Mozambique). The excitement was overwhelming. I stood on Lido Deck looking over the brilliant blue sea which gradually got paler and paler as it faded into shore. The sandy beach was shining white, which glistened in the sun, dazzling me even from that distance. *Paradise,* I thought. The heat was so warm, my skin just tingled as the hairs stood on end. I had been up since 6am that morning watching as we slowed and dropped anchor, holding us in position. I was dress in the cruise uniform. White shorts, red and white stripped T-shirt supplied by the ship. We were cruise staff that day. Our job was to assist in disembarking the passengers from the zodiac boats at shore side. I had no idea what it actually consisted of, but I was up for anything and about to find out. *How hard could it be?* I thought.

We had to be at the crew deck first thing, ready to get on the lifeboats (tenders) that were going to take us to the zodiacs, then drop us off on the beach. *Great, how exciting I* thought. We got on to the tenders, as I turned, I noticed the look of ore on Tam and Rachelle's faces, they were a picture. Both were staring at the site of the beach in all its wonder. The glistening sea, caressing the shoreline, the busy bar staff setting up their equipment, and the BBQ's being set alite at such an early hour ready for the pig roast which followed.

I remember the breeze was blowing through my hair, all my senses were standing to attention. Even the hairs on the back of my neck were tingling from the sun. My sunglasses were on and I was ready. It was a whole new ball game. I close my eyes in my office now sitting in front of the window feeling the sunshine stream through and warm my face as I'm transported back in time.

We transferred to the zodiacs without too much trouble, and after an exhilarating ride over the waves, pounding, and flying through the air, we landed on the beach. Literally landed on the beach with a thud. Brilliant, I couldn't wait to do that again. The three of us stood by the shore watching some of the crew bringing off sun loungers, more food, and some sound equipment they would need for the wonderful beach party later that night. There was everything from toilets, a bar, tables and chairs, cushions and sun loungers. All had to come from the ship as nothing was on the beach at all. I had an insight to how Robinson Crusoe must have felt when he was first on his desert island, minus the entourage that is.

A few of the other staff joined us, Sharmez, Fredrick and Mal the dancers, and shoppies, Hanna and Rod. The passengers were gradually being transferred to the zodiacs from the tenders. What a sight. Nobody fell in, which was really surprising, there were a few near misses. The first zodiacs came to the shore and we all grabbed onto the ropes at the sides to become human anchors. Me being a short arse, stayed at the shallow end, and the taller people, were in the deep end. The passengers got out one by one. They came thick and fast, by the time the fifth zodiac had deposited the next lot of party goers, I had somehow managed to work my way down to the deep end, only to find that I could no longer find my footing on the sandy bottom and was struggling to stay afloat. Suddenly, I couldn't breathe. I was out of my depth and had no foot hold or reference to where I was. I was so frightened. I couldn't get my breath. It felt like an eternity, several seconds in reality before someone noticed that I was struggling. To my relief I found I was getting pulled out by the neck of my t-shirt and hauled back to the shallows. I had a mouthful of sea water and my hair was dishevelled, my t-shirt was up by my neck, thankfully I had my bikini top underneath otherwise that could have been embarrassing. I looked up to see who had pulled me out and to my horror who should be standing there, but dishy officer all tanned and gleaming in the sunlight, white chino shorts, a shirt open to his navel, rather hairy I might add. He had a glint in his eyes, but I couldn't tell if he was mocking me or smiling with me. I felt the colour rise again in my face. Why does this keep happening. I looked at him through my hair, trying to hide my embarrassment, but all I managed to say was grazie (thank you). I Stood up and timidly walked over to where the rest of the gang were, not wanting to look back incase he was laughing at me again. I was motified and frightened all at the same time. Tam came over to check on me, laughing with concern, if that was even a thing. I did see the funny side eventually.

Finally all the passengers were ashore, and the party began. There was singing, dancing, and lots of eating and drinking. The smell of the pig roast was amazing, and the buffet they had set out was stunning. With crab, prawns, fruits crafted into amazing flowers and salads of all the colours of the rainbow. We were not able to join in on that occasion so all of the crew and staff were at the other end of the beach just relaxing trying to catch some sun and enjoy the quiet with some burgers and beer of course that were provided for us on a wood fire made by the cabin boys. They were fantastic usually from South America, they had nothing but would share everything, such lovely people. They would send home money to their families who relied upon their husbands to be away for twelve months to put food on the table. I couldn't imagine how hard that must have been for them.

I was chatting with the zodiac guys Ben and Tim who were just about to go off and do some scuba diving. I hinted to them both that I had always wanted to do scuba, which paid off. Before I knew it, we were getting kitted up, and jumping into a couple of the zodiac's.

I had grabbed Tam, Mal and Sharmez on the way. We were in two seperate Zodiac. Me and Mal in one and Tam and Sharmez in the other, each with our own diver. We took off just bearly touching the tops of the waves, gliding over the surface like a swan of bees embarking on a flight. The feeling was out of this world.

We gradually slowed down and anchored inbetween the ship and shore. The lads got us kitted up and explained a few safty features. I was so excited. Ben would take us down individually. I was the first to go. I looked over at Tam and she signalled that she was ok. I smiled and dropped into the sea. It was so still, hardly a wave in sight. Perfect conditions. Down I went deflating my BCD (buoyancy control device). We didn't go to far down before I reached the bottom, either that or I just sank like a stone. I equalised my ears which was holding your nose and blowing out to make your ears pop. I knelt on the bottom with my arms across my chest looking into the abyss. I felt like I was in space, the only thing missing was the stars. Ben was right by my side, asking if I was ok. I was more than ok I was in heaven. The colour of the tropical fish that were around us were amazing. I saw Manta Rays, Tuna and King Mackeal plus many others that I didn't know the names of. In the distance I could see a huge shadow, coming out of nowhere, just like in the Jaws movie, heading straight for us. I didn't know weather to swim away or hide. I thought it was a shark, one of my biggest fears, but what I saw was a Giant Travelly. It was gigantic, well alot bigger than me. Bigger than anything I have ever seen except from the outside of an aqarium tank. They can grow to a wopping 170cm and 80 kilo's. It was silvery in colour with black spots. It seemed like it was every inch of the size, but who knows, I felt very, very small in the large ocean. I held my breath, closing my eyes and hearing my heartbeats rapid thuding in my chest. I squinted to see if it had gone, just catching the tail end as it swam by. Ben indicated that it was time for us to go up. I remembered to go slowly, but my in-stinks were to go as fast as I could to get away from anything else that could be coming our way. For those who know about diving, if you do go up to quick, it can be very danger-ous causing a condition called the bends also known as de-compression sickness (DCS) or Caisson disease, occurs in scuba divers or high altitude or aerospace events when dissolved gases (mainly nitrogen) come out of solution in bubbles and can affect just about anybody area including joints, lung, heart, skin and brain. So up we went nice and slowly. Looking up it seemed like the surface was just above our heads. But in reality it was alot further. You could see the sunlight streaming through the waves and melting into a

pool of yellow, enticing us back to the top. Excillerating.

Once back in the zodiac Mal was waiting to go down, she jumped in and off she went I could see her bubbles pop-ing, rainbow colours were left at the surface. Laying there in the boat bobbing up and down, it felt very surreal. I looked over towards the other zodiac, Tam was there waiting for the others to come back. I waved at her and the smile on my face must have said it all, she clapped her hand excit-ingly. Ben and Mal soon resurfaced and clambered back in. I noticed that Tam had been joined by Sharmez but Tim was nowhere to be seen.

Suddenly out of the blue, the waves got larger, not just by a little but by huge swells. Ben started the engine. I was very anxious, I could see Tamsin and Sharmez looking a little distressed. Ben shouted for them to start the engine, but the waves were at a five metre swells by that time and so noisey, crashing down into eachother that they just couldn'y hear us. I was holding on really tight, my knuckles turning white as i gripped to the side of the boat. The last thing I remember seeing was Tam and Sharmez frantacally trying to started the outboard engine, pulling the cord over and over, unsucessfully. The next thing I knew, their zodiac did a vertical ascent to the top of a hugh swell, both girls were screaming and holding on to the ropes, dangling by their arms with their legs doing a mid air running man. Funny now looking back in the safety of my home, but frightening at the time. Ben managed to steer our zodiac out of the way of yet another colossal wave. Calmly pulling the boats around and expertly landing it nice and gentle. All that ran through my head was *what the hell am I going to tell their*

mothers, if we lost them.

As we peaked around the last wave it suddenly became very still, and the huge swells disappeared as fast as they came. *Where were they* I thought looking around frantically. Then in the distance I could hear what I thought was crying, and there they were laughing hysterically, more with relief that fun. We pulled along side and I climmed into the zodiac and gave them both a cuddle, so relieved. Tim emerged from the water wondering what all the fuss was about.

Safely deposited back on the beach we tried to relaxed until it was time to load the passengers on to the zodiac's again. I couldn't help wondering where the nice Italian officer had got too. I hadn't seen him since that morning. Possibly a good thing, the events of the day had diminshed the embaressment of earlier.

The last passengers had boarded the tenders, and the rest of us got in the zodiacs. The party had ended and it was time to head back. The zodiac high tailed it to the ship. It was fabulous until I realised we had to jump from the zodiac to the rope ladder attached to the side of the ships. That would never be allowed now for health and safety reasons, yet there we were waiting to time the swells right. It was so choppy at the side of the ship. The ship went up and the zodiac went down in the opporsite directions. It was so difficult. The first attempt I nearly missed and ended up between the two vessels, that would of never turned out well to say the least. Finally I managed to catch it just right, clingy to the rope ladder trying not to look down, but failing miserably. Catching the sight of the waves crashing against the ship. My heart was in my mouth as I clambered up. When I reach the top it dawned on me that it was a really dangeous thing I had just done, and my legs were shaking, but I was having the

time of my life, what an adventure.

It was getting on for 7pm. Rachelle told us not to bother opening the salon as we had no bookings and people were getting ready for dinner. Great for us. I showered and changed, but my head was killing me. I was struck with a full blown migrain. It was agony, I couldn't move. Tam was a bit concerned so she grabbed the ships doctor. I was taken to the sick bay where I apparently had water caught in my ear canal. The doctor told me that they would need to syr-inged it, which was not pleasant. but it did feel better after. Apparently due to the diving the water had got lodged. I have, had problems ever since I caught an ear infection one holiday to Minorca with my family, when I was fourteen. It had developed into a Paulsie in my ear. I remember being in hospital to get it released. I also seemed to remember the doctor saying something about depths and heights. Guess he meant diving and flying. Should have thought about that be-

fore taking off in the zodiacs.

CHAPTER 12 – STORMY NIGHTS

We were fast approaching Christmas, and spent the next week going back and forth from Durban to Cape town, until we changed and set off on our Christmas and New Year's cruise towards Mauritius. I was so excited about this visit I could just about contain myself. Not only was it going to be a lifelong ambition of mine, but it was also one of my Mum's favourite fantasies of sipping cocktails on the beach. I'm sure that I could manage to do that on her behalf. I'm not sure why she wanted to go there, I never did ask her.

Port Louis was where we were heading too in Mauritius. It became a harbour in 1638 under a French Government. It was also the administrative centre and a replenishing port for ships going from Asia to Europe passing through the Cape of Good Hope. We also passed through here. Sometimes a good experience sometimes not.

I remember one time when we had finished work for the night. There hadn't been any clients in for hours, but that was pretty normal when the sea was so rough. The staff captain who was a very dark-skinned short Italian officer) in his 50's caught us before we headed down for dinner.

"You need to secure de salons as soon as possible. We are heading for a bit of a storm. OK" he always finished with Ok. I tried not to snigger; his accents made me laugh. I couldn't let him see me laugh otherwise things could be made very difficult. The officers definitely had a hierarchy and would not bow down to anyone who was a lower rank than they were. They were all nice enough, but there was a definite air of a foreboding nature about them. They would not tolerate any insolence, which was a good thing. It's what kept us all safe.

We went back into the salon and put everything on the floor. We wedged trolleys and anything which had wheels on into the corners, and laid the chairs down tying some rope around them, which we found in the cupboard. Always wondered why that was there? It soon became clear. Tam had done the same in the beauty rooms. There wasn't much we could do in the gym. The equipment was very large and probably wouldn't move very far. Tam and I glanced at each other, thinking the same. We had not had the staff captain tell us to make everything safe before, and we had, had some bad weather during our time onboard. We knew it was different that night, we could sense it.

Down in the dining room the noise of chattering was quietly elated, with the   excitement of the impending storm. Not sure why as all I felt was dread. We had experienced several heavy storms but nothing too bad since we had left Genoa, just the nine-day sea crossing that was a bit hairy, but that was more down to the alcohol rather than the movement. The ship was beginning to roll a little more than usual, but we took it in our stride. Or so I thought. As Tam and I walked back down to the cabin, we noticed how our feet were no longer hitting the deck but the deck hitting our feet. The last time that happened was when I was very drunk on Yellow Birds, that was me then, not the ship. Inside the cabin we just couldn't stand still. It dawned on me what the seat belts on the bunks were for. I swallowed deeply, a thought of capsizing entered my head, but I flicked it out just as quick. A person would have to anchored themselves to one place and hope for the best. I couldn't think like that. We passed by a porthole and noticed that the deck hand men were tying the doors and portholes down with ropes. There were notices up saying not to go outside. I glanced to the sea and the waves looked angry so high in fact that they were washing over the Lido (top) Deck. I was starting to get worried. The claps of thunder were piercing through my eardrums and the lightening ripped through the sombre grey sky cutting it in half. I voiced my concerns to Tamsin pointing to the weather outside. But she just shrugged and carried on.

We made it down to the cabin without falling over and didn't see a sole the entire way. I stared at the seat belt on my bunk as the previous thoughts were slowly coming back. Blocking them once again we managed to change our clothes, but I couldn't stay a minute longer. I felt as though I was in a washing machine. The walls were closing in on me and I was getting flung about everywhere and felt very sick. For some reason I decided trousers would be best for tonight and perhaps a Jacket. I mentally made a list of what to take in an emergency situation. It was a feeling I just couldn't shake. I had this vision in my head of us losing power. It would have been disastrous in those high seas for that to happen.

By the time we got to the disco it was full of staff. The barman Arturo was securing all the bottles, not having much luck and losing a few in the process smashing on the floor. Meanwhile the staff had found some chairs with wheels on, racing each other from one side of the bar to the other. Well that was one way of taking your mind off things. We could see the waves smashing over the top of us from the large windows that surrounded the disco. It was frightening to say the least. The sealant around the windows started to let water through, just a trickle, but it left me feeling even more uneasy than before. I glanced over towards Sharmez, who was looking very worried. She had been cruising for quite some time around those waters. She was from South Africa, Johannesburg to be exact. It was not surprising that she was concerned, at 24 years old, she had already been on the Oceanos a Greek ship which when down off the coast of South Africa in August 1991. The captain of that ship allegedly thought that he could conduct the evacuation better from the shore leaving the ship, passengers and crew to continue the abandon ship process alone.

The lights flickered on and off as we sat huddled in

a group listening to the storm roaring and raging outside. Trapped in our thoughts of what the night would bring. Our faces spoke a thousand words, yet nothing was said, it was like we were holding our breath willing the ships rocking to return each time it listed to one side. It was so dark with each flicker. Why is it always night-time when things get worse?

In our circle Sharmez retold her story of the night she thought she was going to die!

"The storm worsened as the evening progressed and when the first sitting of dinner was served, the waiters could hardly carry the trays of food without dropping something. Eventually the ship was rolling about from side to side so badly that crockery and cutlery began sliding off the tables and potted plants were falling over, much like tonight" she continued with a sombre look on her face as she carried on with her story.

"Whist we tried to make up time after being delayed at the start, due to a bomb threat, it started to get rough. There had been some repairs to the waste disposal system, but they had not been completed, which meant that a main ventilation pipe was not replaced. Passengers did report that at about 9pm, a muffled explosion was heard, and the ship lost power. The Oceanos started taking in water rapidly flooding the engine room and that cut the power, no engines nothing. I had thought that exact same thing earlier, when I looked at the windowsills.

"We were like that all night. Then by the morning the ship was listing really badly."

"That must have been so frightening" I whispered, trying not to interrupt too much.

"You know there wasn't an alarm, or any announcements given the whole time, so no-one knew what they were doing or what was going on. The ship was in real trouble, several passengers went to the bridge to look for the captain but found it unmanned. It was one of the entertainment staff that raised the alarm by radio. We had 16 helicopters that came to our rescue 225 passengers were hoisted off the top deck." She had tears in her eyes, the account of that terrible time was still very raw.

"Did you know that there was at least 5 people on here that were heading the evacuation that day." She added bewildered as to why they had not been frightened off working on the ships.

"Did it sink?" I asked questionably.

"Yes" you could see that her thoughts were right back there, and tears were cascading down her cheeks dropping onto her hands, which were tightly gripped together. I put a comforting arm around her shoulders, trying to reassure her that lightening doesn't strike twice in the same place. At least I hoped it didn't!

"All of the passengers and crew got off" she added.

I felt her pain and reassured her that things would be ok. Tam cruised over and pushed Sharmez on her wheeled chair across the dance floor. It was great timing. I watched Sharmez tears turn to laughter. The moment had passed, and the sadness had gone. The rest of us no so much, we were left stunned that the similarities were continuing to unfold right before our eyes. I shrugged it off and went to join the others on the rolling chairs. It was the only thing to do, to take our minds off the storm, and not to scare myself silly at the thoughts that were running out of control in my head.

The ship continued to roll about listing from one side to the other. At one point the ship lent so far, I really didn't think it wouldn't ever go back. The next couple of hours were much the same, I had never experienced anything so frightening in all my life. The night dragged on and on with every knock, creek, and bump as the ship hit the waves one after the other, I would hang on praying for it to stop. Even the deck crew and officer were concerned on that journey.

Eventually at 5am we headed off to bed as the weather had calmed a little and we were hoping that the worst was over.

Later that morning we stepped into the salon. It was a mess. Even though we had done our best to secure it, it hadn't been enough. Things were smashed, draws were open, it looked as though the proverbial bomb had gone off.

The Captain popped his head around the door to make sure we were ok. He was a lovely man, tall, grey haired, probably in his sixties, with kind eyes and a soft smile. He was in fact the Captain who was on the Achille during the hi-jacking back in 1985 Captain Gerado De Rosa. Some Palestinian terrorists seized the Achille Lauro on October 7th as it cruised off the coast of Egypt and held five hundred and eleven passengers and crew hostage for forty-four hours. The hi-jackers shot and killed a wheelchair-bound American passenger Leon Klinghoffer from New York and threw his body overboard before surrendering to Egyptian authorities. I had said earlier they had played the film Voyage of terror in the cinema, during our cruise to Egypt. Not a great time to remind people.

He came into the salon daily to check on his girls, as he liked to call us (in a fatherly way of course) having his espresso and a chat. Just before I left the ship, he gave me a copy of his manuscript about the events which took place during the hi-jacking, it was a very interesting read, and inspired me to one day write my story.

I looked out of the salon window and noticed the expanse of blue water that stretched in every direction. The rays of the sun shone through the window, onto the white floor where several pieces of broken glass had shattered during the storm, spraying rainbows around the room. It was like last night had been a dream, but one I did not want to repeat.

CHAPTER 13 - CHRISTMAS DAY

I was up on Lido Deck drinking my hot frothy cappuccino watching us come into Port Louis in Mauritius on Christmas day. It was full of numerous buildings and monuments that felt rich with a diverse colonial history. The Pagoda is a central feature of Port Louis Chinatown, which was and still is one of several China Town. Its entrance was marked by a large "Friendship" gate, just east of the Central Market. The site was the traditional location of homes and shops of the Chinese community, which was dominated by descendants of the Hakka Chinese, who first went to Mauritius in 1826. Chinatown is now home to a more diverse community but preserves its original appearance and contains many small shops and restaurants.

We were travelling to the south of Port Louis to the longest beach on Mauritius, Flic en Flac, which is known for its beautiful turquoise lagoon. Flic en Flac was quite a lively seaside village with its beachfront being conveniently close to restaurants, bars and shops.

I had never had a Christmas like this before. We were off to a nice hotel. That would be a change from rain, snow, sleet or anything else the British weather had to throw at us. I was meeting Tamsin and Rachelle at the crew gangway about eight, but for some reason I couldn't sleep. Not sure if it was the excitement of coming into port or that it was Christmas. I wasn't sure, I had no presents to open, so it can't have been that. I was treating myself to a phone call home to Mum, and Dad, so maybe the excitement of speaking to them was playing a huge part. I had so far experienced some amazing things and had lots to tell them. I was certainly feeling different from when I last saw them. I had grown as a person and my confidence was a lot better than when I left the UK. I had finally found my tribe on board the ship. Lots of people from diverse back grounds all having a story of why they went to sea. Either running away from or running to something. That said we all seemed to understand each other, and respect that our stories were left very much behind, and new ones were being created each day with each new experience. No-one had a bad word to say about anyone else. It was the best place for friendships and trust. The people whom I had met on the ship all seemed to have something in common. I know I was defiantly running away from, arguments with my family, never feeling as though I belonged there, always being on the back foot with everything. Standing on the outside looking in through a mirror. My Mum and Dad getting on with their lives after the divorce marrying different people, not realising that the two people they had created had borne the bruises from the transition. I felt alienated from Mum and Dad, by their choices which were not so great. I had only just turned 15 when they divorced, not knowing who I was, trying to study for my exams. It was a confusing time. A blur in fact. Most people my age seem to remember their exam and the last days of secondary school. For me it's a time I have blanked from my memory, as it was so painful. My world turned upside down and dissolved into the abyss. Everything I had ever known, my stability my home just disappeared over night. I went from being a young child to growing up, in a matter of days, to look after myself whilst Mum lived in a different house and Dad tried his best to work and look out for us. It didn't really turn out like that, as the arguments would take over and the hurt would be thrown into the mix. Looking back, we never really sat down and spoke about things in a calm way. Never relaying how we felt. We just had to put up and except the changes for Dad and us kids. I for one found it so distressing, my Mum was my world, she was my stability and the person who I related to the most. When she left it hit me hard and left a massive gap in my heart. She turned out to be a person I whom I didn't really know until later in life.

I had found my vibe, my tribe and a sense of belonging in amongst all of us different nationalities no body belonged, yet we were happy together. It was remarkable. Being excepted for who I was and loving every minute of it. I felt nothing was impossible and all was acceptable.

I met the girls at the bottom of the gangway where we hopped into a cab. The smells were amazing, very aromatic, it smelt like frangipani (Hawaiian lei flowers) and other flamboyantly flowers. The hotel itself was situated right on the beach front. Large and white in all its glory. Huge pillars supporting heavy walls. Balconies popping out as if supported by thin air. We marched in disguising the fact that we were not guest, acting very confident as if we stayed there, (you had to do this, so you could use their facilities).

We walked straight through the fresh-looking foyer with its flowers and statement pieces to either side and an ornate water fall in the centre. There were enormous doors that opened onto a veranda which surrounded the cocktail bar, the wide steps made of polished white stone, ascended between two marble handrails lined with sweet perfumed hanging baskets. At the end was a jellybean shaped pool which spread out onto another terrace which flowed down towards the beach. There were palm trees and tropical plants everywhere.

"Paradise," I said out loud with a sigh of contentment (I'm sure I said that about Bazaruto?) But again, here I was looking out at this spectacular scene.

We laid our towels out and sat down. Rachelle had disappeared and turned up with three delicious looking cocktails with umbrellas and everything.

"Tequila sunrises all round." She said "A thank you treat from me to you" We put our glasses together and toasted

Christmas day.

We had decided on pizzas for our dinner of choice, not very exotic I know and still Italian, but it was needed and very tasty. We followed with some ice cream of tropical fruit with pineapple bowls and lots of cream sprayed on the top. We sat and looked out at the ocean. Tam was telling us about life back home. She came from the North in Yorkshire a much slower place to us. She had always wanted to travel and see the bright lights of the big cities. Her home life was very similar to mine albeit a few year ahead as her parents split when she was 10 years old. Her Dad met someone else and left her with her Mum. The exact opposite of mine. She explained the hurt she had felt, but they managed to work things out between them and kept things friendly for the kids. She had one brother who was older than he, he had left a few years before she did. He was a bit of a loose cannon and would fly off the handle at the slightest thing. That made Tam very uneasy and a little   frightened. She never quite knew if it would turn nasty and really didn't want to hang around to find out. So, she applied to the ships to make her own way in life and get away from home.

I headed for the phones in reception and dialled Mums number. Mum was a very organised and matter of fact sort of person. She was smaller than me in height, with the most amazing brown eyes. She had short blonde hair, well she did when I left anyway, but who knows, she did like to change her hair colour very often, whenever the mood struck her. Very rarely did I do it. If I did it was usually to sort out a disastrous attempt that she had made herself.

" Merry Christmas Mum, you're never going to guess where we are?" I told her and of course, she couldn't believe it.

She was very emotional on the phone as she worried about me all the time and would constantly think about the safety aspect. Very much like I am now with my own daughter. I reassured her that we were like a big family on board ship all looking out for each other. She seemed happier knowing that, but you know what Mums can be like. I filled her in on all we had done, missing out the bits about the scuba incident and the storms. It would only have made her worry more. She seemed a bit more upbeat than she had on other calls. I thought things may have been sorting themselves out. How wrong I was. They were unravelling at a speed of knots.

I quickly gave Dad a call and wished everyone Merry Christmas, going over the exact same conversation that I had just had with Mum. I did feel a bit like a stuck record, but I knew they would enjoy hearing about my adventures. I could tell Dad a little more as he was not as big a worrier as Mum was.

I had felt a little down walking back to the girls. Even though I was in my version of paradise, I missed them all so much.

By the time we got back to the ship it was time to put on our uniforms and head back to work for 5pm. No rest for the wicked even on Christmas day. There was no such thing as weekends or holidays. It was all the same only distinguished by cruise lengths and ports.

It was Tropical Night crew show time. We had been rehearsing for the last few days a Hawaiian themed tropical night. Where me and the girls would dress up in Hawaiian skirts and bikini tops and dance around in a set routine whilst shaking pom poms, and the lads would do their thing without the pom poms, whatever that was. Usually taking the preverbal mickey out of us.

My darling cabin mate had mentioned to the cruise director that I had been a part of a dance group back in the UK. So, she thought that it would be an idea if I did a solo dance in the middle of this routine whilst everyone looked at me. Of course, I didn't want to do it, but somehow, I got overpowered by the rest of the gang and talked into it, so did the shop manager Rodney who used to do gymnastics.

Before we got to do our dance number, we were back in the salon washing heads and styling hair like it was going out of fashion. Due to it being Christmas we had an influx of appointments.

Mrs Henderson was my next client from Cape Town. She was late 50's, a very robust woman. She was a couple of inches taller than me standing at five-four and extremely overweight. Her bosom was huge, resting on her belly with no definition of where one started and the other finished. She was well spoken, white and a strong Africans twang to her accent. I loved it, it sounded so different to anything I had heard. A real mix of posh and tribal. Her hair was so fine that the light was streaming through it from the window. She wore a colourful orange and yellow skirt with a sash reflecting the same running through it which cascaded down her back like a bride. Looking more like a troll waddling along. She sat down heavy in the salon chair, grabbed the brush from my hand and started to fight vigorously with the vast amounts of hair spray that she had used in her hair.

"Thank you, that's so kind of you to start me off" I said gently removing the brush from her hands. "I can take over now" I gentle carried on brushing whilst she explained exactly how she expected her hair to look. I found that quite a few of the passengers were very direct and intimidating at first. But once they relaxed, they would tell me their life story. Mrs Henderson was no different. She first told me about how she had to visit the doctor on board within the first hour to sort out her extreme constipation. She described the episode in so much detail that I could feel my bum cheeks clenching together at the thought of her trying to exhume the remains of the last few days' worth of waste from her body. Next, she told me about the reason for the trip. She had decided to treat herself and her husband to a second honeymoon. They had been married for thirty years and their sex life had taken quite a knock. Apparently, he had been having an affair with her sister for the last 10 years.

She had walked into the bedroom after a day out with her brother to find the two of them having sex in their en-suit bathroom. She told me that she decided after she had calmed down, she decided not to leave or throw him out, but to ramp things up so he would quit seeing her sister and never want to leave her. I couldn't help but ask what she had done?

"Well, listen up, I went to one of those shops that sells sex toys and thought that I would try a few out on my husband. He never knew what hit him" she was laughing so hard her whole body was bobbing up and down. So much so I thought her chest would give her a black eye.

"Ok, I think I get the picture." I said sensing that she was about to get me song and verse of exactly what she did. That I could not unlisten to and the pictures already congregating in my head were enough to put me off my dinner.

"I take it that he stayed"

"Oh yeah, why wouldn't he now?" she added still chuckling.

"How is your relationship with your sister?" I asked quite stunned at how she could possibly have carried on a relationship after that.

"Oh, I have forgiven her, she was very badly hurt that my husband chose me over her, apparently he had been telling her for years that he would leave me to be with her and never did. She is now paying for it, as she really wanted kids and now it's far too late. The boat left that one behind. So, I truly feel she has had her comeuppance. I don't need to do anything to her that she has not already done to herself. We don't talk now. We just exchange pleasantries if we are at family functions. You know life's too short for argument." She was an inspiration to me. Her view to let things go and to not hold grudges stayed with me for a long time. I wish I could say that it taught me to do the same, but alas we are only human. Some of us better than others. However, it did teach me to look at Mums situation in a different light.

The timed had arrived for my debut appearance in our

Hawaiian night out on deck. The atmosphere was amazing, and the essence of the tropics sung throughout the decor scattered around the passenger seating area. From fake palm trees, to tropical birds of paradise distributed in the branches of the trees.

There I was, dressed in this god-awful costume waiting to go on and do my solo. I was so nervous. Sharmez handed me a drink of Tequila and I promptly gulped back the lot. I could feel the warmth rise up from my legs, through my torso and up my neck to my head, it was like a warm blanket being wrapped around my whole body. The music started, I could feel the thumping of the base vibrating through my body, we were off. Halfway through the routine I split from the group and stood in the middle. We were open to the elements, I looked up to see the sequin-silver stars scattered over the sky like embers of a dying fire winking down at me, illuminating the faces of the audience. A few turns and kicks then down into the splits. Everyone clapped, and then I spotted dreamy Italian officer, standing there in his white uniform looking as gorgeous as ever. He had a smirk on his face as if he were mocking me. I felt painfully out of place, like a pepperoni that had mistakenly made its way onto a vegetarian pizza. I tried to stand, but my legs seemed to be stuck. I was desperate to get the attention of the other dancers when Mal spotted I was in trouble. She led her conger line around me, dancing and waving the pom poms to distract the audience while I clambered to my feet as gracefully as possible. I managed to keep up the facade until I could make my way for the exit. I was mortified, not only had I shown myself up to all the passengers and staff, but to dreamy officer. I was so cross with myself for the way I was feeling, so I stumped off to my cabin to lick my wounds.

Tam had come to my rescue and convinced me to go to the disco, in her usual way. On this particular occasion, I had sulked by pulling the curtains around my bunk, in an attempt to shut the world out. Tam had crept in, smudged her make up over her face, making her eyes black and dark, her face was white with cream. She put a coat hanger in the back of her clothes and poked her head through the curtain. Giving me the fright of my life. I laughed until my ribs hurt. She was such a   nutcase. It did cheer me up though.

We sauntered in chatting and laughing about the events that took place earlier in the cabin. I loved the way that Tam would always make me feel better. We ordered our traditional Tequila slammers and set about finding somewhere to stand. I turned around to find a hiding place and I came face to face with dreamy Italian guy.

He finally spoke to me in excellent English. His name was Enrico, he was from Naples, he stood about six-foot-tall with a dark complexion and the deepest, darkest black hair and very white teeth. The contrast hit me with a tingle in my stomach.

After a shaky start of falling over my words, not quite knowing what to say, the conversation started to flow. He had managed to stay put for more than a few   second.

He bought me a drink and we just chatted all night about his travels and how he loved his job. Looking back, he never really told me much about his family or   personal history, or home life. That was common onboard, you never really pushed that hard about personal matters. That really should have sent alarm bells ringing in normal circumstances, but at that age I didn't really think about those things, and the people on the ship never really discussed their home lives much, unless it was joyful.

I had, had enough drink for one night, I was now on my third or fourth Tequila and feeling the effects a little more than I wanted to. My head was spinning, and I was starting to see a double shadow around everything.

We chatted some more about the differences between Italy and England. I felt transfixed in that moment, lost and speechless by his mere presence. He was so   handsome, a beautiful man. A twinkle in his eyes and a mischievous manner about him. The evening drew on and the music was loud, to the point that we could no longer here ourselves speak, so we made for the outside Lido Deck. The ocean breeze whispered passed my ears and tousling my long dark hair over my shoulders. It had certainly grown a lot since leaving the UK. A piece got stuck in my eyelash, Enrico drew closer to remove it, just close enough that I could feel the warmth of his breath on my lips. Longingly looking into my eyes as if transfixed to the spot. He looks to my mouth following the outline with his eyes. Exploring my entire face, as if searching for something which had been lost to him a long time ago. This was no good. I remembered the conversation that I had with Mrs Chapman earlier in the cruising about how the men on board new exactly how to get what they wanted and not to trust any of them. I had to get out of there. Too much excitement for one night, and with that I made my excuses and left, leaving Enrico bemused and   encouraged all at the same time.

I was drawn to Enrico, but I really didn't want it to take over my adventures. I knew that if I let him in, I would get attached and not concentrate on the reasons I was there in the first place, then I would get heartbroken. It was the way my life had always gone, repeating the same scenario over and over. Not this time, I was the master of my own destiny, and this time things would be different. Was I finally growing up and learning by my mistakes? I hoped that was the case, but only time would tell.

CHAPTER 14 - HAPPY NEW YEAR

I felt like I was trapped in an endless sea of people. There was another crew show planned, not the Tropical Night but a Rocky Horror show. It was as busy as ever with copious amounts of hair ups for the captain cocktails. Mrs Henderson had frequented the salon filling me in on more of her doctor visits and her husband's   obsessiveness over the sex toys she had bought. Quite an eye opener

I had also been secretly seeing Enrico on a nightly basis, breaking my resolve of not getting involved with any-one. He had contacted me the following night asking if I had liked my rose, he had left a while back. That was it I was smitten. It wasn't Tam and Rachelle after all.

It was becoming a regular occurrence that once I had finished my partying with my friends, I would run the gaunt-let to his cabin. Being together with someone on ships for a couple of weeks was like the equivariant of six months on land. It was all very intense. I made my ascent up to Lido Deck, passed the pool, onto the stairs, passed the funnel, up some more stairs, which took me outside the corridor where the officer's cabin was. It was so quiet up there, just the sound of the wind rushing through my hair, and an eerie naughty feeling knowing that I shouldn't be anywhere near their cabins. I would look through the round port hole to make sure no one was coming, then stepping inside the doorway I could smell the wafts of aftershave,   expensive I think, tickling my nose. The smell of men, Italian men. The aroma was overpowering, but the anticipation got the better of me and I continued into the   corridor. My heart was pounding, I had to go quickly, or I would get caught, that could be a difficult one to explain away. The Captain didn't encourage relationships between officers and other members of staff, but there were a lot going on. If we got caught , we would most definitely get disembarked, not the officer. I had committed to the long gauntlet of cabins, with nowhere to hide. Enrico's was the last one before the bridge on the right. I kept going until I reached his door. I turned the key that he had given me and slammed the door shut behind me. Leaning against it trying to recoup my breath. I could hear my heart thundering in my ears, sweating profusely and trying to stamp out the giggles that were trying to escape my mouth. The relief was amazing, I hated it yet loved it all at the same time. The adrenaline rush was hitting me hard. My little ritual had become a bit of a habit. Since the first night out on Deck, I had arranged to meet Enrico at the disco bar later the following night. I hadn't told anyone as I wasn't sure what I wanted to do about it. If anything.

I first saw him lent up against the bar with a beer in one hand and eating nuts with the other. He looked so cool and foreign, standing there in his white officers uniform. I could hardly believe that he wanted to be with me. I gave myself a pinch and walked over. His lips brushed against my cheek as he bid me a very seductive hello. He whispered in my ear how gorgeous I looked, I thought my legs would give way there and then. It didn't take much to draw me in, the words of Mrs Chapmen kept knocking in my subconscious but I just stupidly ignored it and let myself fall for the attention I was given and so, it began, the relationship I never wanted, but really longed for.

Enrico's cabin was large with a double bed and a huge window looking out to the ocean. It was lovely by comparison to mine, and I'm sure one of the only reasons that I continued to go there. Well, maybe not the only reason, he had a private   en-suit bathroom that always smelt so nice with his after shave. The excitement and late nights, early mornings were starting to take a toll on me. I was having around two hours sleep a night. To compensate I started to sleep during my two-hour lunch break in the day. Tam was enjoying having our cabin to herself and neither of us asked the other questions about what was going on. My relationship with Enrico had leapt to the next level and I had started to get attached. Much to Tams dismay. She warned me to keep him at arm's length and not to get too involved. It was time to grow up and except the consequences that I was surely heading for.

I couldn't help thinking back to the time on the beach earlier on in the cruising, when my time was my own and I had walked down to the water's edge on the beaches that we frequented. The sand was gentle and warm beneath my feet. Tips of shells peeked from holes, made by little creatures. Mini dunes gradually crept further into shore as the waves pushed them back up the beach. The sun rays peacefully floated on the warm water, and not a cloud to be seen in the brilliant blue sky. I could feel the tension easy out of my body, and I allowed my toes to touch the turquoise blue water. I loved that feeling and missed it terribly. The freedom I felt was intoxicating. It had all changed when I meet Enrico, my time was no longer my own, physically and mentally, constantly thinking about him. I was becoming a little resentful of my time being hi-jacket like that. Yet on the other hand I was loving the attention and the fact that he seemed to really care about me. He always made sure I was ok and had everything I needed.

We spend many a trip out together, hand in hand v ing through the surf on some amazing beaches and ¹ Watching the sun go down up on the Lido Deck invited to the officer's mess for dinner with th the rest of the officers, which was a little usually didn't encourage relationshi very lovely to me, and spoilt me rot⁺ wine.

It was Rocky Horror night and the salon had been busy with the formal night's hair and make-up appointments again. There was a lot of anticipation for the night ahead, ringing in the New Year on a number of occasions, as we went through the different time zones for each nationality who were on the ship. Passengers and crew.

We were just finishing up with the last clients, when the dancers appeared at the door. They wanted to have their hair and make- up done for tonight's Rocky Horror show, which we gladly obliged. It was nice to do something very different from the monotony of similar hair styles being produced for our slightly older clientele. At some point during their transformation, all three of us were talked into doing the Time Warp dance on stage with them. How did that happen? at least that time it wasn't just me.

Sharmez put the music on in the salon, from our small stereo, and all four dancers got up and started doing the Time Warp. Tam joined in followed by me then Rachelle. It was hilarious, in such a small space as well. The Captain just so happened to walk past at that moment and poked his head in to see what all the noise was about. We all stopped and looked at him guiltily, waiting for his reaction. Thankfully he laughed and found the whole thing quite a spectacle. He left as quick as he came, we could hear him still chuckling as he walked down the corridor . We had been ushered down to the dressing rooms of the dancers and found ourselves being kitted out in black leather hats and jackets, black make up with black lipstick, netted tights and thigh length boots. Well we did look funny, but also very effective.

Off we went to the bar to get our Tequila slammers, some-w it had become a ritual before any show, it also gave us tle Dutch courage.

We leapt onto the stage to carry out our routine it was h fun. All of the cast, entertainers and dancer were full make up and leathers. What a sight, all doing the

Time Warp, amazing.

"With a jump to the left," the music played on, we followed the lead of the dancers and finished to a wonderful applause from the audience. It was magical and exhilarating.

After the show, I needed some solitude. It gets a little over whelming to share every waking hour with people 24/7, 365 days of the year. I stood on the Lido Deck looking towards shore and the lights of the bars and restaurants that were glowing, a warm breeze glided through the fine hairs on the back of my neck. I just stood there taking in the smells and the atmosphere seeping through from the   passengers enjoying their holidays. *What a life I have* I thought. Happily standing there gazing out to sea, my mind wanders to Mum. I wondered how she was. The last conversation I had with her she seemed better, more upbeat. But she was also extremely good at disguising her anguish from the world! I couldn't help worrying about her. I was so far away from her, a lump appeared at the back of my throat, as I pushed the tears back from the little triangles at the corners of my eyes. I was overwhelmed with emotions. I had no place to put them and nothing to calm the anxiety that kept creeping up on me. I had to take my mind off the thought of   impending doom. Where was that coming from? The gut feeling that something bad would happen to my Mum and that I wouldn't be able to reach her. I needed to get out of there, back to the noise that stems the thoughts in my mind.

Tamsin was busy with one of the photographers Ant. *When had that happened? or had that happened?* I thought. I expect when I was with Enrico, Tam may have felt a little pushed out. Gosh I hope not. That's awful. I remembered back to my school days. I had felt that way, when one of my best friends suddenly got a boyfriend and disappeared off the scene. I didn't understand then why or what I had done, and now I was doing it myself. I felt terrible and decided even if Tam had found someone to keep her company, I didn't want her to feel that way. I had to slow things down with Enrico.

He asked me earlier when I saw him at the hotel, to go back with him to the ship, and as much as I was tempted, I stood by my resolution and said no. His face dropped, and he looked kind of angry. That had made me stick by my guns even more. I didn't want my whole experience on the ship to be about him. I felt so overpowered by him, in thoughts and obligation. My own doing of course, but none the less. I wanted to enjoy learning about the places and experiencing different cultures. I had felt myself being pulled into this romance. I had been here before at home with boyfriends. They would wine me, dine me, and then just as I was falling for them, they would disappear, no phone calls, no explanation, just silence. I didn't want that to happen again. Stick to my plan. Decision made.

Rachelle was very serious about her Zodiac guy Ben who she had been seeing, and the magician and his partner, Marco and Chris were going to tie the knot next cruise in the Seychelles, on board the ship, with the Captain conducting the ceremony. Chris was going to have a Hen night in the small room by the disco in the next couple of days, so that was something to look forward to.

The New Year's Eve night was quite something. After the show we had all been given Champagne and glasses to distribute to all the passengers. Wondering the decks. I couldn't help but wonder what everyone was doing back home. It was fast approaching the UKs New Year. So, on a whim I decided to do something about my impending doom feelings, I went to the radio room. I asked the officer if I could call home. He confirmed but told me it would cost an absolute fortune. I didn't care. I needed to call Mum. She was over the moon. It was exactly what I needed. I swallowed the bill and Mum said she would split it with me. She was fine of course, happy to hear my voice as short as it was, I had felt so much better. The trouble with being on the ship, is that you can get so caught up in the torrent of life on board, then when a moment comes of a little peace when you can think, you can get engulfed by feelings of home sickness. That night I could feed the urge to call home and I did, but it was not always possible.

The Celebrations continued way into the night and the next morning and long after the passengers had gone to bed, we took refuse in the crew bar, after changing from our wonderful Rocky Horror clothes. The drinks were about fifty cents each (U.S) and they were no way near the sizes of a standard measure they were much larger, double, triple the quantities. My favourite was Kahlua and milk. It was creamy, a little like Bailey's. Lovely on the taste buds but terrible on the waistline. It was fantastic in there. No passengers, no pretence, just good honest fun. The Latino guys would play their salsa music and be dancing, all hips and thighs vibrating at every beat. Some of the crew from the laundry would be in the corner playing cards. There was smoke everywhere, in those days it wasn't illegal to smoke inside the ship. The air was thick and heavy with it. Some of the entertainment staff were singing and laughing. It was just a fantastic atmosphere. I fell into bed around six, having an hour sleep then back in the salon at eight. Gosh how the months went on like that. Good job I was young.

CHAPTER 15 - THE HEN PARTY

We had a few surprise planned for Chris. The guys in the kitchens were making her a cake and putting on a small buffet for us. Plus, two of the cruise staff Bert and Frank had a surprise for her and us all apparently.

Bert and Frank were two very funny guys. They were both from South Africa, Durban, I believe, and they were always playing practical jokes on each other. These two guys had never meet before joining the Achille Lauro, but they just hit it off.

Bert was around six foot three, short, dark wavy hair, with freckles on his nose. Frank on the other hand was five foot ten, with mid length blonde hair, cheeky smile and the most amazing blue eyes. They were both hysterical to have around. Never looking sad always, a smile on their face. I think they just never took life too   seriously.

We made our way up to the room next to the disco. The curtains had been drawn, to stop the passengers looking in, and the decorations were ready to be hung. We set about the tasks at hand of decorating and making the room look amazing with streamers and balloons pinned strategically around, some looking like phallic symbols. Max the DJ came in with some music and mobile disco lights for us. Max was Italian, unshaven, large brown eyes and very tanned. Whinny one of the petite pursers on the reception desk had eyes for him, she was south African also coming from Durban, lovely bubbly girl. At ten O'clock we had finished. The decorations were up, the music playing, the cake and food in place and all the girls were there ready for Chris to make her entrance.

Hanna from the shop brought her in   blindfolded.

The lights were off, and you could hear titters and whispers coming from every corner around the room. Suddenly everyone let out a loud

"SURPRISE" and the blindfold dropped to the floor. The look on Chris's face was priceless. The music went up and Hanna pulled out a piece of see through fabric to put on Chris's head, representing a veil.

All the light went off and the room was plummeted back into total darkness, the music changed to 'You Can Leave Your Hat On' by Joe Cocker. Back in the 80's the soundtrack was taken from the movie 'Nine and Half Weeks' with Mickey Rourke and Kim Basinger. Now it was more well-known from 'The Full Monty.' Max appeared from nowhere, pointing the red spotlight to the door. In walked Bert and Frank in black suits and Trilby Hats. The music carried on with

"Baby take off your coat and take off your shoes" so that's what the lads did. They crept into the middle of the room, in a sultry manner, still only lit by the two red lights. At that point we realised what was going on, and a chair was pushed onto the dance floor for Chris to sit on. Everyone was laughing, not quite believing that Bert and Frank were about to do a strip. All eyes were glued as the song continued.

"Raise your arms in the air" the boys did that and slipped off their ties. They danced around rubbing their bodies up and down Chris who was mortified, but really enjoying it just the same. She giggled whilst turning a crimson red. They walked around one by one getting her to undo their shirts, which fell to the floor. The girls went wild. Laughing, we started to clap in time to the music. Some of the girls were screaming

"GET 'EM OFF". Frank put his hands up as if to say, calm down all in good time. Then laughed and joined Bert back beside Chris. They lifted her up and gently put her on the floor, laying her down so they could pulsate, their bodies over the top of her. It was a good job that Marco wasn't there as he was a very jealous guy. The song was reaching a climax to

"You can leave your hat on" whilst the two lads pulled off their trousers and landed on their knees in front of all the girls, who went bananas with screams and laughter. It was hysterical. Thank goodness they stopped there as I think they would have caused mayhem amongst the girls if they had gone any further. We cheered and clapped and went wild when the lads finished. Bless Chris she took it all in her stride, I would have died with embarrassment if it had been me. The night ended on a high with us all talking about how brave Frank and Bert had been and danced until the early hours of the morning. I felt for any passengers that had walked past listening to us lot carrying on, there was a sign on the door saying 'Private Function' so hopefully that cleared things up.

We had to get ready for embarkation the next day in Durban, and I wanted to call Mum to clarify that she was ok and wasn't hiding something. Plus, we were sailing earlier that day, we were heading to Mozambique and the Seychelles.

CHAPTER 16 - TWO-WEEK CRUISING

It was finally my turn on the phone, so I quickly rang Mums work number. She picked up on the first ring. I filled her in on all the exciting stuff we had done and informed her of our impending departure to the Seychelles. Mum had some awful news, she told me that her and Al had to move back to Stevenage, as the company in Cornwall wasn't making enough money. Al wanted to go back and work for the sunblind company that he was at before. Al was the M.D for this company and it was there that the two of them had meet. Mum went to work there as his secretary. She had in fact divorced my Dad to be with Al. He had a really bad reputation for the ladies at the time. Everyone tried to warn her, but she didn't listen. She had sounded so deflated on the phone. I knew how much she loved it in Cornwall. She had moved down there when I was 18 and lived in Car-green and I had moved to Plymouth to be close to her. At the time I couldn't bear to be parted from her, she was my rock. I knew how much it was hurting her to go back, she had said she would never return. Now for some reason, she was some four years later doing   exactly that. Something was not right. I couldn't put my finger on it, but she was not letting me in at all. Al had been commuting back and forth for the last few months, which has taken its toll a bit. Looking back, that's really when Mums problems started.

Her relationship with Al was always a bit strained. When I left for London after the fire at the store I worked in, I was convinced something was up. Mum seemed distant and distracted but I shrugged it off. I couldn't help wondering what she wasn't telling me. I got that same feeling when talking to her on the phone. The impending doom was back with vengeance. When we hung up, I couldn't help but feel really sad. I missed her so much, my heart was heavy like a brick that had been made out of gold

Time passed so fast, especially when we had been rushed off our feet with embarkation days, booking appointments, sail-a-way's, and the day to day hairdressing. The clients were fantastic, all very happy and willing to chat about their daily lives back home. Yet you always get one client that surprises you.. I had my sixth client of the afternoon, a lovely lady called Martha from Kentucky U.S.A . She was in her seventies, small and frail in a shell suit with bright yellow and blue birds printed on the material. She was so cute that I just wanted to gather her up and look after her. I bet she has saved all her life for this holiday. So, I went to work and gave her a beautiful set and a mini facial explaining everything I had used to create her new look. She was over the moon. On the way to the reception she dropped some money in my hand as a tip. Not wanting to look at what she gave me I just slipped it in my pocket and carried on giving the bill to Rach as she was on reception. I asked if she was happy with her service and that I had written down everything I had used on her docket in case she would like to pick something up at a later date. With that I left her to pay. I was just cleaning my section for the next client when Rach came bounding over skipping and clapping. I wondered what she was doing .

"Oh, Jo you clever girl. Your client Martha has only gone and bought everything on the list you recommended. Her bill was over five hundred dollars. I can't believe it. How did you know?" I had no idea what she was talking about. Apparently, Rach told me that she was one of the wealthiest people on the ship, occupying the penthouse suit. I would never had believed it . I was shocked, I stood back leaning on the chair for support, just digesting what she had said. I smiled and thought *good for you Martha* I slipped my hand in my pocket and felt the cash she had given me earlier. When I pulled it out, I nearly fell over, she had tipped me a crispy one-hundred-dollar bill. It was and still is the largest tip I have ever received from one person.

It was no time before we docked in Hell Ville Nosy Be just off the northwest coast of Madagascar. Nosy Be pronounced 'Nossy Bay' meaning big island is a very popular beach destination with clear turquoise water of the Indian ocean 'paradise'. It was renowned for Omura's whale spotting, (later in the year July – August time) all year-round dolphins and turtles could be seen.

We anchored off the coast and began to see small boats in the distance .These were a few of the natives paddling towards us in some of the most primitive boats I have ever seen. Some had home-made sails and many of the boats had been hand carved from tree trunks.

We boarded a tender to shore. We were starlight cruise staff on that day (tour guides), taking care of passengers, who were on an excursion to a small part of the Island. Back in our stripy t-shirts with starlight logos and white shorts, we ushered thirty passengers each onto buses. We had responsibility for our passengers making sure we counted on and off exactly the number we started with. I had been given a brief the night before, about the island and what sort of things to point out, we travelled to local villages and markets. I had never done anything like this before and suddenly became very nervous. I had however mastered my demonstration technique on board the ship, so I thought it best to apply the same tactics.

The passengers were settling in their seats, and we set off. I frantically looked at my sheet to see what was first, by the time I looked up, we had passed it. *Oh god this was harder than it looked.* Again, and again this happened. I needed to say something. The passengers were starting to look bored and irritated.

"Good morning ladies and gentlemen and welcome to

our excursion around Nosy Be." I said convinced that I could wing it. I stated that the name Nosy Be meant Big Island. That's it I thought I would read from the sheet giving some information out. Thank goodness they couldn't see me as I was at the front talking into the microphone. It seemed to be working as the passengers were starting to take an interest through the windows as I told them what to look out for. I've cracked it I thought. I got a little cocky on the way and thought I would make some jokes. I pointed out some of the local women washing their clothes on rocks by the water's edge, stating that it was the local laundrette, and that a shack on the other side of the Road was a super- market. A couple who were from England found it funny, but the South African passengers did not. Maybe my sarcastic British sense of humour was not called for on that occasion, but the Brit's appreciated it. I should have just stuck to the plan and read from the sheets.

We stopped just outside a village entrance near the beach. I stood there   momentarily looking down the first narrow street, well dirt path, it was about 15-foot wide riddled with potholes, mud and protruding trees roots. I counted off the   passengers one by one to make sure I could count the same back on.

On each side of the path were native dwellings, some made of grass with thatched roofs, and some were made of cinder and trees. There were no windows, and no doors. The floors were just dirt.

The native people were all going about their daily activities, washing clothes, on the rocks scrubbing them by hand, some were bathing young children in what looked like large cooking pots, and some were working on carvings that we could buy. All were bare foot. I could feel the heat from the dirt track through my trainers, how could they stand on it? Sometimes some of the dust would get kicked up and land on my leg like blistering ashes from a fire. They looked at us with the same curiosity as we looked at them, the difference being that we were in their world.

Patricia our cruise director was feeding a banana to a small monkey. She had been a cruise director in the area for over fifteen years, she certainly knew her stuff. Rob one of the other cruise staff on board had an Iguana on his shoulder, it was bright green, the Iguana not Rob. The native people had snakes around their necks, hanging there like it was an everyday occurrence. The hustle and bustle from the market was quite something, I bought some figurines from a local carver on the side of the Road, but I did not pay with money, I swapped my earrings for them. I did tell the chap that they were not real gold, but he didn't seem to care.

The image of the man had stayed with me until now, poor thing, he worn thread bare clothes and broken sandals on his feet. He was so filthy, and the smell was not pleasant, it was a cross between body odour, human wee and petrified fruit that sticks in your nostrils. I tried not to gag. I learnt not to take anything for granted and reminded myself constantly how those people had nothing and were so grateful for the smallest thing. *Has modern life spoiled us*? I think so. I thought as I wondered around.

Some of the passengers had gathered around Patricia and Rob to take pictures, it was like the little guy was used to it, he was relaxed, basking in all of the attention, quite happy with Patricia feeding it the banana without a care in the world.

I counted my passengers back on the bus, all were present and correct. I gave Patricia the thumbs up, but I noticed that Tamsin wasn't quite so calm, scurrying around like a headless chicken. She had lost one, a passenger that is, she was distraught. We wandered around the village trying to locate him, up and down the street we patrolled but with no joy. No sign. Rob gave us a whoop and a whistle, when the passenger was spotted wandering down the dusty track without a care in the world, totally oblivious to the trauma going on around him. He was suddenly surrounded by the local children. He was dishing out sweets like Charlie out of the Chocolate Factory. *Bless him* I thought, but I think Tamsin could have hung him out to dry judging by the look on her face.

The cruise director frowned and ushered him back on the bus with a full head count. Finally, the calm was restored, and the world was at peace with itself again.

We climbed back on the buses and took off to our next location. Lunch was being served in another village, local children from the small village school were going to do a rendition of an ancient dance which has been passed down through the ages.

I continued on with my explanation of the sights and local knowledge from my papers along the way until we arrived. The vision of the village was like something from 'Out of Africa'. Huts made of mud and cinder blocks and brown leaves for the roof tops on all sorts of different size buildings. All were decorated in brightly   coloured flowers and vines which were intertwined in the leaves and around the walls.

The smells were wonderful, my nose danced around with the sweet vapours of the local foods being cooked on an outside fire. It made my mouth water. Children were lined up outside their schoolhouse, (again made of cinder blocks) dressed in native yellow and red skirts and matching tops. They couldn't have been more than five or six years old. They were fabulous and so cute. They performed their local dance it was wonderful seeing the tiny kids doing their traditional dances. It lasted a good five to ten minutes and the passengers loved it. A huge applause went up at the end and some were even standing up clapping with excitement. The children were   beaming. It was a fabulous sight to witness.

What a happy lot of people I had. The trip was a complete success even with Tamsin losing a passenger. Patricia was so happy and impressed with our work and attitudes that she asked us to do another one in Mombasa. I had better research better and be prepared for that one.

Once we boarded the ship, we were so busy, Rachelle and I were conducting our artistic skills by putting hair up into beautiful chignons and buns for the formal captains cocktails, whilst Tamsin would complete their looks with breath taking transformations.

The passengers did laugh at me, when I opened my draw not only did, I have mousse, hairspray and such like, but I also kept a can of cockroach spray. Sometimes in the middle of doing a client's hair one of the little beauties (cockroaches) would scamper up the mirror quite oblivious to where they were let alone the effect they had on my clients. Inevitably I had to quickly neutralise it to stop it multiplying and releasing its babies to produce even more of the dam things. Apparently, the ship was crawling with them. At night I would lay awake thinking about them, with both my fingers in my ears and a peg on my nose, holding the sheet across my mouth to stop them climbing in to a warm and secluded environment like my ear canal a lovely sight I was. I was so worried that they would crawl in whilst I was asleep. Silly I know, they never did. Not that I was aware of!

CHAPTER 17 - CROSSING THE EQUATOR

We arrived at Mahé the largest Island in the Seychelles, twenty-seven kilometres long and eight kilometres wide. It was and still is a dramatic island of granite outcrops and mountains rising from the sea. Mahé is surrounded by coral reefs, which protect the beaches and ensure tranquil seas and Azure lagoons. The coastline is crinkled with picturesque coves, stretches of sugar-white sand and beaches crisscrossed with bird footprints and littered with shells. Coconut palms stretch over sculpted granite boulders. We decided to head off on our own and hire a jeep for the day. Tamsin and I had not really driven since we had got onboard for obvious reasons, but here they drove on the same side as us in the UK. So how hard could it be?

It was amazing, we had no roof so totally open to the elements. The Roads were quite rough and most of the residence treated it like a racing track, a little scary at times swerving out the way of a local trying to get somewhere in a hurry. The coves were incredible, white sandy beaches with palm trees protruding out over the red-hot sands .The heat waves rising up and the ocean just gently caressing over the   shoreline. Not a soul to be seen. We stopped at an inlet, staring out at the   magnificent paradise. We were just standing there digging our feet into the hot sand and letting the small particles of crushed shells slide through our toes. It was out of this world. I kept pinching myself to make sure I was not dreaming. It was   everything and more that I had ever dreamed about from my bedroom window back home as a kid.

After a couple of minutes, I was starting to feel a little hot so I bunny hopped down to the sea. The sand was so hot you couldn't bear to leave your feet on it for more than a few second. It must have been a funny sight. I looked out to sea taking in the tranquillity of the it all, looking at where the stunning blue sky merged with the clear blue waters of the West Indian Ocean. It was so difficult to tear ourselves away from there. I never wanted to leave, not a care in the world. In fact, the world seemed a lifetime away. Reluctantly we got back in the jeep and carried on around the Island as much as we could before it was time to head back to the ship as darkness started to engulf us. The chap in the hire shop did warn us that night-time fell very quickly and there were very few lights on the Island. He was not wrong sure enough the sky was black, and the tiny specks of stars descended on us like a blanket with holes punch in it. The amount of stars was phenomenal. I had to stop myself looking at the sky and concentrate on the road ahead. The light pollution In Mahé was hardly anything compared to the UK. Mesmerising.

Over the course of the next week we stopped at a few of the Islands around the Seychelles each one out did the last with its paradise views and tranquil settings. Hard to imagine now looking out onto a dull, wet October day, sitting at my laptop again staring out of my window telling you all about my adventures. It was all that you would imagine it to be. We had experienced a glass bottom boat trip where the tropical fish were stunning with their fan tails and spinney fins and incredible colours and shapes.

The best was a bike ride around one of the Islands where no cars were allowed, and Aldabra giant tortoise lived. These ancient creatures can weigh well over 400kg and grow to be roughly 1.3m in length. Some individuals have grown over 250 years old, but most live between 80 and 120 years. Due to their long lifespan, they only reach sexual maturity at around 30 years old. Once they mated, the female will lay roughly 25 eggs in a dry, shallow nest.

Incubation takes up to 8 months. All this I learned from accompanying the passengers on excursions from the ship, and the best thing about it all was being paid for the pleasure.

Fantastic. I remember back to the training academy no one had mentioned that I would be doing this at the interview. Good job otherwise there would have been many more people applying for the posts.

On the way from the Seychelles we had the crossing of the equator ceremony. The tradition originated with ceremonies when ships passed the headlands that become a "folly" sanctioned as a boost to morale or have been created as a test for seasoned sailors to ensure their new shipmates were capable of handling long rough times at sea. Sailors who have

already crossed the Equator are nicknamed Shellbacks, Trusty Shellbacks, Honourable Shellbacks, or Sons of Neptune. Those who have not crossed are nicknamed Pollywogs, or Slimy Pollywogs. Anyone, passengers, crew, officers that had not crossed the equator before, went through a ritual. They were stood in the court of King Neptune and his court (usually including his first assistant Davy Jones and her Highness Amphitrite and often various dignitaries, who are all represented by the highest ranking seamen), who officiate at the ceremony. During the ceremony, the Pollywogs (people not been across before) undergo a number of increasingly embarrassing challenges, mainly for the entertainment of the other guess, and sentences to either the hairdressers, the doctors or dentist (on our ship). Where they would have horrid stuff such as spaghetti or beans pored over them or put inside their clothes. Then sentenced to the pool to finish with. Obviously, this was for passengers that were happy to take part, but the crew not so much of a choice, but an absolute necessity. It was great fun. Tamsin Rachelle and I oh and our want to be Steiner Stan the puppeteer all dressed up in white dresses with large red ribbons in our hair. The people that were sentenced to us had spaghetti poured on their heads and massaged in by all of us. It was hysterical. They then got taken to the poolside and thrown in. As you can imagine the pool was in a terrible state by the end. It did get cleaned thoroughly after.

Once all the passengers had been dealt with it was over to the crew. If you can imagine Simon, the comedian who was Neptune was standing on his royal chair commanding the
ceremony to take place he was dressed the part , no shirt, very tight shorts and staff (fork) he certainly looked the part. To one side there was a commotion going on as some of the officer had grabbed a rookie and placed him in front of Simon (Neptune) They went to town on this poor guy, he had to experience all three areas. It was the dentist that was the worst. He had eggs in his mouth with spaghetti. How he did not throw up I will never know. Us Spa girls were laughing so much we didn't hear the call of our names. When we realised that everyone was looking at us, it was like a comedy sketch. It fell silent for a moment, and then we just ran, in all different directions to escape the inevitable wrath of Neptune. The crowd roared with laughter. I never saw Tamsin run so fast or where Rachelle and Stan had disappeared to. I knew a few were in hot pursuit of me. I made sure they didn't catch me and ran down to my cabin. I really didn't want to do get caught. Unfortunately, someone must have predicted that would be where I would head for and the soldiers of Neptune were already waiting for me. My fate had already been sealed. I got marched up to the Lido Deck, my head hung low ready for my sentencing. The crowd were loving it. Clapping and laughing. The passengers that I had so readily heaped lots of spaghetti on , were now very willing to repay the kindness I had shown them. I got covered, and it was everywhere, in nocks and crannies I never knew I had.

After my soaking in the pool, everyone dispersed back to their cabins to get ready for the evening's entertainment. I certainly had had enough excitement for one day.

We all received a certificate to say we crossed the equator, and it was all in good fun. Needless to say, the pool needed a complete make over after.

CHAPTER 18 - A FAR CRY
FROM PARADISE

It had been three months since New Year's and time had started to drag a little, especially after we had finished the cruising around the Comoros, Zanzibar and Mombasa. Coming in and out of Durban and Cape Town had worn a little thin, as the passengers were not spending their money or time in the salon anymore, it was so boring most days. The sea days were the worst. I spent a lot of time in the crew bar at night and walking around up on Deck, trying to get fit. My bar bills were astronomical, the tips from passengers were non-existent. Not to mention I could no longer have advances on my wages as I had used them all up. Things were looking a little grim.

I hadn't seen Enrico for a few weeks, especially after I had told him that day that I didn't want to hang out with him, I only meant to slow things down but now it looked as though we had finished. I tried to past the time by doing demonstrations and joining in with the fashion shows, our tropical nights and sail away were always good fun. Singing and dancing around the pool as we departed Durban or Cape town with the next lot of victims , I mean passengers, but that was about it. Time in paradise was coming to an abrupt end. My heart was also starting to shatter in many directions, what with the worry of Mum and now the worry that Enrico didn't care about me at all.

Standing up on Deck with Tamsin we watched as the ship sailed into Southampton, a UK port. It was actually very exhilarating. The warmest clothes we had were those which we arrived onto the ship in, we had not needed much else other than shorts and T- shirts for the last six months.

Tamsin was jumping up and down waving her arms like some crazed monkey playing charades with her counter parts, she was also shouting really loud in my ear.

Our families were at the dock side. We could see them so easily. I don't know what I was expecting, but defiantly not to see them until I got inside the terminal.

I could see my Mum, her husband Alan, Dad and Trisha, Lily and her sister from Plymouth, and my brother, all standing there waving excitingly. It was amazing. I felt the emotions overflow and a big lump in my throat gave way as the tears stung my checks as they started to flow uncontrollably. The last six months had been quite a roller coaster of emotions. I had grown as a person and changed so much. I had finally grown up, I guess!

I joined in the shouting with Tamsin. The Captain popped his head out by the bridge and looked up laughing at us clapping his hands with joy, realising how happy we were. Our surrogate Dad had shown such warmth and consideration to us over the months, always looking out for us, even when we didn't realise it. He was such a family focused captain and could totally understand our excitement. Lovely man!

We stayed there watching and shouting until we had pulled alongside the dock and our throats had silenced us, closing up, dry and horse. We could actually speak to them from this point, without too much shouting. I told them to go and get a cuppa as we had a coast guard drill before we could get off. I would see them in the terminal. I quickly ran down to sort out the passes for them to get on board ship. They would love it. Perks of being crew.

I ran to my stations, just outside the salon. The emergency sirens went off about two minutes after the last passenger had disembarked. My heart always leapt out of my body when they started. They were so loud. I could only imagine the adrenaline that would run through my veins if I had to deal with the emergency for real. Thankfully that never happened to me.

We were the first to be inspected. I remember the coast guard saying,

"Ciao come stai" (Hello how are you in Italian) he said.

"Molto bene grazie" (very good thank you) I replied in my best Italian accent.

The coast guard asked me to name what was in the fire extinguisher in English.

"CO2" I said confidently. I had been practicing for the last week, we knew this was coming and it had paid off.

"Your English is fantastic" he said, very impressed by how fluent I was.

I chuckled.

"I hope so, I am English" I replied trying to wipe the smirk from my face. I could have got into trouble; I was obviously not taking it seriously enough.

The man blushed and grinned embarrassed that he had not realised his mistake.

Tamsin was trying not to wet herself as she had tears running down her face with the hysterics building inside her.

I had played this trick on a passenger before, who came into the salon and impressively in his pidgin English asked very loudly if I had any appointments available for his wife to have a blow-dry. I just couldn't help myself as I played alone pretending to not understand this poor chap as he repeated his request over and over getting louder and louder. In the ed I relented and put him out of his misery, when the frustration started to get out of hand, when he turned to his wife and said

" How on earth am I going to ask for a simple blow-dry, if no body speaks English" he said.

" Just ask me nicely and quietly and in English and I will see what I can do for you" I said smiling and laughing. He was a good sport and saw the funny side. It could have been very different but thankfully all was well.

My skin was very dark as was my hair and eyes I realised why he had made the mistake, but on the same level very impressed that the English officer had spoken in fluent Italian.

After the coast guard had left, we made a bolt to our cabin, grabbed our passes and left running to the gangway. We flew to the terminal not waiting for anyone. I spotted my family and leapt into my Mum's open arms. I had never been so happy to see them all. Tears rolling down our faces I gave her the biggest hug ever, trying not to squeeze the life out of her. The familiar smell of home engulfed me. I wanted to stay there forever, safe and sound.

In turn I hugged everyone. By that time there was not a dry face in the building. I guessed they must had missed me just as much. That was a surprise!

I lead them onto the gangway and up onto the ship. My Mum said she could already feel the boat move. I corrected her and said

"It's a ship Mum not a boat"

As I showed them around , the crew were greeting me in Italian, French and Spanish. My Dad was absolutely flabbergasted that I could speak so many languages. He didn't know that those were really the only words I knew, except for a few fraises in the salon. I didn't like to burst his bubble and tell him. I managed to take them onto the bridge and meet the

captain, which my Dad especially thought was brilliant. By the time we had had coffee and caught up on all the gossip it was time to say our goodbyes. The time speed passed like it had been sped up on one of those Benny Hill shows. On that occasion it was not fun.

We not only had to say goodbye to our families but

to all the south African friends who had spent the last six months with us. They had to disembark. The dancers and the crew staff. What a wrench. My heart strings were being pulled in so many directions. My true family and my surrogate family were leaving me left right and centre. I couldn't cope and just crumbled into a heap with tears tearing at my eyes.

It was so difficult, I had never experienced such friendship, nothing would be the same again.

The time just flew whilst my family were with me and it seemed like no time at all , that Tamsin and I were back up on the top Deck waving, a complete reverse to us coming in,

She looked at me with a half-smile unable to talk. She didn't really have to say anything as her face said it all. She had done this many time and obviously still found it just as hard as me. We walked back down to the cabin arm in arm in total silence.

We didn't do much for the next few days, we had travel agents on to report back to the different travel companies who advertise the cruises. The best night was watching Simon the comedian in the lounge bar the night before we docked into Genova for our last cruise before heading to Egypt and Israel. The ship was due to go into dry dock following that. All the crew were allowed in to sample the other side of life. It was great to see all the cabin staff and rope Deck crew, bar staff and cooks. The Chinese from the laundry and the South American's from the kitchens all dressed up to watch the show. Simon was on form he was really funny and so blue (rude) it had us all in stitches. It was a great night and certainly cheered me up.

CHAPTER 19 – VOYAGE OF TERROR!

Getting off the ship in Egypt was amazing. Port Said is a city that lies in the North east of Egypt extending about 30 kilometres along the coast of the Mediterranean Sea, north of the Suez Canal, with an approximate population of 603,787. The city was established in 1859 during the building of the Suez Canal. We had gone through this a few days before, I was really looking forward to it. Unfortunately, I did embarrassingly find the whole thing very boring. I guess you have to be an engineer or of that nature to appreciate the enormity of just what technology it took to build such an amazing phenomenon, just not my thing. It was and still is a very long and very slow artificial sea-level waterway, connecting the Mediterranean Sea to the Red Sea through the Isthmus of Suez. Constructed by the Suez Canal Company between 1859 and 1869, it was officially opened on November 17, 1869. The canal enabled ships , boats and such like a shorter journey reducing the journey by approximately 7,000 kilometres. The landscape didn't seem to change much during the whole time, but we were working so it didn't really matter too much to us. My Dad would have loved it, so I took as many photo's as I could in between clients, to show him when I returned home . Funny really when I look back on the photos now, they all look very similar.

We finally disembarked in Port Said the sun was scorching hot, but we had to remain covered up due to the culture. Women needed to cover their upper arms, cleavage, midriff and legs when visiting holy places. In tourist resorts, modesty was definitely the best policy, or you may attract unwanted attention, and we didn't want to upset the locals. The ship was dropping all passengers and crew who wished to disembark in Port Said and was picking us up in Port Alexandra. It was quite common apparently. Never the less it left me a little uneasy when we collected our passports and made our way through the customs into the terminal. Well shed, not exactly a terminal as such. The currency was Egyptian pounds, but we had to be careful of unscrupulous people who may have tried to give us piaster notes instead when giving us change. The bills look quite similar, so we were encouraged to get familiar with them before going ashore. We never gave them money until we had agreed upon a price. We got extremely good at this on our travels. Egypt's largest city is full of traffic, glorious mosques, palaces and bazaars, where shopping was excellent - as long as you bartered, haggled and then haggled again! The selection of museums was incredible. The most famous being the Museum of Egyptian Antiquities, which holds more than 100,000 relics and the

Archaeological Museum, where you can see the face of Tutankhamun, the boy king. We were heading in that direction and I was so excited about it, but I had to be patient. Just outside the city was one of the Seven Wonders of the ancient world - the Pyramids at Giza.

We teamed up with two of the shop assistance Charles and Hanna. We thought it would be better to travel in numbers. I don't think I would even attempt to do it today. We managed to get a good price with a cab and set off towards the Pyramids and Cairo. It took us quite some time to get there, travelling through some very arid terrain and some extremely dangerous check points. The soldiers carried huge machine guns and were dressed in black. They stopped the cab every time we came across one asking us if we had cameras or video cameras on us and wanted to see our passports. We denied having the cameras and nervously gave them our passports all on instructions from our cabbie. He told us that they would either destroy the film or even the camera on some occasions. This was mainly because we were not on an organized tour, and they didn't want any police or military accidentally or deliberately in your photos. It could be equated to spying. There was a presence of spiked wheel puncturing devices just in case anyone needed to be stopped quickly. Even within the cities and resorts police and tourist police (those dressed in white uniforms) were present in abundance.

The reason for the apparent police state was that Egypt was under a 'state of emergency', as it has been since 1981. The state of emergency was first imposed following the assassination of Egypt's president Anwar Sadat after he signed the peace treaty with Israel. Sometimes we heard that you would get a police escort through some of the area's mainly to protect us from these dangers, it could and did slow us down for hours. We also got our passports stamped several times. This was great as far as I was concerned, I was trying to get as many stamps as possible put in there, so later in life I could see where I had been. A little like collecting postcards.

The aroma in the air smelt a little stale, the Road ahead was bone-dry, not a trace of moisture. The particles got caught in my throat which made it so hard to swallow. If only I had brought some water. As I look out over the barren landscape to the horizon, I could see the shimmering heat waves rising from the dessert, no sign of life. Why would there be? I thought.

It felt like an eternity in the sweaty back seat. There was no air-conditioning inside, all we had was a faint breeze coming through the window. I stuck my head further out to try and capture it, but unfortunately there was nothing but warm air that lifted the damp hair from my temples.

One of the strangest smells I remember was Shisha smoking. This was also called water pipe, or Hubble bubble smoking. Sounds like a past time from a Harry Potter book. It's a way of smoking tobacco, sometimes mixed with fruit or molasses sugar, through a bowl and hose or tube. The tube ends in a mouthpiece from which the smoker inhales the smoke from the substances being burnt into their lungs. It smells like the incense Catholics burn in church.

As we came into Cairo in the street dozens of coffee shops, places where men traditionally went after hours to play backgammon, dominos, and smoke shishas. There was a definite lack of female presents.

We stopped and got out of the cab, we literally couldn't move without being approached by some vendor or another, from taxis (which was bizarre as we had just got out of one), to camel rides and horseback riding. It was unbelievable. I felt as if I had stepped onto a movie scene in the Raiders of the lost Ark. On one hand it was extremely irritating to be bothered so much, but on the other hand I couldn't help thinking how desperate these poor people must be to earn some money. They were only trying to make a living after all. Egyptians are very proud people. They refuse to beg. Instead, they operate under a concept called baksheesh. Some people think baksheesh means bribery, or an aggressive form of tipping.

Loosely translated, baksheesh means share the wealth. Kind of like if you have it, and I don't, you give some to me. Baksheesh can be taken to ridiculous heights. If you ask directions from someone on the street, chances are that person will expect baksheesh. We didn't ask. Our Cab driver called Ashmed, arranged for us to be taken to the Pyramids via camels. Once they had haggled a fair price, we were rounded up (literally) between a small group of men, with turbans and ushered into some dark stables in the shadows of the Pyramids. There were half a dozen camels and stallions' horses, they were used to give us tourist rides out to the great Pyramids. I must say that none of the animals looked in great shape. The horses had ill-kept coats, and bones that showed plainly through it, the knees knuckled over, and the forelegs were very unsteady. I felt so sorry for them. One came and nuzzled its head into my arm, so I stroked it carefully, being very weary of this huge animal. I was suddenly brought back to reality by a handler pushing me out of the way, so the camels could lay down to enable us to sit on them. Talk about no manners. I was yanked, and pulled, and thrown up onto the saddle with a thud as my bottom hit it with some force.

Tamsin was laughing as she so elegantly got on hers. Hanna the shoppie who was British, was as bad as me. She was slightly bigger than me, height more so than width, luscious long dark hair, which had been tied up in a simple top knot and beautiful olive skin.

The camel leaned forward until I was looking face down to the dirt, as it raised its rear legs first to stand. At that point I was holding on for dear life. There was only a small area to hold onto that was attached to the huge saddle. The camel tipped me backwards in the same unsightly manner until it was up on its feet. I tried to get comfy, but it was impossible. The other camels rose to the screams of the girls and Charles, much to the handler's surprise and amusement. Charles was Stans gay friend, we never did know if they had a thing going or not. The handlers lead us out towards the great Pyramids, wow what a sight it was. The dust rose from under the camel's hooves as they slowly ambled their way around, with a forward, then backwards and side to side motion. Yes, just like a ship, which I thought, was why they were called the ships of the dessert. Now it all made sense! Unfortunately, this was neither comfortable nor easy to manage and I hoped it would be a short journey.

The trip was a little longer than hoped and my rear was so painful I could hardly bear it, but the sights were amazing. The city of Giza was directly below the Pyramids and somewhat spoilt the view. I was under the impression that the Pyramids were in the middle of the dessert far away from everything. I was disappointed about that, but not so much now I was on a camel. However, the pyramids themselves did not disappoint. They were colossal structures which were built 3000 BC to 2300 BC. The largest and most remarkable of the pyramids were in several groups. The Great pyramid stands at an amazing 450 feet, burning into the dessert sky-line. It was a fantastic piece of engineering and remained the tallest structure in the world for some 3800 years. The pol-ished limestone shone in the sun giving it an eerie glow with what looked like electricity beaming from its summit, but in fact it was the heat ascending towards the blue cloudless sky.

We approached from the rear, so the camels could at least be in the shade for a moment. The heat was intensive to say the least, especially in the long trousers we had to wear. We were to be left there for a while, so the handlers could go and fetch some horses for our return to Ashmed. We entered one of the pyramids and had to crouch down for quite a distance until we got to the main area where the broken Sarcophagus resided. There was nothing else in there.

We looked at each other as if to say is that it. Shrugged and made our way back out again. It was cold, dark and a little eerie inside, again, that eeriness I seemed to feel around there was freaking me out a little.

We headed to the panorama area at the far side of the smallest pyramid (Menkaure) as it was a popular spot to take photos to get all three pyramids in one shot. Next, we headed to the Sphinx which looked as large as the pyramids but was very small. Near the Sphinx, you can walk through the Valley Temple of Khafre (next to Sphinx) & the Solar Temple (in front of Sphinx. The Valley Temple is interesting architecturally & also gives you a good vantage point for viewing The Sphinx.

We had just about finished our tour of the site when Ra-chelle noticed the handlers coming over. They had brought five stallions with them. Now I was much better at horses than camels I thought to myself. I had ridden a few times as a child on a friend's horse. My confidence was growing by the minute, only to be plummeted into the deepest roots of despair and outright horror as the handler slapped the horse on its backside and took off across the dessert with me holding on for dear life screaming at the top of my lungs. No matter what I tried I couldn't stop the dame thing. It obviously knew where it was going because I was not in control one iota. To my utter relief the horse finally came to a mild trot, back into the stables. I must have looked a complete sight. My hair was in my mouth, I had tears streaming down my face and my cheeks were burning red from the sun and fear.

I slipped out of the saddle praying that my legs would hold me up and not turn to mush as I hit the floor. I straighten myself up, brushed myself off and confidently walked to one side where I casually leant up against the fence while I waited for the others. When really, I just wanted to kiss the ground and curl up in a corner shouting for my Mum.

Tamsin and Hanna appeared around the corner amazed at my incredible riding skills. I didn't have the heart to tell them how petrified I had been and ruin their illusion. I was exhausted and welcomed the hot leather seats of the cab to takes us to the museum in Cairo.

The Egyptian Museum of Antiquities contains many important pieces of ancient Egyptian history. It houses the world's largest collection of Pharaonic antiquities. It was first built in 1835 near the Ezbekeyah Garden and later after several moves it finally ended up in Tahrir Square where it still is today. We were hoping to see the treasures of King Tut Ankh Amun and the golden mask of Tutankhamen. On arrival we headed into the great building and straight to the toilets. This was an experience in itself; the attendant gave out tissue that you were expected to pay for before you could use them. Good job we didn't need much. I also desperately needed some water and chocolate from the gift shop. The museum was not disappointing it was huge and the amount of antiquities inside was incredible. The collections were vast from burial tombs with manuscripts of the book of the dead, carriages, weapons and sarcophagus. We had picked a quiet day more by luck than judgment, but what an amazing experience.

When we left no one spoke until we were well on our way. We passed the unpainted and derelict buildings, vendors on the streets accosting the cab every time we slowed down wanting us to buy their gifts. We visited a Papyrus store and Egyptian cotton store on the way back to the ship, but we found them to be very aggressive and had a hard time leaving. We had heard of tourist being locked in the shops until they bought something, however our humble cabby made sure we were safe and ushered us out of the shop quickly before things got out of hand. The air in the cab was quiet on the way to Port Alexander, I think the events of the day were starting to catch up with us.

By the time we arrived at the harbour (which at the time the new cruise terminal hadn't been built) it was dark, I mean pitch black, and all we could see was lots of people milling about. We gave Ashmed a generous tip on top of his fee for keeping us safe and looking after us so well. He was a very happy and humble man. We negotiated our way through the throngs of tourists and street vendors towards what looked like a floating jetty leading out towards the ship which was just the other side of a large walled area. This was lined with small fishing vessels packed full of articles to sell, and smelts like an old fishery. We were being grabbed, pushed and pulled, left, right and center. There were chickens, goats, and an assortment of other paraphernalia all the way along the walkway, it was pure chaos.

The small illuminations from lanterns were hanging from poles above our heads and didn't provided much light to our already overpowered senses, they were more like glow worms hanging from a seamless poll. The scene was not a pretty one, in fact It was quite frightening. To my relief we reach the ships gangway, being greeted by our security who were on tender hooks. They were from Israel, so not a great time for them as the two countries were at logger heads back then. A sense safety once again filled my whole being, I hadn't realized how tense I had been during our trip. The relief seem to be reflected at us from the security guards, they looked as though they had been waiting for us.

To our surprise and horror allegedly the ship was intending to stay overnight when we left, but due to some issues, the captain decided that they wanted to leave early and didn't want to pay the overnight charges and were ready to depart and leave us there. How true that was I'm not sure, but that was the story we were told. Allegedly again they didn't want the publicity of leaving passengers ashore, so they stayed put because they were not sure how many had gone off alone and a couple of the excursions were not back in time. They would have seemed to be happy to leave us out there! In that chaos. A shiver went down my spine at the very thought of it trying to find a port agent in the madness outside, would have been a total nightmare. Not to mention we would have had to pick the ship up in Israel. Thank goodness for small mercies.

CHAPTER 20 - THE PILGRIMAGE

After our eventful day in Egypt we arrived safely in Ashdod, Israel ready for our pilgrimage to the holy city of Bethlehem. The same five of us meet outside on the dock and used our well learnt negotiation skills yet again with our new taxi driver named Yosef. He would take us as far as the check point in Bethlehem, where we would have to walk the rest of the way. We were getting used to and understood the people from that part of the world by that point and seemed to feel happier with our plans.

We arrived in Bethlehem after about an hour, the cab ride was nowhere near as bad as Egypt, thanks to the wonderful air-conditioning system. We walked through the check point and stopped at a small shop to get some water. We were surrounded by white building of all different shaped and sizes, some with steeples, some with court yards. There was a sweet smell of incense wafting through the air. Looking up we could see the Church of Nativity, which housed the cave where it is thought Jesus was born. We covered our heads with scarves we purchased earlier, not knowing if it was an appropriate thing to do or not. We entered the great church and a sense of calm just enveloped me like a warm blanket. It was quite bizarre. The smell of the incense surrounded us, and the quietness was deafening especially considering how many people were in there, a busy day.

The church itself was shared by Catholics and Greek Orthodox people. The Half which was Greek Orthodox was said to be the oldest church in the world that is still used as a church. We stood in a line waiting to descend to the crypt where Jesus was thought to be born. As we got nearer, I'm not sure why, but butterflies started to manifest inside my stomach. I was nervous. I placed my hand on the stone where the manger is marked by a fourteen-point Silver Star called the star of Bethlehem. It was cold and hard to touch but I felt very humbled and blessed that little old me was here visiting this holy site. I was never that religious, just spiritual. I could understand why so many people went to the site from all over the world. It was mesmerizing.

We left the Old City and walked through the Armenian and Jewish quarters. The steps were very step and uneven under foot. The Road was lined with shops and vendors, again trying to entice us in with their sales patter. We just smiled and nodded walking past. I did purchase a cross whilst I was walking down. I felt it was the right thing to do. The journey down was very hazardous and long. I could only imagine the pain Jesus was in carrying the immense cross on his shoulders for his own crucifixion. Once at the bottom we were faced with the Wailing Wall. It was and still is one of the holiest sites in the world. The translation of the Arabic term *el-Mabka* means the place of weeping. The name was based on the Jewish practice of mourning the destruction of the Temple and praying for it to be rebuilt at the site of the western wall. Three times a day, for thousands of years, Jewish prayers from around the world have been directed toward the Temple Mount, where it is situated. The practice of writing notes and placing them in the cracks of the wall has been going on since it was first recorded in the 18th century. We witness this going on, people standing close to the wall rocking backward and forward reciting prayers. The notes are collected twice a year and buried on the mount.

We kept our distance for a while, not wanting to intrude, it really didn't seem appropriate for us to get to close. I manage to take some fantastic photos from where we were stood. The time was getting on, so we retraced our steps back to where the check point and cab was waiting for us.

My feet were aching, and I was ready to visit the highlight of the lowest point on earth, The Dead Sea. After our whirlwind visits of the past couple of days we were well and truly ready for a change of pace. We headed through the remote Judaean desert to wonderful beaches at the Dead Sea. Yosef dropped us at the Roadside where we walked down to the beach and stripped down to our swimming costumes and entered into the sea. Wow how magnificent it felt. The water devoured my body, but I didn't sink I stayed floating at the surface. It was like being in space but without the darkness and twinkling stars. It was because of the high mineral content in the water. We floated effortlessly around laughing and enjoying the coolness after the hot and dusty day. We smothered ourselves with the mud from the seabed which had a natural exfoliating and rejuvenating effect on the skin. It was fantastic.

An hour passed, and we had managed to dry off enough to get dressed and back into the cab, where Yosef was waiting to take us back to the ship.

How lovely I felt very relaxed, quite different from yesterday.

CHAPTER 21 - THE LAST LEG

Over the last 6 months it had been quite a roller coaster of emotions and events. Not only did I have to say goodbye to some great friend and fantastic people, but I had to deal with most horrendous heart ache that blew me away.

After doubting that Enrico and I were no longer together, out of the blue he arrived at my cabin with some flowers and a bottle of wine. He had been so busy with the running's of the ship that he had not had much time off. Why he couldn't have said that to me , but they are a different culture. I had continued to see Enrico during the rest time on the Achille Lauro. We were having such a great fun together, so much so we were started to make plans once we were off the ship. The other officers on board knew we were an item as did the Captain. No-one batted an eye lid and it all seemed very natural. I had completely fallen for him. His tenderness and gentleness. He was kind, thoughtful and passionate just how I thought it should be. From all the happy ever after films, I was convinced that my knight in shining armour would sweep me off my feet someday and take me away to a para- dise Island where we could live in total harmony for the rest of our lives. Naive I know, but that's how I thought things were meant to be back then. I had thought that Enrico was the one for me. The one to spend my life with. The following cruise sailing around the Mediterranean changed all of that.

It was embarkation day again back in Genova. At the time, we had predominantly Italian passengers onboard, some French and German as well to mix things up a bit. Hardly an English person amongst them. I didn't mind because we were on an Italian Cruise ship after all, and my Italian had improved immensely. So much so I could finely hold a short conversation with some of the passengers in the salon.

We were playing guess the nationality as the passengers came on and tried to get them to interact with us to see if we were right. It did make things a little more interesting and made the time pass very quickly.

On Lido Deck our sail away was happening as usual, but this time it was very flat. A great hole had emerged since our friends had disembarked in Southampton. We always had so much fun singing and doing our funny dances getting the passengers involved. What a laugh. However, it had been a real effort to muster the same momentum that was so apparently missing.

I walked to the bar area of Lido Deck already feeling in a solemn mood and turned to see if Tamsin was coming up behind me .

My heart sank and the blood drained from my face , I felt like an earthquake was about to swallow my car with me inside it, my world had come to a grinding holt. Enrico was walking hand in hand with another woman heading straight for me. My hands were clammy, and I didn't know where to look, I wanted to look away, run as fast as I could, anything to stop me seeing the nightmare that was in front of me, but I couldn't move, I was cemented to the spot. I stood there with my mouth wide open, unable to move. The way he was looking at her, The softness in his eyes, the body language between them. I knew she was not just a friend. Who was she ? and why was she holding my boyfriends' hand in that way? It took all my will power not to go and knock her off her feet. I couldn't I was in a public area. All I could do was watch.

He saw me, and in that moment our eyes locked, knowing that the end was insight, our beautiful relationship was over. I couldn't believe it, he did nothing, he just looked away and carried on, not even trying to hide the fact that he had been caught. My heart was heavy, and I was so confused, what was happening? I stumbled backwards, only being propped up by a table. I watched transfix following them as they disappeared in the direction of Enrico's cabin. I felt sick, suddenly my legs moved, and I walked as fast as I could, trying not to bring attention to myself, before I could reach the salon. I was mortified, tears pricking the corners of my eyes, ready to flow in a torrent down my cheeks, I could no longer hold back, I found the salon empty and sat at the backwash and sobbed, staring out to sea trying to make sense of it. What was happening? My head was rushing in so many directions, I felt dizzy and sick. I put my head between my knees, trying to stop myself from passing out.

"No, it can't be true" I shouted.

Enrico must have caught hold of one of the officers on the quiet and requested that he come to see me, hoping that I was heading for the salon. The officer Maurice entered in his white uniform looking very dapper, he heard me shouting and could see the sadness in my eyes, he knew that I knew something was amiss. He told me that the lady who Enrico was with , was in fact his wife. That he had been married for 5 years and had two children, a boy of three and a girl of eighteen months. He explained that in Italy it was commonplace to take a mistress, as long as the two worlds didn't meet. He said that Enrico really didn't expect that he would feel the way he did about me and that it was unfortunate that I had found out the way I had. He expressed that Enrico was very sorry and that maybe one day I would forgive him for what he had done. He made it very clear that Enrico's wife must never know about the two of us. He told me that I should stay away from Enrico and his cabin and that he would come and visit me, at my cabin later that day, to explain!

I was so angry and upset, I told him to tell Mr Enrico to stay away and that I have nothing to say to him. He did make it also very clear that nothing was to interfere with his wife and that the other officers would make sure she never got to know about Enrico and me.

I could not believe what I was hearing, they were closing ranks and I had no choice but to do as I was asked. I vowed there and then never to get so involved with anyone on the ships or my life again. I was so hurt. I couldn't stand any more heart ache. Why all the plans? Why not just tell me? I could have had the choice to carry on or not, and it would have been my choice, not his. The alarm in my voice was rising as I realised that I had said all that out loud. Maurice walked away shaking his head, like it was my fault. How can I trust anyone? So many times, before had I been betrayed by so called friends and boyfriends.

It brought a hurtful memory flooding back to me. Back in Surbiton before the house, I had been living in a bedsitting flat in the basement of a large house. My Friend Lily was living in the attic room of the same house. We had moved from Plymouth together. We had been in a relationship with two brothers, who were twins. Not identical , that would have just been weird.

One of our other friends Carmel , came to live in a bedsit in the adjacent house. The houses must have been so grand in their day. She had been living there a couple of weeks, when I decided to go out for the night with my boss's daughter. We had an amazing night, dancing and chatting. I had, had great fun. I got back in the early hours of the morning. My boyfriend, Jason usually stayed with me as his brother was upstairs with Lily.

That night I thought it was a bit strange as Jason wasn't there. I assumed he had watched a film with Lily and his brother Will.

The next morning, I went up to see them, only to be greeted at the door by Lily, not allowing me in, saying that Jason was asleep. I thought it really odd, as that hadn't happened before. Just as I was walking down the stairs feeling really confused, she came after me.

"Jo" she said with concern in her voice. "Jason isn't here, I can't lie, he is with Carmel at hers. They got together last night. I'm so sorry"

I couldn't believe what I had heard. I ran downstairs, only to run straight into Jason.

"Is it true" I asked him

"Yes" he said looking away.

I couldn't speak, a lump had formed in my throat. I just walked past him. He followed me into my bedsit, where he was trying to make excuses. I couldn't bear to look at him. Not only did I feel betrayed by him, but with my other best friend, I couldn't believe it. The two people I thought that I could trust the most. Upset was an underestimate. That same feeling was with me again. The absolute betrayal is sole destroying. Why? It seemed to be a constant reoccurring situation in my life. The trust I had in people, who were closest to me, I just got trodden on. From my Mum leaving for another man and not taking me with her, to my Dad's ultimatum when his now wife moved in with her boys and there being no room for me, to my friends cheating on me. I couldn't take it anymore. No- one taking my feelings in consideration at all. It was like I didn't matter. Anyone could do what they liked to me; I just didn't matter at all. It was one of the reasons I left in the first place. To get away, start afresh. Become the person I longed to be. But again, I put my trust in someone undeserving, only to be taken for a fool again. It had to stop!

During the cruise I felt like I was pulling teeth, my heart just wasn't in it. I had to endure a week's cruising to some great places and witness Enrico and his wife walking around hand in hand without a care in the world. It wasn't right , it wasn't fair. Talk about rubbing salt into the wounds. So similar to Surbiton. Jason and Carmel carried on seeing each other for months. I had to suck it. I felt so alone back then as I couldn't bring myself to hang around with them anymore.

Our friendships were over. I was lost.

I so wanted to tell her what her husband had been up to, but I dared not say a word. The consequences, I didn't want to risk it.

I decided instead that I would make the most of my time left on the ship and enjoy it as much as I could. Keeping myself to myself. Tam was great, she felt for me so much. I started to smile again, when Tam, got up to her normal antics in the cabin. Messing about , pretending to hand herself up in the wardrobe with a coat hanger, literally. It was hilarious. Just the medicine I needed.

We had a telex through from H.Q notifying us of what to expect once we got back to Genova. Telexes were the only way to communicate without encompassing to many costs. As I said this was all pre mobile phones and internet. I suppose it was like texts now a days. The radio officer brought it down to us. He gave me a such a sad, heartfelt look as he walked out the door. Gosh I felt like everyone knew what was going on, except me.

H.Q informed us that Rachelle was to disembark and return to the UK as her contract had finished and Tamsin and I were going to join the Costa Daphne in Genova, staying overnight in a hotel and picking the Daphne up in the same port the following day. That was a turn up. Tamsin and I going onto another ship together. Just for a few months to finish our contracts, great, at least I didn't have to say goodbye just yet. Rachelle joked that she would notify the Daphne and warn them that we were coming.

" Very funny" I said.

I was so excited to get off of here but sad all at the same time. It was time for a change. Things were not going to be the same as they had been in South Africa. I wondered where the Daphne would take us. I guess we would have to wait and see. Mind you it would have to be some cruise to top this one.

We stopped on the island of Capri before going to Naples.

Capri was an enchanting and picturesque island made of limestone rock. A favourite with Roman emperors, the rich and famous, artists, and writers, it's still one of the Mediterranean's must-see places. It was wonderful . Marina Grande is the island's main harbour it's where we anchored and used the tenders from the ship . The ship was far too large to get to close. The beaches are scattered around the island. There are only two towns - Capri, just above Marina Grande, and Ana Capri,

There were some wonderful places to visit, such as Faraglioni, rock formations, one of the island's natural wonders. The Faraglioni make up the classic view associates with Capri. On the shore, the Faraglioni beach is one of the island's most beautiful beaches. There are several other unusual rock formations in the sea around the island, including a natural arch. Anacapri, the highest town on the island, has incredible views of the harbour below. Near the central square there's a chair lift to Mount Solaro and a street lined with shops, several of which have limoncello tasting.

Villa San Michele, in Anacapri, was built by the Swedish writer Axel Munthe in the late 19th century on the site of a Tiberian villa. Bits of the Roman villa are incorporated into the atrium and garden.

We had decided to just settle in a bar overlooking the water's edge of the marina and watch the world go by. Other crew members joined us, but no-one really spoke to much. We ordered our food and settled down to a relaxed dinner before heading back to the ship. The dusk fell quickly turning to night and my body ached with the emptiness. I couldn't take it anymore, it was no good, I refuse to feel this way again. From then on, I was going with my original plan , enjoy the travelling , forget the relationships and concentrate on having fun. Life was far too short to get caught up with all of the drama. It would not happen to me again...

We were up with the larks to get off in Naples just to get a few essentials before leaving Genova in a few days' time. A lot of the Officers and Italian crew disembarked here with all of the passengers. It just left a skeleton crew to see us back to our home port. Where the Achille Lauro would return to wet dock for repairs.

Enrico was one of the officers to disembark. I was up on Lido Deck looking down on the crew who were leaving, when I felt someone behind me. Those dark passionate eyes burning into the back of head.

" Enrico " I said out loud before turning around.

" Jo" his beautiful Italian accent, oh how I had missed that." Come stai? He added. (How are you ?)

I turned on the spot, making sure I kept a distance between the two of us .

" Where's your wife" I said trying to keep from spitting it at him.

" She is waiting for me dock side, I told her I had some business to attend to"

" Oh, so I'm business now, that's a low blow even for you Enrico" As if he hadn't hurt me enough, he just could stop himself. " What do you want Enrico" I added scornfully.

" Jo, bella, I want to express to you how sorry I am for hurting you so much, I did not intend to let things go as far as they did. I'm sorry" I could see the remorse in his eyes, as his gaze dropped to the floor. His head bent low. " Can you ever forgive me Jo?" he added.

" I'm sorry too Enrico, for allowing myself to believe there was ever a future for us. As far as forgiveness, I'm sorry but that is not mine to give. You will have to live with the burden of what you have done. Not just for me but every time you look into your wife's eye's, you will know that you betrayed her. Her Love and the love of your children, the trust that they give you. Their hearts would shatter if they knew what you had been doing. I hope you have learnt that love is too precious to play with and should not be given away that lightly. You don't deserve them"

I walked away, not looking back not giving him the chance

to answer. I could feel those eyes following me as I disappeared into the Lido Bar. My heart breaking with every step, remembering back to when we first met, those eyes, the anticipation, the excitement. To have all of that crumble at me feet. I was mortified. I felt a fool to have been taken in by such lies. Never again!!!

I watched from the rope Deck as he left with his wife, he looked back and saw me watching, with remorse in his eyes, and head hanging low, I felt justice had been done by not giving him what he needed, the forgiveness, even though I had forgiven him, but I knew I would never forget him. I was hurt by the way he had handled the situation; it could have been so much better. My heart was heavy, and I felt an emptiness inside as tears rolled down my face . He vanished into the building across from the ship. I never saw him again

I couldn't say I was sorry to see him go; it had completely upset the apple cart and I felt an idiot for being so naïve. I always seemed to get caught out and get so involved. Getting carried away with a situation and imagining that this time he could be the one. I was such a romantic at heart. I think that steamed from watching Cinderella at the cinema when I was really young, and still hoping for my happy ever after and my prince Charming to come along. Yeah right, never again !!!!!

As we set sail and watched Naples dissolve into the horizon, the three of us stood up on Deck with a few drinks and watched the sun melt like an ice -cream on a hot day, dripping into the sea. None of us said a word, our emotions very mixed. My heart was broken, the future looked quite sad from my vantage point, but Rachelle was full of wonder, her eyes sparkled, she going to see her Zodiac guy during her holidays and maybe return for another contract. She so excited about her future, and I was happy for her, it was nice to see such delights amongst my darkness. I wonder if their relationship lasted. I hope so.

CHAPTER 22 - END OF AN ERA!

The crew gangway was down and the three of us were standing with our suitcases ready and passports in hand. That was it for our time on the Achille Lauro, and what an adventure we had. Some beautiful places that I could have only imagined in my wildest dreams. The sights, the sounds, the smells and the animals were all amazing and memories that would last forever. I wanted to remember every detail of my exploits, imprint them into my mind forever.

We descended the gangway and saw Rachelle off into her taxi. I felt so sad and deflated, yet excited and exhilarated all at the same time, looking forward to our new adventures ahead. I sucked in every detail of the ship as we left, committing it, in all its glory to my mind's eye. As we watched her cab fade into the distance, I couldn't believe our time had gone so quickly. Amazing really the things we had been through in a relative short period of time. They say a few months close confinement on a ship is equivalent to a year or so land based. Maybe this is true!

We waited for our cab, to take us to our hotel for a night of luxury. Gosh I was so looking forward to ordering the food I wanted and to have a bath. The feeling of immersing my body into a warm soapy indulgence was overwhelming and one I hadn't had for over six months. I gave a heavy sigh of the sheer thought of it. I would be so refreshed before we joined the Costa Daphne the next day.

Out of the blue a tear trickle down my face, the thought of all the people, friends, colleagues and relationships we have had in the last few months, now having to say goodbye to all of them was somewhat overwhelming. Was it the waving goodbye to Rachell that got to me , or maybe the fact that I knew I would never be able to re-live the highs and lows, the sights, the people and experiences which I had enjoyed so immensely on a ship that was my first the Achille Lauro.

Our cab arrived and with one last glace to my beloved Achille Lauro, we left it behind. I couldn't help feeling as if I had left a piece of my heart there, just like a first love.

I smiled to myself knowing that I would always hold a special place in my heart for that ship. My first ship at the start of what became an adventure of a lifetime for the next 4 years. One that would never be repeated but would never be forgotten.

Standing at the gangway of the Costa Daphne Tamsin and I knew a whole new chapter in our lives were about to open. Some lessons had been learnt and some lessons really had only just started to embellish and make a mark inside of us.

We glanced at each other, hand in hand we stepped onto the gangway of the Costa Daphne. A twinkle in our eyes and a smile just dusting the top of our lips, we made our first step towards our next adventure......

CHAPTER 23 -THE COSTA DAPHNE

What a difference a day makes, in no time at all we had gone from one ship to another, setting sail to Cannes in the South of France, The Costa Daphne was half the size of the Achille Lauro. Still Italian officers but a lot quieter. The clientele seemed more refined and a lot older. It was such a different atmosphere. It was cleaner on the inside and white on the outside. The Daphne was built in 1955 as the refrigerated cargo vessel in Port Sydney for Port Line's, sailing from the UK. She was laid up in 1971, then sold to Greek-owned Carras Cruises, who renamed her Akrotiri Express. She was completely rebuilt into the deluxe cruise ship Daphne, entering service in July of 1975. She sailed for Costa Cruises from 1979 through 1996, I knew her in that time frame. She was then sold to Leisure Cruises and renamed Switzerland. In 2002, she was purchased by Majestic International Cruises and renamed Ocean Monarch , in 2005, Ocean Monarch served as a hospital ship off the coast of Sri Lanka affected by the tsunami and in the late 2007, Ocean monarch was sold to Lisbon-based Classic International Cruises (CIC), who refitted and renamed her Princess daphne. When CIC went bankrupt in 2012, the ship was seized at Souda and offered for sale. Sadly, the only takers were the Alang shipbreakers who were able to fire up the ship's original Doxford diesel engines for a final voyage to the Indian scrapping beach, where she was delivered under the name Daphne.

Our cabins were at first a major disappointment they were smaller than our previous one on the Achille, which I never thought to be possible and the girls from our company who were on the ship before had left it in a right state. Tamsin and I got to work to make it feel like home. Putting pictures of our families over our bunks and cleaning up so at least it smelt better.

Our manager Flo short for Florence was a nice girl, a little older than me about twenty-two , from Wales. A beautiful accent, quiet, and shy personality, so different from Tam and me. She had masses of long curly red hair and applied our glow powder a little too much, that she gave off an orange radiant skin tone, rather than a bronzed one. She did get the mickey taken out of her a lot for that reason, which was such a shame, but she took it all with a pinch of salt. Her cabin was situated in the salon. Strange I know, but there was a doorway behind our reception desk that lead straight in. As managers you didn't have to share. Now that really appealed to me. Not because I didn't enjoy sharing with Tam, but I really liked my own space sometimes, and that was something of a rarity.

The Daphne's salon was set out very different to the Achille's, for a start the salon was on the seventh Deck. On cruise ships generally the higher the number the lower you were on the ship. The Daphne only had seven Decks available to passengers, so that meant we were down at the bottom, well not quite there were two crew Decks below, one being the engine room. We had no windows, and it was laid out in a T shape. Reception area first then hidden in a long galley area was the styling stations. Very gloomy. Tam's beauty room was a few doors along from the salon in an old passenger cabin. As usual she did her magic and transformed it into a luxurious aromatic treatment room.

I felt very strange on the Daphne at first getting to know the different routine and crew, staff, and officers, it was all a bit daunting, but something I learnt to adjust to over the years. We had settled in quickly in comparison to our major wait on the Achille. It was a case of dumping our stuff, get things set up, uniforms on, ready for embarkation day. Just a few hours this time.

I had about four months left of my contract. I had heard from Mum just before leaving the Achille and she was back in Stevenage at her old company where she had started with Al at Aegina Blinds. She was now made secretary to the limited company and Al and the accountant George were both directors. She was waiting to move into a house they had bought just around the corner from Dad's, which was a little odd, but there you go they were now all in one place and I was thousands of miles away. I know Mum would be heartbroken at the move, but what was her alternative at that time. She had no money to herself, no-one to fall back on. When I think about it, she must have been so depressed about the situation. I didn't know quite how depressed and how close she was to breaking until my last contract.

We had met a lot of the crew staff by the second night and was already in the swing of things. We had been to Cannes in the south of France and was on our way to Palermo on the Island of Sicily. Lots of conversations were flowing about not getting off alone, staying in large groups, girls to be accompanied by guys etc, etc. Tam and I thought they were overreacting a little after the dangerous liaisons we had been through in Israel and Egypt but decided to keep it to ourselves.

We always seem to gel well with the entertainment and shop staff on the ships and this one was no exception. Our new bestie was Noah, he was about twenty-four, blonde hi lighted hair, very attractive and very gay. He was a lovely guy who always had time for us salon babes as he like to call us. He was originally from Australia but had lived in London for a while before embarking on his dancing ship life.

Flo had got really friendly with the chief purser Pedro from south America, he was very dark and stunning looking with bronzed skin and a very passionate Latin way about him. He was twenty-five also a gay man. This was great for me that there were so many gay men on this ship, because I had no interest in developing a relationship at all on here.

It was all about the cruising. We had a lot of girl power around us too, we had four wonderful shop girls Tina, the shop manager, Cassandra, Poppy and Debbie. They all worked in the gift shop and were an absolute scream. On our first night onboard, they had us up on the Lido Deck in the bar doing Tequila shots. What was it with the shots all the time?

We arrived in Palermo, early in the morning, and on that occasion, there was an army of us getting off to explore together. The three of us, the four shop girls, Noah, Pedro and we had also been joined by Alfonso the contortionist and Stephan the cruise director. Alfonso was the bendy man as we renamed him. He was in his early thirties, from Madrid in Spain and was married with two kids both under 4. Stephan on the other had was in his early forties with a typically English gentleman nature and extremely well spoken, but great fun to be around. He always made me smile. He was also gay, and his partner was onboard as assistant cruise director Tony, he was from England, but not with us today as he had to work.

Our gang left the ship and manage to locate a few cabs to take us to the centre. In a world where so many places have become tourist-friendly to a fault, visiting Palermo was still somewhat of an adventure and dangerous to us the tourist. We couldn't find many restaurants with menus translated into different languages and we had trouble communicating in English in many places, and some parts of the old town centre had remained untouched since they were bombed during the war. There were lots of back streets that had opened up to those from the outside, and it is still often difficult to obtain any information worth having that explains about the surroundings. It was a good job we had so many that spoke fluent Italian with us. The lack of English spoken was very apparent. The Felling I got from Palermo was one of secrecy and intrigue. It was said that the Mafia had a massive presence there, but I wasn't so sure how true that was. I did feel that I needed to keep my wits about me. I found this piece from The Guardian about the state of Palermo the year before we were there, a little frightening:

Every city, at some stage in its history, reaches a tipping point. For Palermo, it was one sweltering afternoon in July 1992, when more than 1,500 soldiers armed with automatic weapons took up positions on every corner of its eerily quiet streets in a show of military force unknown to Italy since the end of the second world war.

On that day, 24 July, the war was against the mafia, and Italy was losing. Six days earlier, a car bomb had killed Paolo Borsellino, the chief justice investigating the godfathers of Cosa Nostra, the Sicilian mafia. The five officers in his police escort also died. In May, the car of another judge, Giovanni Falcone, the mafia bosses' number one enemy, had been blown up. The 300 kilos of TNT that killed him along with his wife and three escorting officers opened up a 15-metre crater in the motorway connecting the airport to the city.

"Palermo just like Beirut" was the headline splashed across the front pages of Italy's leading newspaper at the time. Italy's mafia wars marked the lowest point in Sicily's history. Many thought Palermo had reached a point of no return, but its ability to bounce back from crisis has become a trademark of a city that has been invaded more often than any other in the Mediterranean.

That report really hit home to me, of how dangerous these places were and how naïve we were to its catastrophic demise over the years, and its impact on the local community was horrendous.

We finally stopped for some food after looking around the old town with its Arabic origins and the now familiar aromas and colours that hung around in the air, the narrow labyrinthine of streets and the exotic array of food on display. We soaked up the atmosphere around us. The food was particularly good there, the succulent beef in a delicious tomato sauce and vegetables on the side was absolutely outstanding. My mouth is watering now as I remember its smoothness and delectable indulgence seeping into my taste buds. Our bill arrived and we were working out how much each of us had to pay when Flo announced that her bag was gone. Someone had stolen it.

" Where did you see it last?" Pedro asked concerned she may have left it elsewhere.

" I put it on the back of my chair" as she said it, she had realised that it was a really stupid thing to do. The colour rose in her cheeks as everyone looked at her. She started to cry as she had all her money and credit cards in her bag.

We paid between us covering Flo's costs and Pedro and Tina said they would go with her to the police station to tell them about what had happened, so a crime report could be sent to her credit card company to inform them of what had happened. The rest of us hustled back to the ship as quickly as we could, no longer feeling safe to continue our exploring. We headed up to the bar on Lido Deck for a well-deserved drink and after a couple of hours Flo, Pedro and Tina returned to tell us what had happened. They said that they had to wait ages before someone would see them. Thankfully Pedro spoke fluent Italian and made it clear what had happened.

They told them that it was commonplace for tourist to have things stolen. It didn't reassure them that they would ever see the bag returned but I think Flo learnt a valuable lesson.

CHAPTER 24 – IT'S A HARD LIFE!

The next sea day was a formal night, on here people did tend to dress up far more than the Achille. We were full to the brim in the salon with blow dry's and hair ups. Mainly from the Italian women who had masses of long dark hair that was really thick and curly, all wanting it to be blow dried straight. Of course, in the early nineties hair straighteners were not around. So, it was good old fashion arm power, and boy did my arms hurt by the finish. Both Flo and I had around twenty blow dries' in each, from early afternoon through until eight, when we finally packed up our brushes.

A couple of Italian women were so insistent that we could do their hair that they disregarded the fact that we were too busy, and whilst we were with other passengers, they went ahead and shampooed their own hair and came and sat down next to our clients who we were working on and waited for us to start on them. We couldn't believe what they were doing. Flo had to call the pursers desk to get Pedro down to explain to them that it was not how we did things on the ships and that they needed to make appointments in future. He sent them away back to their cabins saying that we would do it for them the following night. They were not happy. Our two clients that we had in were lovely Italian ladies who spoke perfect English, they told us that the women were laughing and saying that they were trying to get the service for free.

They did come back the following night and sat together whilst we blow dried their hair. They were very rude, I understood everything they said about us. They thought that we didn't until I corrected them, telling them that I under-stood Italian a lot better than I spoke it, and that I knew what they had said. They soon shut up and left with their heads low and very embarrassed, apologising for everything that they did. Honestly it takes all sorts to make a world.

That night we had to put on a fashion show in conjunction with the shop girls . We had the pick of the dresses in the shop. Wow was all I could say. They were amazing and so heavy with diamante sewn into the fabric. I picked a black dress, knee length full of diamantes, a silver fringe at the bottom and a very Spanish/ Latino type collar which draped across my shoulders and down to the bust line in a v, that was in white with white diamantes incrusted in a paisley de-sign. It was amazing and I felt so beautiful wearing it. Debbie kept telling me to be careful as it was worth a lot of money. She never did tell me how much.

'How the other half live!'

Tam had a black diamante dress with a v neckline and long sleeves, it had a high cut fringe around the bottom, thigh length, hiding the fact that it was actually quite short. She loved it and she had the legs for it. Flo choose a com-pletely different dress that was golden, covered in sparkles. She just shone and dazzled as she walked. We all looked stunning.

Before we could do the catwalk in the formal attire, we had to adorn the sportswear and ship wear too. These all had cruise ship themes of anchors and waves upon the lapels and cuffs.

We were joined by Noah, Pedro and Stephan to escort us down the runway on the stage. We were at the same level as the passengers rather than a stage which was a little unnerving.

It started with the obligatory tequila slammers now with our new barman Oscar who was from Guatemala. He lined up a few of them shaking his head in amazement at us silly Eng-lish girls giving me a wink as he did so.

"Here we go again" I said to Tamsin, laughing in amazement of the things we got talked into. My role was very small in comparison to Tam's. I was escorted down our make shift runway by Stephan during all my casual wear, and whorled around the dance floor to a big band number for the formal attire. Stephan looking very dapper in his tuxedo. I didn't have to learn any of the step's as I just followed Stephan's lead. He was so good at dancing and very easy just to let go and have fun. Which I did.

Tamsin on the other hand had to start on stage for her formal debut, with just her undies on. Sold in the shop for a small price. (I might add) She sat on a stool in front of a mirror which was perched on a table. She pretended to apply her make up to some very seductive music. She continued to do a reverse striptease. She put on her shoes, then stepped very carefully and sexily into her dress, all in time to the music, making sure she was on que for the big finish of Pedro coming on to zip her up and spinning her around to a climax of the bands crescendo of music. It worked so well that the audience went mad for her, standing ovation was amazing. She looked stunning.

As she came off the stage, I planted a tequila in her hands, which were shaking so much the drink spilt over the edge. I gave her a big hug, she just smiled with relief. They did try to get her to do it again on the other cruises, but she wasn't having any of it. Once was enough for her. The night was a success, and our friendships onboard had developed into a close-knit family. I was starting to feel quite at home and looking forward to our cruising. All was well.

We had an overnight stop in Istanbul, we visited the Bizarre, full of men trying to grab us to buy their merchandise. I did buy a hat a small memento of our visit. It was all very busy and not a woman to be seen, other than the tourist. That night a group of us decided to go off to a night club we had heard about. The cab ride to the venue was a white knuckle one, tearing around the streets like we had been shoot out of a cannon. My heart was in my mouth as I sat between Tamsin and Stephen. I couldn't hold onto anything to support my weight and crashed and bumped into both of them in turn, crushing them against the doors. After what seemed like an age we stopped just as abruptly as we had started, I was trying hard to hold down my dinner from earlier. We piled out of our cabs and made our way to the entrance of what looked like a car breakers site. I was worried and turned to Tam to see her reaction.

"Its fine Jo" she said reading my mind before I had opened my mouth. "one of the crew was telling me about it before we left."

Re-assured by Tam's words we paid the equivalent of five pounds and followed the others through an open aired wreckage yard. Up some step steps all open to the elements, with search lights, dancing across the old cars in a multitude of colours. It was quite something, nothing I had ever seen before. We continued over a high bridge and descended into a circular half demolished building, with a bar, tables and dance floor enticing us in. The lighting was amazing. Springing out from old rumble and smashed windows. (no glass) the sound system was defining. No wonder we were in the middle of nowhere.

Tam and I approached the bar to get a well-deserved drink. Stephen grabbed my arm and pulled me back.

"Grab Tam" he said I looked at him puzzled, but did what he said and followed him to a seating area,

" What's up Stephen" I said, curious to know what all the fuss was about.

He told us that it was not the thing for women to approach a bar here in Istanbul.

We looked up and took in our surroundings, noticing that there were very few women actually in the club. All of them were mainly from our ship. The ratio of male to female must have been at least fifteen to one. Approximately that is. I had no idea, but never the less the night was fantastic and went without a hitch, even the cab ride back wasn't as bad as before. My head hit the pillow about five thirty am, exhausted I drifted into a deep sleep.

I had managed to write to Mum and Dad to let them know of the change of ship and it's itinerary. Also, I needed a cash advance to buy some clothes for the colder weather. I only had with me what I bought onto the Achille six months ago. All summer clothes.

I was hoping that they would come and see me again in Dover, but I wasn't holding out much hope. We were going to be there on a weekday. Everyone would be at work. I couldn't help thinking back to seeing Mum and how much older she appeared. We had only been away six months, but she had seemed to age a decade in her appearance. Something was defiantly amiss there. I decide to write to my brother to see if he could shed any light on it. By the time I heard back from him. It didn't matter, he was unaware of any problems. He had enough of his own worries.

We continued onto Candice, Vigo, La Coruna, before we docked in Dover, unfortunately none of my family could make that one as I had previously though they were all working, But it didn't matter as I received lots of post from them and managed to get off to buy some warmer clothes. The weather was starting to change, and it was pouring with rain. It was a nice change to be honest, I hadn't seen rain for six months.

Our cruising had started to get a little tedious, or maybe I was getting a bit tired of the same thing. See it doesn't matter what you are doing, if things repeat themselves too much anything can become boring. Life took a turn around just after we had docked in Amsterdam. We had gotten off for the day, just the three of us and wandered into the main part of town. We decided to walk but the main form of transport were bikes and or trams. We were careful not to get run over by the trams, because they were very quiet.

Wondering around a few shops, Tam came up with the idea of finding the red-light area in Amsterdam, I was horrified, but by all accounts it was very famous and a lot of tourist just went to have a look, she thought it would be an experience. We all agreed and set off. To our surprise we were not far . We turned a corner and was greeted by brothels, sex shops, museums, and café bars. The Amsterdam red light district had it all. But contrary to what a lot of people might think, it was a very friendly atmosphere and not very dangerous. The sights were shocking to me. The ladies (prostitutes) were stood on show in the windows, flaunting their bodies and showing just enough to attract their next punter. On the whole the Dutch in Amsterdam had very liberal and tolerant attitudes, embracing the fact that people may be into prostitution, soft drugs and pornography, and that it was only human. So instead of criminalizing everything, they enjoyed the honesty of it all.

We on the other had tried not to stare to much yet couldn't help ourselves. We had dived into the nearest coffee shop giggling like schoolgirls. Only to find that where we had ended up sold marijuana in lots of different flavours, in lots of different forms, such as coffee, chocolate, cakes (space cakes) to name a few. Needless to say, we did try a space cake, but it had no effect on us at all. We later found out that some cafes say they put it in but actually do not. That was fine by me. You could even buy it out of a vending machine. I was totally stunned, but that wasn't the end of my fascination with Amsterdam. We grabbed our things and carried on a little further to a museum of arts.

Not what we were expecting, the arts were of phallic symbols, sex toys and a peep show hidden down at the rear of the shop. Well what a laugh. I was intrigued, embarrassed and disgusted by everything I saw. What a torrid of emotions, I had to leave. On my heels were Tam and Flo looking the same as I felt. We decided not to bother with anything else but to carry on back to the ship. Or so I thought . Tam had disappeared for a couple of minutes to get some water and a snack to take back onboard, but that's not all she came back with!

To my horror later that evening in the crew mess, she handed me a present that she had wrapped up for me, in front of everyone. When I opened it , I found a vibrator placed in a love silk case. Everyone laughed! I was mortified!

CHAPTER 25 – IT'S COLD OUTSIDE

Over the next couple of weeks, we cruised up to Stowaway, Oban, Dublin, Iceland and the fjords, carrying on up to the most Northern point where we hoped to see the midnight sun and some Northern lights. I was so glad that I had bought few warmer clothes, it was turning colder by the day.

To past the time onboard we had quite a few parties. Some in the cabins and some on rope Deck. Rope Deck was exactly what it said on the tin. Just outside our cabin was a door which lead onto a small half Deck full of ropes and lines. There was a staircase rising to the upper Decks which then went on up to Lido (The top Deck)

On one particular night, on our way to our first really cold port Reykjavik in Iceland, we had a party that evolved like most did back then out of boredom. There must have been about twenty something people, with drinks flowing and cigarettes being thrown overboard. Something that just would not be tolerated now. A sound system had been brought out by one of the Deckhands, it had loud Latin music thumping from its speakers. Somehow it didn't have the same effect on me now being in the colder climate than it did out in South Africa, where the passion and the heat from the sun seemed a distant memory.

There was a lot of laughing and joking going on in the corner that involved a chair. I really didn't know what was going on , but I was about to find out. Derrick a twenty-year-old dancer from Manchester, England came over and asked if I wanted to play a game. Being a little suspicious I reluctantly agreed and followed him to the other side of the Deck, where Afonso and Stephan were standing. They looked very guilty about something, but I was a little tipsy and threw caution to the wind and agreed to sit on the chair. Whilst they blind folded me, I could hear Tam shouting

"don't do it Jo, you daft cow"

But as usual I paid no attention to her at all. It's very true though that when one of your senses is halted the others do tend to go on high alert. I was desperately trying to hear what the whispering was about. All became very clear very quickly. Stephan asked me if the blind fold was too tight which I confirmed that it was not. He said.

" Ok Jo, I want you to hold on as tight as possible. Just promise me you won't let go until we ask you to"

" Ok" I said with a tinge of sarcasms in my voice. So, I tighten my grip on the arms of the chair slightly afraid to move. I had no idea what they were up to.

" Do you trust us" Stephan continued. What a funny thing to say, I thought, but agreed, as he was the cruise director after all. That said I felt myself being lifted up in the air. I felt like I was being lifted for ages, all the time being told to hold tight. My head then hit the ceiling or so I thought. Then all of a sudden Stephan shout's,

"JUMP, JUMP, JUMP, quick now JUMP"

Alarm was in his voice. My feet were dangling, and I had no idea where I was or how high. Stephen's voice sounded far away. All that happened in a split second and I just leapt off my seat waiting for the falling sensation and hitting the ground hard. I was so frightened, to my utter relief I was just inches off the ground and stepped onto the floor without falling to my utter demise.

Everyone was in hysterics at my expense of course. I took the blindfold off and started hitting (playfully), anyone that was close, more out of adrenalin and embarrassment than anything else. I did see the funny side after a while and saw the large piece of wood they had used for the ceiling, where they had actually brought it down to my head rather that the other way around. I felt incredibly guilty, when an unsuspecting Flo walked out onto the Deck. The boys looked at each other and said

" Flo, what you up to" I knew what was coming and stood to one side, shamelessly not wanting to be the only one to experience the chair of horror. The games continued far into the night on any unsuspecting crew member that sealed their fate by stepping onto the 'ROPE DECK'

I stood with my back to the crowd that was now congregating around the chair of terror. The noise of their voices faded into a distant hum, as I ascended the stairs to the Deck above. The wind was chilly around my ears, I pulled my jacket close, to cut the frosty feeling from my lobes. I lent on the side rail and looked out to the darkness. My thoughts wondered back to Enrico, I missed him so much. The world seemed to stand still , the feeling I had never felt before, one of total sadness. I felt slightly faint and dazed as if I were falling or dreaming. I knew that It was going to happen, but I could never had been prepared for the total emptiness I felt inside. No tears would come. I had to get out of there, to escape, runaway anything to make this feeling fade. I didn't want to believe it had happened after everything, all the plans we had made. Part of me wanted to cry my heart out and the other wanted to hit something with the anger that raged inside. Then the tears came in a torrent , like a dam that had burst wide open. I looked to the sky asking , " why god, why," but I knew it wasn't his fault. I buried my head into my arms, rocking back and forth trying to comfort myself. I hadn't really let the last few months sink in until then. I had to hold it together, but at that moment I just couldn't stand it any longer, all the hurt and deceit hit me harder than I had anticipated. Perhaps not just that deception from Enrico on its own, but the many I had suffered before could be catching up with me. I didn't want to face it, I couldn't face it, I was afraid to face it. I refused to face it.

Right on cue half a dozen party growers clambered up the

stairs, grabbed my arm and announced that we were off to the disco. I let myself be washed a long, anything was better than standing there alone.

CHAPTER 26- MIDNIGHT SUN

I was up early the next morning, watching one of many fjords slowly passing by the ship, sluggishly the ship ambled to our next port. We had been cruising around from Burgan to Gravdale, in Norway passing across the Arctic circle. It was amazing really that I had in the space of seven months gone across the equator and the Arctic circle. Unfortunately, this time there was no ceremony to mark the occasion, just a certificate to state that I had achieved the status as a crew member. We were heading to the Nordkapp the northern most point of Europe. We were to see the midnight sun in all its glory. I was actually looking forward to the experience because I had never been anywhere that would demonstrate the sights that we saw that night.

The excitement was felt amongst the crew. A coach was hired especially for us, separate now from the passengers. On the Daphne we were not involved with the trips as we were on the Achille. That was fine by me. It made a nice change just to sit back and enjoy it. It was June and very cold out. The summers in Norway and Iceland had a lot to be desired. I was dressed in a coat, jumpers, hats and scarves.

As we climbed the mountains to the summit the snow was laying like a thick blanket over the surface. No grass could be identified through it. I spotted a wigwam at the Roadside. Surely no-one would be living in that this time of year. For centuries Nordkapp has been the great adventure for travellers. The majestic landmark has challenged explorers to the north.

The mountain cliff rises three hundred meters above the

Arctic ocean and marks the end point of the European continent. Tam was huddled next to me trying to keep warm. Even though the heaters were on, it was still very cold on the coach. We were so excited to get to our destination; it was a once in a lifetime trip. We had seemed to have had a lot of those lately.

Our coach pulled up in front of a huge building. The Nordkapphallen was built in 1959, mainly out of stone. In 1988 work began to expand the buildings complex. To protect the visual experience of Nordkapp, large parts of the building were placed inside the mountain, a plateau, a cinema, and a huge grotto. After we had visited a new entrance was added in 1997 and today the building centre is able to accommodate several thousand of tourist at one time.

We could see the famous Globe monument which became the symbol of Nordkapp. It shows that you are at the end point of Europe - the northernmost of the continental mainland. We descended from our coach and got ushered into the building, it was very welcoming, as it was warm and airy. Unlike the coach which was stuffy and cold.

Our experience took us on a journey of the four sessions in the incredible building. We followed the pathway up to the a breath-taking top level of the buildings centre where we found a restaurant with stunning panoramic views of the mountain plateau and steep cliffs that plunge into the Arctic Ocean.

I took a sharp intake of breath at the enormity of what I was witnessing dawned on me. The sky was like twilight for a few minutes, my eyes followed the horizon until they settled on the wonderful array of floating lights. The shimmering beauty of the northern lights would forever captivate me. Dancing through the sky like ballerinas on the stage. Delicate and angelic, a powerful force, yet gentle to the touch. Floating on the aura's through the sky, the colours were mesmerising. I glanced over at Tam, her face shone in the glow from the lights, twinkling from her watery eyes as a tear trickled down her cheek and splashed to the floor in slow motion. The moment was fascinating. The feeling was one of rebirth, tranquillity and still.

I put my arm through hers and as we stood, we were transfixed to the spot, frightened to move not wanting it to be over. As the moment faded the crowd that had gathered on the balcony turned in silence to return to the warmth of the restaurant. No- one spoke, the silence was vibrant yet eerie. Looking around, the expressions on the visitors faces were immense, full of dreams and hopes.

" Amazing" I whispered to Tam

She glanced at me " What is" she answered in a low voice.

"look at the people's faces Tam, they all look similar" She laughed a silent laugh, not wanting to draw attention to herself as we followed the flock inside.

"hot chocolate" she added breaking the mood and transporting me back to reality.

"Sure" I said crossing over the room to join the rapidly lengthening que.

After our welcome refreshments we headed back down to the gift shop to purchase our certificate to prove our attendance, which I still have today, sitting on my lap in fact as I fondly reminisce about our trip. Just as we exited the vast building above the globe the soft glow of the midnight sun was in full bloom. Gosh I checked my watch and there it was sure enough, telling me that it was midnight.

It never did get dark the whole time we were in Norway or Iceland. Such a strange feeling. Sitting out on the aft of the ship, on rope Deck Tam and I used to have many chats about our life, our dreams, our fears.

We were very similar in lots of ways , both coming from a broken home, about the same age, wanting to travel and see the world. I think Tam was a little more adventurous than I, always seemed to have lots of energy about her. But she was after all my big little sis. 'Taller than me but a few year younger.'

We had some memorable times on the costa Daphne, making some good friends, visiting the Geysers, seeing some incredible places in Iceland, and Norway, some of the names were very difficult to get the tongue around, such as Eldfjor, Ny-Alesund and Longyearbyen to name a few. It was time to think about home and what lay ahead for me there.

Would I do another contract, or would I put my sea legs to bed. I was tired and exhausted from my travels, but finally looking forward to going home. I had heard from Mum a few times, but nothing of any substance to give me an idea of how she was feeling. She always kept her cards close to her chest. I know that she would never worry me on purpose, but her lack of saying nothing at all was a cause of great concern for me. I knew her relationship was strained, and she had very few friends in Stevenage. All her great friends were back in Cornwall.

My Dad had well and truly moved on with his marriage, but he was always concerned for Mum, because Al's reputation had preceded him. He was well known for his many affairs with women. Trisha Dad's wife knew of him when she worked in a pub, where she had met my Dad. He used to go in and out of there with a number of women, married, single, he really didn't seem to care. My Mum ended up being one of those married women with whom he took up with. Which lead to my Mum leaving my Dad. I supposed some would say that she was getting her just deserts, but Mum was very naïve to Al's charms. She had only ever been with my Dad since school. No other relationships to speak of, and I think she was so flattered by his advances and being noticed as an individual, rather than just our Mum and Dad's wife that she was drawn to him very easily.

Dad was working very hard to bring in the money for the house and Mum had discovered a new sense of freedom after getting a job as Al's secretary. A new feeling of self-worth which a lot of women in their early forties go through when the kids suddenly don't seem to need you quite as much. In my opinion after being one of those kids that was in the middle of that intense trauma, kids don't ever stop needing their parents. In fact, during the secondary schooling period, I think from all my experience over the years of this and watching the kids in my family and others, the children still need their parents more than ever, to support them and have their corner.

No matter what fight they put up; you have to be there for them regardless. Directing advising and guiding them through the good, bad and downright ugly highs and lows of the teenage years and beyond. So many parents give up and think their kids can carry on without them, to allow the parents to get back to a life of their own, and to see these children suffering and crying out for help, not knowing which way to turn or whom to turn to, that they end up lost and alone. Playing up their parents to get the attention so desperately needed and wanted. The parents wonder why their kids are finding it difficult to cope, when they don't see any further than the surface.

My heart breaks even now , when I think back to how venerable I was and scared to face my fears, I am still trying to cope today with the losses I have had over the years.

So now the time was fast approaching that I would be amongst the very situation I ran away from when I joined the cruise ships. The constant arguments with my Dad and the situation I found myself in. Having to leave home before I was ready, but so incapable of realising that. Everything is wonderful in hindsight. I knew that I was a different person to when I left. I was hoping that I would be allowed to be that person by my family and not the one I had been painted to be. I had felt that nobody really understood me, and I was getting it all wrong. Or was I?

CHAPTER 27 – HOME

It was a bright sunny day as we pulled in at Tilbury docks. The seagulls were swarming around the ship and the pilot boat had navigated us in. The anticipation of the day was swirling around in my head and the anxiety was building in the pit of my stomach. Even though I had seen my family since I left eight months ago, I still wasn't sure of the reception I would receive. Plus, it was the day to say goodbye to Tam.

Sadness filled the air with a very dark cloud hanging over my head, the memories came flooding back of all the fun we had on the ships. I hadn't been so happy in so long. It had been a wonderful experience, one I never really repeated. I have held onto the memories throughout my life. I watched as the Daphne pulled along and settled dockside, easing in like the last piece of a puzzle that had been missing.

I could see my Mum standing next to Al waiting for me and my heart filled with love at the realisation of how much I had missed her.

Tam came up behind me shouting at her family to get their attention. Nice and quiet as usual. She put her arm around my shoulder and gave a small squeeze.

"Well, this is it kiddo, time to go. Are you ready?" the sadness was quite apparent in her voice. Even though she was trying her best to hide it.

"Come on let's go and meet our public" she was always the joker. It was just Tams way of covering up how she really felt about things that mattered to her. Her steely exterior of fun and madness was a great cover up to the hurt and pain that she carried. Her parents divorced when she was young, which left a massive gap in her life. She seemed very close with both of her parents, but her Mum was also a great worry to her. Not in the same way as mine, but she was always striving for perfection, which I think was extremely hard for Tam to achieve all the time. She put a lot of pressure on herself to look a certain way and her clothes always had to be just right. She really didn't see herself in the same way the rest of us did. We are all different I suppose, that's what makes us so unique.

We said goodbye to our friends on the Daphne, which was really hard, our surrogate family were splitting up again. We descended the gang way arm in arm, just as we had left all those months ago at the airport. But this time it was us who would be going different directions.

We stopped to say goodbye, I had a feeling that it wouldn't be the last time I would see her, my partner in crime, my big little sis. A lump was in my throat so big I thought that I would choke. I couldn't cry, because I didn't think that I would ever stop. Her eyes were full of tears as were mine. The ship life was so amazing in every way, but there is always a payoff. Saying goodbye to people in your life, who are constantly changing, the people who become family.

" Well Kiddo" she said " let's get it over with"

We hugged, hi - fived and left, not looking back. Couldn't look back. We had decided the night before to make it simple and easy, a swift exit. Not dwelling on a long goodbye.

It was all too much I fell into my Mum's open arms and sobbed. My emotions had caught up with me when the familiar smell and warmth of Mum enveloped me. I was home, and that was such a great feeling.

The journey back to Stevenage seemed really long, but I was so tired I slept most of it. Having a touch of nodding dog syndrome, where my head kept jolting up and fell again. The car pulled onto the drive and for a moment when I opened my eyes, I was confused, disorientated and just didn't recognise anything. Mum's voice came sliding into my eardrums, like nectar to a bee.

"Love, we're here, wake up Jo" the familiarity of her tone brought me too, in an instant, and the events of the day flooded back.

Her new house with Al was nothing special, a three-bed semi in a cul-de-sac just off of Mossbury Way. A new estate, well new to me, it had been years since I had been here. This was part developments which were popping up all over the place. Expanding at an enormous rate, it had become quite the commuter town.

Emma, Mum's Labrador came bounding up, jumping all over me like a long-lost friend. It was so good to see her. Full of energy as usual. Licking my face, turning around and round, so surprised that she had remembered me.

Entering into the hallway, it was kind of weird being inside a house again. Carpets on the floors, stairs leading directly up to the bedrooms on the level above. I walked into the spacious living room where the large couch and TV lived. Al had put it on straight away to watch the cricket. He was a massive fan. Mum went to the kitchen and put the kettle on.

"Tea, Jo?" she said as if it was the most natural thing in the world for me to be there. To me it was surreal. One minute I had been cruising the Fjords, the next I was in Mum's front room having a cuppa. Life was so bizarre in the most luscious of ways. A cup of tea, that was a novelty.

We chatted all afternoon, about my adventures, showing her photographs that I have got developed along the way. No digital cameras then, well not that I could afford. It all seemed so long ago now. Al Mum's husband had ascended to the bedroom to watch the cricket; he just wasn't interested in anything I had to say. He never was, he put up with the fact that Mum had two kids. As I said before, he was an awkward man, tall and slim but his manner was, well, awkward! When he stood, he would be resting on one straight leg with the other bent and his hip pushed quite far out and his hand on his hip. His teeth protruded out and his lips came together like a parrots beak. He looked uncomfortable in so many ways. I really couldn't understand what my Mum saw in him.

I watch Mum for a moment and the sadness was back

"Mum is everything ok here?" I blurted it out a little too loud and abruptly that it took her by surprise.

"Oh, yes of course, why do you ask" she fidgeted on the sofa, crossing and uncrossing her legs, eventually getting up to make our fifth cup of tea. She lit a cigarette and inhaled the smoke deeply, sighing as she exhaled.

"What is it Mum? what's going on with you, I can see you're not happy , and your letters were, so, well, non-descript." I couldn't help it; it just came out. I needed to know!

" Nothing Jo, I was just sad that we had to leave Cornwall, that's all. I really loved it down there" she seemed as if there was more to it than that, but if there is one thing I knew about my Mum, if you keep on, she will just clam up. Slowly, slowly worked best.

"Ok, you would tell me if there was anything else, wouldn't you?" I added hopefully.

"Yes, Mum," she always said that when I started to mother her. We both knew she was not telling me everything, but what could I do?

It was four thirty in the afternoon and Mum had swapped the tea for some red wine. She was already on her second, I put it down to me being home, that can put stress on anyone. Now, I can see that it was the first time I noticed that there could be a problem. But as most twenty somethings, I didn't pay too much attention. I couldn't really say too much, as I had drunk the equivalent of a small ocean whilst on the cruises. The saying was if you didn't have a drink problem when you got on a ship, you certainly would by the time you left!

The next day I phoned my boss at head office to let them know I was home safe and that I would like to go back out on a second contract in a couple of weeks' time, I asked if

I could go on a larger ship in the Caribbean, not thinking for one minute that I would. Sure, enough a few days later a letter arrived with my contract details, flights hotel and ship. I was so excited, I rushed into Mum to tell her the news.

"I am going, drum roll, to the M.S Fantasy, picking it up in Miami, Florida, staying overnight in a hotel and joining the next day. Can you believe that Mum" I was jumping up and down at that point, holding Mums hands at the same time.

For the second times in as many days I saw that sadness back in her eyes.

"Oh Mum, are you ok?" I said suddenly brought back to earth with an almighty thump.

"Yes, yes, it's fine, I'm just being silly. It's wonderful news, I'm so happy for you." She wiped her eye, trying to hide the tear that escaped. I gave her a hug confused, with the excitement of my new adventure and hurt to see Mum so distressed. I hadn't realised she was so upset by it. She re-assured me that all was well. I wasn't convinced!

We headed off to the shops to buy some new clothes and anything else I needed. I wasn't going to get caught out with the lack of preparation. I knew what was coming.

The rest of the holidays I managed to catch up with Dad and my brother David. The arguments that I was dreading, didn't seem to arise. Dad seemed really interested about the places I had been. He actually seemed really proud of me. That was a different feeling. Maybe we had finally hit some common ground. Maybe it was the fact that I had put some distance between us, or maybe I was just growing up. It was nice either way. My brother was like a whirl wind, not quite understanding what all the fuss was about. Stopping for a cuppa and leaving within the hour. Not sure what was going on there with him.

I was trying to take everything in around me, trying to process what was going on with everyone, that it had taken my mind off my own heartbreak. I had told Mum about En-rico, and that I had vowed not to get mixed up with anyone on the ships again. She smiled that all knowing smile, and with a glint in her eye she just nodded. She knew me better than I knew myself. It seemed as though it was Mum and I against the world sometimes. She would always back me up, without questioning my decisions, but always giving her opinion without forcing the issue. She was clever like that. You ended up thinking that it was your idea, but she had in fact put it there without you realising it in the first place. Clever lady!

The time passed quickly and before I knew it Mum and Al were driving me back to Heathrow to catch my flight to Miami. I was a little nervous because it was my first transatlantic flight, and I was doing it alone. Mum did her normal, don't talk to strangers, be careful, stay with the crowds speech.

As we said our goodbyes, I whispered in Mum's ear,

"I'm only a plane flight away, you can reach me quick by calling head office, and they will get me off in the next port. I will call you when I get to Miami. Please don't worry about me, I'm in safe hands, Mum! Look after yourself, the time will fly"

She squeezed me tight and I inhaled to lock in the familiar smell, and I was gone. Next stop Miami.

CHAPTER 28- MIAMI HERE I COME!

The fight was long but quite enjoyable, watching the latest moves and chatting to an American girl who had been visiting England on her holidays. The aircraft was so different to anything I had ever been on before. The plane was huge, it had an upstairs as well, who would have thought that. Mind you that was definitely not for the likes of me, cattle class only where I was. It was for first and business class up there. The flight was uneventful and smooth thankfully and the approach to Miami was amazing, I could see the palm trees, swimming pools in gardens and beautiful blue sea. It was so tropical. I felt a tinge of excitement as we landed.

August was 'HOT!' and when I disembarked the plane, I got that oven feeling, when the doors to the aircraft opens and the heat hits you like a furnace. That was at five pm, ten pm U.K time. They were five hours behind us. I was exhausted, but I still had to go through customs, and mid-summer it was going to be busy.

Two hours I stood in that que waiting to pass into the U.S.A. Crickey what a bother that was. The officer didn't like the Israeli stamp or the Russian stamp in my passport. I had got them at the end of our Daphne cruise. He eyed me up and down, I felt so guilty and I'm sure my face was flushed. He asked me what my business was, and I showed him my letter of employment. He was satisfied and I carried on through. I collected my bags and jumped in a cab amongst all of the hustle and bustle. So busy, I was surprised that I found my way out. I headed for the Travel lodge only nine dollars by cab, plus tip of three dollars it wasn't too bad. I knew I had to tip a lot, but I was never sure how much.. I changed some money at the airport, not ideal, but I had forgotten to do it before.

The hotel was nice, and the bed, wow, I had never seen such a size. Extra queen size I think it was and there were two of them to choose from. I could lay full out with my arms above my head and I still couldn't touch the tip of the bed.

The TV was thirty inches at least, or that's how it seemed. Massive, by the nineties standard that was large. I felt like I had just stepped into the land of the giants where everything had been supersized. I threw my bags on one bed and ran a bath. Sinking into the hot water was exquisite. Just what I needed. The aircon was doing its job, in fact it was quite chilli. The water tingled on every inch of my body. I indulged for far longer than I intended, but a bath was going to be off the agenda for the next eight months at least.

I put on the robe supplied with the room and ordered room service. I was famished, but I didn't dare step outside the room alone. Not quite that brave. I did feel so grown up. Just like those American movies I used to watch. I giggled to myself as I devoured the large pizza. Of course, it had to be large !!

The cab arrived to take me to the port where I picked up the Fantasy. I was so excited. This was one of carnivals largest ships at the time , with two thousand and fifty-six passenger capacity and nine hundred and twenty crew, this one was going to be a large one. How large didn't dawn on me until I was dock side, standing right next to her.

She was built by Kvaerner Masa-Yards in Helsinki, Finland, she was floated out on December 9, 1988, completed on January 27, 1990. She was formally named on March 1, 1990, as Fantasy by Tellervo Koivisto, the wife of the then President of Finland, Mauno Koivisto. During 2007, she had the prefix "Carnival" added to her name. She is currently the oldest vessel in the Carnival fleet.

I looked up to the summit of the vessel, she was humongous. I recon the Daphne and the Achille could have fitted inside together. Well maybe not, but you get the idea. I approached the gang way nervously and suddenly feeling really shy.

I handed over my documents and waited for my manager to come and get me. Two hours I waited, so typical of my luck, that all the crew had coast guard drill. Nobody was allowed any further until it had finished.

"Hi Jo, I'm John" A voice came out of nowhere and made me jump. " I'm your manager and welcome to the Fantasy" he gave me a suave smile. He was approximately five eight in stature and slim frame, hi lighted hair and a typical hairdresser look about him, if ever I had seen one. He turned out to be ok, fair but firm.

He led me up through the Decks to the salon. The ship was amazing, the atrium was impressive, with a glass lift running up the outside of different levels, lit up like light house on a dark night. On the upper levels where the lounges and disco where, there were strategically placed larger than life baked bean cans and soup cans ready for a photo opportunity. Quite random really. The lighting throughout the ship were loosely based on Vegas and the casino facade . I found it all overwhelming and very loud. He led me to the salon where he introduced me to the team one by one, of which there were twenty in all. Ranging from hairy's to beauty and fitness. We also had massage therapist and spa therapist on the ship. It was a completely different ball game. It was no longer about the cruising but about the money, and lots of it. That's the passengers, not us. The Americans tipped everything and everybody it seemed, much to my delight. Finally, I could start earning some decent cash. It had been a little sparse up until then.

The hair salon was so bright and incredibly busy with the amount of furniture and equipment. The sections consisted of a mirror which had light bulbs all around the edge, looking like a dressing room mirror of a theatre. Also, we each had our own sterilizer and hairsprays, mousse and other products which were needed to create the fascinating styles that were required of us.

John introduced me to Tina my cabin mate, she was Irish, tall and blonde, the complete opposite to me. There was just the two of us in the cabin, so we headed down to settle me in. Tina filled me in on all the info I needed about rotas, cruising and dinner times. The rules were simple on the ship. Always dress to the required days, such as formal, informal etc we can go anywhere on the ship, but no dancing in the disco and no seating on stalls if there were passengers around. We had a bar bill as normal to be settled at the end of each cruise, which were just three and four days to Nassau and Freeport in the Bahamas. Oh, the hardship. PARADISE again, could I cope, what do you think? I had hit the jackpot.

I had to change straight away and join in with embarkation, showing passengers around the spa etc, learning on the go. The spa had a pool in it with massage room set to one side. I didn't know half the stuff myself, but I winged it until I did. The fun had started and so did the amazing difference in the English and American language. We speak the same, but somehow so much got lost in translation. The Americans are wonderful people, but very literal in their terms, and sarcasm was not on the radar then.

Up they came in their droves to book appointments and see what's what. Life jackets in one hand ready for boat drill and a cocktail in the other. The questions were amazingly cute, I had only just joined the ship, but 'how long was a half hour massage?' really did top the all-time favourites of mine, along with ' What time was midnight buffet', 'does the elevator go from the front to the back of the ship?' (no sideways lifts have ever been made yet, not to my knowledge) and the Biggy was ' how does power get to the ship is it via a long cable?'. Classics and well known in our world. But all that aside they were lovely people , so friendly and forth coming.

I got shoved into the demonstration, which I welcomed with open arms, only to be faced with and auditorium of a capacity of two thousand people. I suddenly wanted to bolt for the exit. What a show though. Yes, a show! The fitness instructors ran on opening the extravaganza to demonstrate their classes, with John comparing and introducing the staff. Just like something out of Vegas. What a rush. I didn't have to speak which was a bonus, so I just put a formal night hairdo together and spun my client (passenger I had accosted before) to showcase my skills. I was buzzing. It beat our little gatherings on the other ships.

By eight o'clock I was exhausted, we had started hair around three as the ship set sail for Freeport, the first stop on our four - day cruise. It was now eight pm when we hit the crew mess. Busy was an understatement. The tables were set out in long rows. All of us salon staff were on the same long table and the food was delicious. From burgers and chips to pasta, it was the same food that the passengers had. I was looking around at all the other staff, when I caught the eye of a photog called Lucas and his counterpart Jim. They looked very dapper in their Carnival suits. Lucas was around twenty-five with short dark hair. I was just thinking that he reminded me of Enrico, when he looked at me and winked, my tummy did a somersault as I realised, I was staring.

Tina elbowed me " he fancies you, so he does" Her northern Irish accent sang out at me.

" No Way, I'm off men" I said and explained what had happened on my first ship.

"Well you've got to keep um' at arm's length don't ya know" She added. No, I did not know that then, but I was certainly going to make sure that happens in the future.

We headed back to the cabin . It had all the essentials, clean, comfortable and a lot bigger than it was on the Achille Lauro and Daphne combined. The bunk beds were slightly wider and a lot newer. The bathroom was larger and not so metallic. With a few soft edges and finishes.

We were just around the corner from the gang way, I

thought that might be quite handy for when we were in port, but it turned out to be really noisy, especially when we didn't want to get off early. We were at the end of a corridor where all us spa girls and boys cabins were. Easier for our manager to find us.

Tina asked if I wanted to come to the crew bar, but I was done in. I wanted to be up early in the morning to watch us dock in Freeport. I was working but not until three pm. I had arranged to get off with Tina and Thomas (massage therapist who was American and around twenty-two) and Karen another hairdresser who was from London. She was the same age as me. Very quiet girl, very different from Tam.

I was on the top bunk again, but it was fine, something I was used to. I had put my pictures up above my bunk of Mum and Dad, but now Tam was added to my little family. My head hit the pillow and I was out like a light.

Tina woke me the next morning as I had forgotten to set my alarm. I could hear a lot of hustle and bustle outside our cabin as crew were waiting to get off. I dressed and met the others on the gang way fifteen minutes after the masses had disembarked. It was a lot calmer at that point. When I stepped off the smell was crisp and clean, I could smell the engines of the ship amongst the fragrances of the flowers which were close to the dock. The sun beat down around thirty degrees, already at nine am. It was going to be a hot one.

We headed to a beach close by. Xanadu Beach it was the closest to the
cruise port, so it was an easy option for a quick beach jaunt. Its sheltered
curve protects the beach from strong wind , the water was shallow and clear
enough to paddle and snorkel without getting bombarded by large waves.

The setting was idyllic, reminiscent of those waters and beaches in the
Seychelles. Yet another paradise island. Thomas was filling me in on the gossip from the ship, who was with whom, who wanted to be with whom and who to stay away from. It was quite the character assassination in the nicest possible way. Tina told Thomas not to be so harsh on his fellow ship mates. He of course thought it was hilarious.

After a nice gentle start to the day we headed back for lunch and a shower to get ready for the onslaught of the formal night ahead of us. Going around the ship was a nightmare I kept getting lost. Tina reassured me that I wasn't the only one. The other new girls who had started the week before me were still getting lost now. Somehow that didn't help.

I approached the reception area of the salon to collect my paper for the day. This was a timed itinerary of who I had in and what they required. My first appointment was at three pm and then every half an hour until eight pm that night, mainly full of blow dries and hair ups, plus a few mini facial thrown in for good luck.

John came over to ascertain if I was ok , and to remind me never to judge my clients on the way they look for the amount of money they may have. I thought was a strange thing to say but became very apt soon after.

CHAPTER 29 - FUN & GAMES

Of all the places I had visited over the years I think Nassau in the Bahamas was up there as one of the best and most exciting I had come across. Not so much for the sights or even the people but for the fun factor. I had met up with quite a few of the other girls and boys from the salon at a bar just off of the main cruise line area. It was reminiscent of Carlos 'n' Charlies in Mexico. The name escapes me for the moment, but there were barrels full of beers and music belting out of the sound system. Calypso music with a bit of reggae pumped in for effect. That was at ten in the morning. We were overnight whenever we hit Nassau and on that particular day, I had had quite a wild adventure. (not the animal type)

I started off with Tina at the bar calmly drinking a virgin strawberry daiquiri. and eating a bagel for my breakfast. The sun was beating down like a grill on an oven. I was watching the wavy lines jumping off of the Road outside, where the heat was so intense, I think an egg could have been fried on it. I was watching the passengers and crew meandering around the shops being accosted by the men and women trying to get them to hire anything from jet skis to jeeps and hair braiding of many a form. We found this highly amusing over time, so much so that one of the Fitness instructors Steve got a t-shirt made with 'No I don't want a jet ski,' 'no I don't want my hair braided' and 'No I don't want a jeep hire'. I am surprised that the locals let him get away with that.

To my surprise I see Lucas and Jim approaching the bar in the distance. They wondered over and invited themselves to sit and drink with us. I didn't mind as they were like a double act. Very funny. Cracking jokes every five minutes and trying to ply us with drinks. Before I knew it, Tina had to go back as she was working.

I decided to stay with Lucas and Jim as they decided to head off to Paradise Island. Paradise Island was exactly what it said on the tin. It was formerly known as Hog Island, with an area of two hundred and seventy seven hectares and located just off the shores of Nassau, it is best known today for the sprawling resort Atlantis with its extensive water park rides, pools, beach, restaurants, walk-in aquarium and casinos. Paradise Island is connected to the island of New Providence by two bridges that cross Nassau. The James Bond film Thunderball (1965) was partially shot on Paradise Island as was Casino Royal. It was first built in 1966 by Resorts International, and then added to in the late 1990s.

We were going to play in the casino. I had never in my life been to a casino and I was so excited that my stomach was turning over and over with anticipation. I had only seen the ones on the cruise ships, but because I had known the staff it really didn't seem to matter. As we approached the complex, I was suddenly worried about my attire. I had some half decent shorts on with my bikini underneath and a flowing white top. I whispered to Lucas if I was ok going in looking like I did, but Lucas just smiled and said " you'll do very nicely" and squeezed my hand for good measure.

I was mesmerised as we drove up to the Atlantis resort, back then I was only half of its amazing resort it is today. The hotel looked like the mythical city of Atlantis. Lucas and Jim showed me some of the lagoon beaches with hammocks and loungers surrounding the crystal-clear waters.

We headed into the casino , which like everything else in America was far larger than I could have imagined. It wasn't the first time these two lads had been to the casino and a neither would it be our last trip here. It became one of my favorite places to relax.

We sat at a black Jack table where Lucas ordered three pina coladas for us. He gave the croupier his money and received chips back. I was amazed at the sights I was witnessing. The drinks arrived and I went to pay. Lucas covered my hand with his.

"You don't pay if you're playing a table " He said smiling, slightly mocking me.

I flushed with embarrassment I didn't know the format and was well and truly out of my comfort zone, but slightly enamored by it. It was noisy and bright, and the atmosphere was one of anticipation of a big win. Unfortunately, neither Jim nor Lucas won anything but lost quite a bit. A couple of hundred dollars I believe. I couldn't imagine losing that amount of money.

Reluctantly we called a cab and headed back to the bar near the docks. I knew that I would be back here again, not for the Casino but for the tranquility of the water and the subdued relaxation on one of the hammocks.

Back at the bar the party was starting to get going. It was now about nine and I headed back to the ship to change. I adorned some jeans and vest top with my trainers. That was much more comfortable. Lucas and Jim were still in the bar when I returned, slightly more drunk than I had left them. Lucas was dancing and Jim was chatting up some poor unsuspecting girl from another ship the Amsterdam that had pulled in with us.

I headed to the bar and this time ordered a beer from the barrel. I had a lot of catching up to do. Tequilas were next on the agenda, as always on the ships, which I gladly joined in with. I had lost both of the boys at that point but tagged along with John my manager and a couple of the other girls from the salon.

I was starting to get really drunk by midnight, but I didn't want the party to end. I was chatting to some other American guy called Sam who was very smartly dressed and quite handsome, he asked a few of us to join him at a party on a resort nearby.

Stupidly I agreed thinking the others would come along and soon realized that it was just me with a few other stranger, a mix of women and men. We boarded a large people carrier and headed off.

My vision was starting to merge and become very muffled and odd by that time. I looked out the window trying to recognize where I was going. When I asked Sam, he said we were off to Millionaires row. I thought that it was just in Miami, but unbeknown to me we were heading back to Paradise Island. I found out the name much later.

We headed into a pool complex and there was a band playing and dancing and lots of drinking. Sam seemed to enjoy my company until I turned him down on an invitation to head to his private boat in the marina. With that he left me standing alone and pounced on some unsuspecting young girl who accepted his offer, walking off down to the marina hand in hand laughing as they left.

In the meantime, I was lost and in an area I didn't know. I looked around to fine that there was no-one else left. I looked at my watch and it was five thirty in the morning.

"Shit, Shit and double shit" I said to myself. I had to be back on board by six. The ship was due to leave at six thirty. Bile rose up in the back of my mouth at it dawned on me that if I didn't find a cab, I would miss the ship.

I ran around like a headless chicken trying to locate the reception. I stopped and calmed myself, suddenly finding a signpost indicating where abouts of taxis.

'Thank you, thank you god' I said to myself, and promised never to do it again.

I hoped in a cab, who sped me back to the ship , when I explained how much trouble I would be in if I missed it. He was lovely and got me back with minutes to spare. I dropped him a twenty-dollar tip as I was so grateful.

The security guards were laughing at me as I ascended the gang way. They knew I had only just made it and wagged a finger at me whilst shaking their heads. I darted into my cabin just in time for a shower and breakfast, before heading to the salon for work.

CHAPTER 30 – HERE I GO AGAIN

Everything moves along very quickly on the ships, another couple of months had passed in a wink of an eye. My party antics in Nassau were never repeated, but a date with Lucas was . I swore that I would never get involved again, yet here I stood arm in arm with Lucas in the crew bar. We had got together during a party in one of the entertainers cabins. Well when I say a cabin, I mean a whole host of cabins down on the lower Decks. The salsa music was very loud, and everyone was dancing in the corridors, swinging their hips to the music, trying to replicate the Latin waiters, who were amazing dancers. I felt so alive during those parties. No-one judged you or spoke badly of you. It was a happy family, where you could be yourself.

Lucas and I certainly took full advantage of that as he swung me around in the small space trying not to bang into the walls. My feet felt as if I was gliding along an iced lake, laughing and singing. I was having the time of my life. The troubles of home seemed a distant memory. We had got together that night, under the stars, radiating beams of light onto the upper Decks. I had never seen a sky like it. There wasn't any light pollution in the middle of the ocean. Lucas had reminded me so much of Enrico in the way his dark complexion glistened in the moon light, and the way his eyes twinkled when he looked at me. Had I learnt nothing from my encounter before, obviously not, I had fallen hook, line and sinker. What was it with these guys? Lucas was from L.A, near Hollywood, believe it or not he hated it there. He said everyone was so false and non-genuine it made him so uncomfortable . He had started off as an art student but started to lean towards photography at the end of his studies. He had tried to get into the Hollywood studios but, when he went along to find out about it, he realised very quickly that it wasn't for him.

He had accepted the role on the cruise liners to tied him over until he could decide what he wanted to do with his life.

Apparently, I had now thrown a spanner in the works. Things do move quick on board as I had felt the same.

I had called Mum at her work a few times filling her in on my travels, even though there wasn't too much to report on, as we did the same three and four day cruising, to the same places, and like creatures of habit we visited the same beaches and bars every time. I had told her about Lucas, and she was happy for me. Especially when I told her that he had put a red rose on my station in the salon one day. Very romantic. I was so happy, but still Mum sounded so sad. She had told me that there was a few difficulty with the business, but nothing too much to worry about. I wasn't so sure.

We had wet dock coming up soon in Miami, it was just four days, but we would stay on the ship whilst crucial maintenance was carried out. I had to say goodbye to Tina my cabin mate, but I had another girl called Kerri come on. It was nice not to be the new girl anymore.

I had been selling extremely well in the salon and I was made Head stylist. Which was great for me, a little extra pay and I managed the team of stylist which there were six. They didn't like it at first as some of them had been on a lot longer than me, but hey they needed to sell more. Unfortunately, money spoke louder than anything. If you took more, you got more benefits. My manager had told me to think about doing management training before I come back out on another contract. I said I would think about it. I couldn't think that far ahead at that time.

We were just seeing off the last of the passengers when an announcement came over the loudspeaker that the air conditioning would be turned off for a few days starting from midday and that we should make necessary arrangements if needed. We had all decided to stay on board as head office would not subsidise us to stay elsewhere.

Kerri and Sonia who were my new partners in crime decided to go roller blading along South Beach, which was an amazing place and something we had been talking about for the last couple of weeks. So that's where we headed. The sun was beating down hard, and the temperature must have been somewhere in the late thirties.

We had our cut down jeans and bikinis on covered by crop tops. Oh, how I could get away with so little clothing back then. It was very funny when we all turned out looking the same, but we didn't care. We jumped in a cab and headed for Long Beach. Amazed at all the sites and music which were blaring from windows along the way. Miami was very built up but in a tropical stroke, Latino way. There were so many Latin people in Miami. It is now the sixth most populated city in America. Miami is a major centre and leader in finance, commerce, culture, media, entertainment, the arts, and international trade. Also known as the Capital Latin America, with Cuban's being a large part of the population.

It was an event that I would never forget, gliding along South Beach like a swan on a lake, cruising with the breeze flowing through my hair. The sun was bright, but with my shades and baseball cap, I felt right at home. We had hired the skates from a bar up the other end of town. What a feeling. We had the most fantastic day, stopping for lunch in the renowned Hooters bar. I wasn't sure what to make of it. Girls running around with skirts just covering their bum's and tops cut so low that it never left much to the imagination. I could see why there were so many men there. Lucas and Jim being two of them. I did laugh when I saw them.

"Busted" I shouted as we walked past heading towards our table.

Lucas looked up startled at the outburst. But his features

soon softened when he saw me. They wondered over and asked if they could join us.

" Are you sure I'm not going to cramp your style" I laughed

" Nah, they're not my type anyway" He winked as if trying to prove I was the only one for him. I didn't believe for a minute but appreciated the thought. The food was amazing, I had decided to go for something light. A salad with chicken and guacamole. But when it arrived it was in a massive taco shell. Filled to the brim with cheese, guacamole lettuce and tomatoes, it was large.

"My goodness" I said with my mouth wide open. " I only wanted a small salad, not to feed an army" I added

Lucas thought that it was hilarious, as did the others until there's all turned up just as big. Kerri's was a burger and fries, but the burger was the size of a dinner plate on its own and the fries were enough for three people not just one. We sat back and looked at the left overs. There was enough to feed a family of four.

" That's terrible" Sonia said shaking her head with the amount of food left.

"I know right, we could feed so many homeless" Karri added

" Come on girls, next time we need to order between us" I said feeling quite sick at the thought of eating anything else. Lesson learnt.

We stopped at a few bars on the way back to the ship and had a dance or three. All of us being whisked off by other people. Not meaning anything, it just the way of the people, they loved to dance. It was a great night. The music the atmosphere was hot and happy. The air was a light with possibilities, rushing in. I had the feeling that anything was possible, and sky was the limit. They say that America is the land of the free. Well that's how it felt. That wouldn't be the last time I got that feeling, but that didn't not have a great outcome.

Back on the ship we headed to our cabins. Kerri went to her boyfriend, who was an engineer on the ship from Italy. I did warn her about the Italian men, but she didn't care. Sonia headed back to her own and me and Lucas headed to mine. We headed down towards my cabin, and the temperature was getting hotter and hotter.

"Oh No, the air con. It's not on is it?" I looked at Lucas. "It's going to be so hot, can you stand it" I added thinking that I couldn't breathe already as the hot air was seeping into my lungs.

" Come on " he said, " Grab and blanket off your bed and follow me" With that we headed up to the top Deck, where to or surprise and amusement, all the other crew and staff were already.

We were lined up like sardines in a can. I spotted Sonia and Jim up by the funnels. They were waving like idiots, trying to get us to get a givvy on. They saved a few loungers but were afraid someone else would take them.

"Oh, guy's thank you, can you believe how hot it is down there" I said to Jim and Sonia, looking from one to the other, wondering how they had managed to get up there so quick and together. What a coincidence. Or was it.

They both started to laugh when they saw me putting two and two together, Jim put his arm around Sonia.

"I knew it, how long have you two been, you know to-gether?" I pointed at them individually. I turned and looked at Lucas. He smiled

"I don't believe it, you knew, didn't you" I started playfully hitting him.

"Ok, ok you got me, yes I knew, but only because I bumped into them both kissing behind the photo studio the other day" he said blushing.

" You should have told me" I couldn't help thinking why he didn't.

"Sorry baby, I didn't think it was a big deal" he was shrug-ging his shoulders in a don't kill the messenger type of way.

Lucas and I pulled our beds together as close as we could. It was so hot. We didn't need the blankets, so we used them as pillows instead. What a feeling it was to fall asleep under the stars. The air was humid and there wasn't a single breeze around to relent the heat that was all encompassing. I couldn't imagine what it would be like in the cabin. I didn't care, Lucas was beside me and my friends were close by. I looked up to the starry sky and thought of Mum looking up into the same sky. The words she had always said to me. ' If you get home sick Jo just look up to the stars and remember there is only one sky above this earth, think of me as I will be looking into the same sky as you. That thought had always brought me comfort.

Waking up on Deck was really wired, looking around it must have been early , but the sun was up and the noise of lorries and trucks making deliveries to the ship started to gain momentum. I turned to my right where Lucas had slept, to find an empty bed. I sat up right and saw him looking down on the commotion below.

" Hey Jo, you sleep well" he said squinting from the sun that was glaring in his eyes.

" Yeah not bad" I replied, wiping sleep from my inner socket.

"I'm going to head off now and check on some deliveries that are being made today" he said gathering up his stuff. He kissed me on my forehead and with that he was gone.

I couldn't help but think something was amiss. Call me over cautious but after my track record I couldn't be sucked in again and then be let down without noticing anything. I was becoming quite cynical. I headed back to my cabin, into the stifling heat. The sweat was just starting to bead on my forehead when I heard the wonderful swish as the air con came rushing through the ventilation unit. The relief was instant and very welcoming. I jumped into the shower and washed off the sand and aromas of the day before. Karri entered the cabin, beaming with joy.

"You ok?" I asked, knowing why she was full of jumping beans.

"Yeah I'm good" she replied looking up into the ceiling ,

smirking out of the corner of her mouth.

" What are you not telling me Kerri"

"Oh nothing, just that Fabio asked me to spend two months with him in Italy, when we leave"

"Wow that's great" I said " Now, don't shoot me, but are you sure he is not married"

"No" she jumped at me slapping me on the arm" Not everyone is a creep" She laughed.

The four days in Miami flew by, but we were all ready to move on, after shopping until I dropped and smuggling on some food and drink in the cabin, which was forbidden, we were all set. I had bought a new formal dress whilst at one of the shopping malls. It was just plain black, fitted like a glove with a slot taken out of the middle. There were strappy sleeves and a small slit from the floor to the knee. I loved it and couldn't wait to wear it.

The ship sailed without any passengers to Fort Lauderdale, which was going to be our new home port. Fort Lauderdale was a stone throw away in American terms from Cape Canaveral, where the Rockets launch from. I was excited that we may see one. We were a little far away to witness one from there, but I did, go over to Cape Canaveral Later to experience a launch and it was thrilling, although it was a little like seeing a giant firework go off, from where I was standing.

Our cruising was still going to be the same unfortunately, but I suppose at least we knew all the good places to go.

The passengers started to embark, and to our surprise there were a lot of younger teens coming on, eighteen plus. We had a telegram come to all departments warning that there were a lot of underage kids coming on and warned us that under no circumstances were we to mix with them or sell them alcohol. I did, chuckle to myself thinking yeah good luck with that. Thankful for what I thought would be a quieter cruise. Gosh how wrong I was.

It started the minute they arrived; the salon was heaving with giggling girls wanting their hair done for formal night.

We obliged as much as we could, but tempers were starting to fray, when a few were standing ridiculing us for our uniforms.

I could stand it no longer and promptly asked the girls to leave the salon unless they had an appointment. They did so under duress. I knew I wasn't going to like this cruise. Not only that but we found out our area manager was going to meet us in Nassau and there were going to be some changes.

We hit the ground running, kids(16 to 19-year olds) everywhere all screaming and shouting. We heard that some of the boys who were seventeen, got caught drinking, fighting and having sex on the outside Deck with some of the girls. They had got put into the ships prison, yes there was a holding cabin down in the lower Decks, for such incidences. The parties were wild and noisy. The staff were so busy trying to keep order. It was utter chaos.

We finally arrived in Nassau, and to my surprise there was the Statendam in port. It was Tamsin's ship; I was so excited that I couldn't wait to get off. It was also unbelievable that the area Manager was an old friend of mine from Plymouth called Jules. I walked up to her and said

"Hey Jules, fancy seeing you here" trying not to give the game away she turned and her face lite up

"Jo, wow, my gosh I knew you were out here somewhere, but I hadn't checked all the names on the inventory" She gave me a massive hug.

"Well you're a sight for sore eyes" We laughed as we explained to John that we worked and hung out together when we worked in Plymouth for the same company years ago. I arranged to meet with her later up in the bar for a catch up. But for then she had to go and have meetings.

Who would have thought it, area manager for such a large organisation? Jules wasn't exactly management material when I knew her, quite the opposite in fact. Always challenging the salon managers and not really meeting the required standards as far as her attitude. But she was fun, and a great hairdresser, we had such a laugh going out in Plymouth to the night clubs. She shared a flat on the Barbican with another girl Fran from the salon. I used to crash there regularly after nights out.

I was heading out for a coffee on Lido Deck, but I decided to walk up the other way passed the funnels and down the other side to avoid the crowds of teenagers, as we couldn't get off just yet, the ship hadn't quite cleared.

I approached the first funnel, and I could hear some giggling coming from behind it. Oh no I thought not another two kids at it. I tried to mind my own business as I walked past, when I heard Lucas's voice. I stopped in my tracks and a cold rush of ice-cold blood ran through my veins. 'No, it couldn't be, no, he wouldn't. '

I dared not look but found I had to. The draw was too intense to ignore. I looked to my left and saw Lucas with one of the teenage girls, kissing half clothed. Holding her up against the funnel. I was rooted to the spot. I couldn't move. I just stared. The girl turned to meet my gaze, and shouted pervert. Lucas followed her gaze and looked straight at me. He stopped and dropped the girl like a stone. His faced flushed with embarrassment. This time I had caught him. My mind was swimming, I felt as if I was going to throw up. I didn't know whether to cry, run or just hit him, but I couldn't do any of those. I couldn't move. Lucas turned his back on the girl and started to walk towards me with his hand on his chest, shaking his head saying he was sorry. The girl was shouting at him and me demanding to know who I was.

I stood looking at him through steely eyes, we were inches apart. The disbelief that it could and did happen again to me was unbelievable, so much so I started to laugh. Large out loud laughs. Had I gone mad or was I just mad as hell. The later was in fact where I was at. The girl came rushing over tucking her top in her trousers. Demanding to know who I was again. I turn to her and in the calmest voice I could muster, I told her that I had been his girlfriend. Emphasizing the had been. I turned on the spot and walked away, head held high, until I was out of sight.

As soon as I hit the steps I ran back to my cabin. My mind was blown, all sorts was rushing around my head. No way could I put up with seeing him now after that. Not like Enrico, where I had to keep seeing him, rubbing salt into my wound. What to do, what to do. In an instant I knew.

I got changed and headed for the gang way. There were lots of crew hanging around, but we were finally let off. I had to get away before Lucas came looking, as I'm sure he would, to try and clear his name if nothing else.

I ran to the Statendam's gang way and waited. I was sure Tam would be getting off soon, and there she was. My big little sis. Oh, how I had missed my friend. She saw me and screamed.

" Jo, Jo, bloody hell girl, where did you spring from" We hugged and as she looked at me, she knew something was wrong.

" Are you ok luv" she said

" Have you got time for a drink" I said wishing that she could come with me.

"Yeah chick, come on let's go"

We headed to the nearest bar where I filled her in on what was going on. She couldn't believe it and told me that I must be one of the unluckiest people she had known. That didn't make me feel any better.

"What can I do, Tam, I can't wait six months watching him play around again"

" I have an idea, one of our guys wants to go to the Fantasy, her boyfriend is on there"

I knew instantly where she was going with it. At that moment her mates turned up to the bar. She introduced me. I made small talk for half an hour, then left to track down Jules. I found her in the piano bar, with John and the manager Karen from the Statendam

" Hi, I said sheepishly, so sorry to interrupt but have you got a minute."

"Who do you want Jo" John interrupted

" Well, all of you I think" Jules looked at me oddly. I told them what had happened about the girl on the Statendam who wanted to come on here. They understood. I told them that I didn't mind swapping, not mentioning Lucas.

Jules left saying she would contact head office in Miami and check to see if it was ok. The others agreed that it would be a good move for both of us girls. I hung around until Jules returned getting to know Karen who was twenty-eight and from my neck of the wood in Hertfordshire.

I saw Jules enter the piano bar, my stomach was in my mouth, with the anticipation. She nodded and it was all systems go. Karen located the other girl and informed her of the transfer if she still wanted it, then it was all systems go to get off. I only had until five as the Statendam wasn't over night and was leaving at six.

I gave Jules a letter for Lucas, explaining that I couldn't be on there with what I had seen. I then went to the salon to find Sonia and Kerri. I filled them in and made a hasty goodbye. They were so shocked, but they got it. We exchanged home addresses and promised to stay in touch, and we did for many years.

I packed my stuff and headed to the gang way where I picked up my passport and met up with Jules to take me onto the Statendam. I crossed paths with the girl who was heading to the Fantasy. She gave me the biggest smile and thanked me for transferring. I don't think she knew why, but I'm sure she would fine out in no time.

Jules gave me a hug at the gang way and told me she would see me soon in another port, where she was due to catch up with the staff on there for her four-monthly meeting. So, there I was about to follow Karen to my new cabin. I couldn't wait to see Tam and tell her. The twosome was back together. I took one last look at the Fantasy, not quite believing how quick it had all taken place and how shocked

Lucas would be when he found out. It was the best way to survive for me. I knew I couldn't take any more heart ache.

CHAPTER 31 - REUNITED

Rose was my new cabin mate, tall slim, very attractive. Long dark hair which touched her waist and olive skin. I was a bit disappointed that I couldn't share with Tam again, but I was grateful to be on the ship and away from Lucas, even though I missed him terribly. My cabin was better than any of the previous ones I had had before. They were passenger cabins that were not used anymore. Slightly larger than normal crew quarters and we actually had carpet on the floor and a TV. Unfortunately, we couldn't get any channels on it, just stuff about the ship. Rose was from Brighton, not far from the beach front. She had never been away from her family before and at twenty-one it was quite hard for her. She often got home sick for her large family of five brothers and two sisters. I couldn't even begin to imagine that many, with just my brother and I in ours.

After chatting to her for a while, it was the fact that she had so many siblings that brought her to the ships. She was the oldest and never got a look in on anything she wanted. Having to look after the young ones all the time. Coming in from her day job in the salon to start again when she got home with chores. She had felt more like their mother, than their sister. She came for some peace and to follow her dreams. Her family were happy for her but disappointed also.

The rules on the Statendam were different to anything I had encounter before. The passengers were older, with money and the officers were Dutch. It was after all a Holland American cruise ship. Holland America The Statendam was the fifth in the company's one-hundred-and-thirty-year history to bear the name. It was the first of a new class of ship when it debuted in 1993. Alternative dining, updated spa facilities, great entertainment. At the time it was in a league of its own. .Holland America treated Statendam to an extensive makeover in early twenty ten. It came out of dry dock on March the twenty sixth, 2010, with a dynamic new showroom replacing the traditional Van Gogh room, the outstanding changes to Deck 8 (Upper Promenade), with new lounges and new public areas and some new touches in all the cabin classes.

Unfortunately for us we could no longer treat the ship like our second home. We were required to wear our uniform at all times in the public areas. Unless we were on a day off, then we had to wear our fitness gear, which entailed the company logo on all items. On formal nights we had to dress is cocktail dresses that were of a modest nature. Bang goes my nice new dress I thought. Not very modest with the slit in the middle where my belly was.

Rose led the way to the salon; the ship was about to depart, and we had to start work. I found Tam slouched over the reception desk, obviously regretting an onslaught of alcohol the night before.

"Somethings never change" I said laughing as I approached the desk.

"Jo, I didn't think that you would pull that off" she said giving me a massive hug.

" Well you know me I have friends in high places." Which was true but I didn't say anything else as Karen our manager was walking through the spa to where we were standing.

She smiled " All set Jo?"

"Yeah, no worries" I told Tam that I would catch up with her in the officers mess, later for some food. I followed Karen to my workstation and was greeted with a panoramic view of the ocean. I took a sharp intake of breath.

"I will let you settle yourself in, you have fifteen minutes until your first client is in" she laid my work sheet on the side and walked off smiling to herself.

I found it hard to take it all in. The Fantasy was full of equipment, bright lights and quite garish. But this was on a different level. We were situated on Lido Deck, with a large window stretching the full length of the salon. All the stations were placed at an angle so that every passenger had a view of the ocean. If was breath taking. I knew this was luxury. I could understand why it was a world cruise ship. The other girls were lovely, there were eight of us altogether. Not the same size as the fantasy but where it lacked in quantity it made up with quality.

The cruising on the ship was better than I could have imagined. We were going around the Caribbean incorporating St Thomas, Martinique Barbados, St Lucia St Maarten, Grenada and curacao, plus the Panama Canal, and Acapulco, not in that order. It was out of this world. They were all the places that I could only have dreamt of from my window in the bedroom when I was young. Who would have thought it, little old me now cruising the world?

Sally coughed releasing me from my daydream, she was one of the other stylists letting me know my client was here. It was another busy formal night, with plenty of clients and sales made. I had become quite good at selling the products, but it was because they were extremely good, and I used them myself.

I met Tam in the petty officers mess, where we had our dinners. It was a lot smaller than the other we had use. It was staff and petty officers only on here. The crew were somewhere else, and the senior officers had their own bar. The petty officers mess and bar we could go in how ever we wanted but the officers bar we had to be in uniform. It was very strict on the dress code.

Tam and I seemed to carry on where we left off all those months ago. If was quite funny really. We went off in every port with the others, hired jeeps to see the islands, and snorkelled in the magnificent clear blue ocean and saw some wonderful wildlife. I felt that I was back on Track. The bar was the same with tequila slammers, but the Dutch Officers were welcoming but not as laid back as the Italians.

CHAPTER 32 - NEW YORK, NEW YORK

We certainly had some fun, with parties going on late into the night(Next morning actually) I was starting to get tired, but I wasn't half way through my contract yet. Christmas came and went with out to much fuss and word soon came that we were relocating and heading to New York. To get there we passed through the Panama Canal stopping at Puerto Vallarta, Huatulco, Puntarenas (Puerto Caldera), Cartagena (Colombia) Key west, Charleston then onto New York. Karen told us that to win a day off in New York we had to hit the most sales out of hair and beauty. Well now, that was a challenge if ever I heard of one.

I managed to call Mum in Puerto Vallarta in the crew phoning centre. It was slightly cheaper from there than a normal phone. I filled her in on what was happening and apologised for the lack of writing. I found a lot harder to find the time due to being so busy with work and sightseeing. She didn't mind so much as long as she was kept informed about where I was in the world so she could put a pin in her ginormous map on the wall. She was tracking me apparently. I thought that was sweet of her. She didn't have much news about anything, other than work was busy and she was walking the dog a lot, due to Al being away on business.

"I thought that he didn't have to do that so much now you were in Stevenage. That was the whole point of you going back there surely?"

"Yeah your right, but he had to go where the work was , so that meant him travelling around the country again" she was so down in her voice, my heart was breaking for her. She had very few friends and I think she was lonely.

"Do you need me to come home Mum?" I said half hoping the answer would be yes. But she said no, in fact but there was a small pause as if she was thinking about it.

"No, your fine dear, nothing wrong here" I'm not sure who she was kidding but it wasn't me.

After the call ended, I tried to call my brother , but as always there was no answer, just went straight to voice mail. I left a brief message stating that I would write to him in due course. I had to get him to see Mum more, but after the split with Mum and Dad, he had taken it really badly and wanted nothing to do with my Mum for two years. I was hoping that it had all blown over, but he didn't see her as much as he should have done that's for sure.

Puerto Vallarta is a Mexican beach resort city situated on the Pacific Ocean with dozens of nightclubs, hundreds of restaurants and some of Mexico's best beaches. The original colonial town shines through an endless selection of shopping and art galleries. I didn't go on anywhere as I had to be back for eleven to start my shift for the day. I wasn't that bothered, which is terrible really. When do you get a chance to go to Mexico? I just wasn't feeling it that day. My mind was focus to much on Mum.

We finally reached the Panama Canal; I knew my Dad would have loved to see this with all the engineering and history attached to it. is an artificial eighty two km (51 mile) waterway in Panama that connects the Atlantic Ocean with the Pacific Ocean. The canal cuts across the Isthmus of Panama and is a channel for maritime trade. The Canal locks are at each end to lift ships up to Gatun Lake, an artificial lake created to reduce the amount of work required for the canal, which is twenty - six metre (eighty five feet) above sea level, and then lower the ships at the other end. The Canal has since been widened to allow the larger ships to export more cargo.

I was working for the eight to eight shifts, but because we

were lucky enough to have the large window with uninterrupted views, I could witness the whole thing, as did my clients. It gave us so much to chat about, sharing it with the lovely people was wonderful. So many of my clients were of the older generation so they knew so much history which they were kind enough to pass onto me. Such as the construction of the Panama Canal was where the expression "Another Day, Another Dollar" came from, as the workers were rumoured to be paid a dollar a day for their labour. I never knew that. We learnt something new every day. I expect that originates from somewhere also.

It took us all day to get through it ten hours to be exact. It was slow going and to me the scenery was similar all the way through. I guess you had to really appreciate the whole engineering aspect of how long and how many years it took to build the vast canal. At that time, I did not appreciate any of the history, but now I think it would be fascinating. That's what age does for you.

We had to docked in Cartagena Columbia a gorgeous fishing village on Colombia's Caribbean coast, has excellent beaches, a historic old town and beautiful colonial architecture. It is also one of the safest places in the country. We got off at the port and was inundated with vendors hawking souvenirs. Tam and I had shopping on our minds so together with Rose and Sally we headed off to the nearest shops. Cartagena is the fifth-largest city of Colombia and the second largest region after Barranquilla. It was a bit pricey but if you are a shopaholic like Tam she didn't care. There were narrow cobbled lanes and markets selling unique handcrafted items, charming antiques, gemstones, silks and silverware, and different varieties of imitation goods. There was also some of the well-known night markets such as the Bazurto market and Portal de Los Dulces where you can find a variety of shops selling clothes, antiques made of wood, gold, jewellery, eateries, and upscale restaurants that attracts a lot of tourists every year. But we had to be out of there by five.

The aromas of Columbia were that of coffee, typically around every corner was a coffee house. Not like we know it here to be today, costa on every corner but of a traditional nature. Tables outside with lots of men sitting watching the world go by. The typical white canopy which gave a small amount of relief from the sun, and the wooden frontage of the shops looks like trendy pallets that had be stuck to the outside walls. Plants hanging down with their lush greenery, just being hit by a slight breeze that trickled through the gaps of the wood. It was a beautiful contrast of the two colours.

We headed back to the ship laden with our bags, some of us (Tam) had a few more than others. We dropped them into our cabins and made our way back to work for a couple of hours before dinner.

We had a day in Key west which was nice to get back to more of an up to date environment where we received mail from home. Mum had sent me a long letter telling me about bailiffs turning up at the door threatening them with prosecution of not paying some bill. I couldn't believe what I was reading. But she did finish with, it had all been a big mistake in her last paragraphs, and that she was to keep a better eye on the accounts.

She also informed me that unfortunately my uncle had died suddenly. He was my Mums brother in law and that he had been unwell for a few day but later died of a heart attack. Well that was some cheery letter I thought. I wonder how she is coping with it all. I planned to nip off later to call her if I could. Unfortunately, I didn't have time as we had a quick turn around and stock to bring on board. That was a massive undertaking bringing it up from dock side on trolleys and checking and putting it all away. Our next stock delivery was due in New York, in five days' time. We had a lot of sea days between now and then and I didn't have much time off.

It wasn't too much of a problem working so hard. Tam and I had made a packed that we would aim for the day off in

New York together. It would be a tough call as we didn't know where anyone else were with their sales. So, we just kept pushing. Bag after bag went out of the salon full of hair products and facial creams. Berets and sun glow were my best sellers and at fifty dollars a pop for each I was on a roll. I just hoped no one else was.

The night before we were due to dock in New York, Karen called a meeting just after port clean. That was traditional on all ships to do before we headed into a major or home port, to start a different cruise on a clean note. We sat around some of us on the floor huddled around the hood dryers waiting for the announcement of who had one time off. My heart was in my throat as I really wanted that day off to see the sights, what a thrill.

Tam and I were sitting hand in hand holding so tight I think the blood circulation was cut off for a minute.

" Drum roll everyone , I have the results" In no particular order she read out the first five of us. " I won't drag this out to long" she said grinning from ear to ear. She left it for what seemed like an eternity, the salon had never been so quiet, so much so we could hear the slot machines chiming away in the casino.

" Ok for the Beauty we have a tie, so I have decided to let the two highest to have the time off in beauty, Its Tam and Maisy" I looked at Tam as her arms flew up to the ceiling whooping as she did it. Her and Maisy did a gig on the spot. I thought my head was going to explode with anticipation, but I felt in my heart that I wouldn't get it.

"Ok ,ok you two calm down" She said to Tam and Maisy who were about to hit the mirrors with all their dancing.

" Ok for the hair....... Ok Jo I will put you out of your misery, I can see you are about to explode if I don't tell you. You have done it, well done Jo" I looked at her in disbelief, I pointed at my self

" What , me , what, I have done it, I have won the day off" I couldn't believe it I was sure that I had not achieved anywhere near where I wanted to be , but apparently I had smashed it by double the amount that the others had done between them. Karen congratulated me and I joined the other two dancing and singing around the salon.

After they joys of the news had settled down, we headed to the mess to plan our day. Starting off with watching us sail into Manhattan passed the Statue of liberty. Once our itinerary of the day had been sorted, we headed back to the salon to find something warm to wear. The weather had been getting cooler over the last few days. It was January after all, and it was snowing in New York. We had planned ice skating in Central Park, A trip up the Empire State Building and shopping of course. I managed to dig out some jeans I had , a hooded jumper and the only jacket I had was part of the salons fitness wear. I grabbed a scarf from one of the other girls and hoped that the shop would sell some gloves. Lucky enough they did, probably the most expensive gloves I've ever bought. At thirty dollars a pair I couldn't afford to lose them, but they were much needed.

We were up on the top Deck at the front of the ship at the crack of dawn. Five am to you and me. The weather was freezing, and I was thankful to the for layers of clothing that I managed to fit under my jumper. The wind was wiping around my ears and my nose had turned a bright red. Very attractive. Tam had the same on except hers was in purple , mine was blue and Maisy's was red. We looked like something out of a girl band. But none of us had coats. How ridiculous was that.

As the sun rose the sight of the Statue of Liberty came into view. I took a sharp intake of breath as it was astounding. I had seen it so many times on TV but never in the flesh. So, to speak. "The Statue of Liberty Enlightening the World" (the full name) was a gift of friendship from the people of France to the United States It stands at a colossal one hundred and fifty-one feet from the base to the torch. Not the largest structure in New York but one of the most iconic.

Sailing passed the monument was amazing and I couldn't help but snap away on my camera trying to get as many shots as possible. The day was unfortunately hazy, so the full impact of the sky line was hidden by low cloud. But as the sun came up the full impact suddenly took hold of me.

As soon as we docked the three of us were ready to disembark. We jumped in a yellow cab and asked to be taken to Central park for ice skating. The cabby told us that it didn't open until nine am and reminded us that it was only seven thirty. We had been so keen, we forgot about opening times.

We asked to be taken to a proper diner to get some breakfast, so he dropped us off at his favourite place Joe's café just up from the cruise Terminal.

We headed in and sat at the dinners enclosed tables, just as I had imagined it from the TV. In fact, I felt as though I had just walked onto a movie set of Starsky and Hutch back in the dat. I was expecting 'Huggy Bear' to walk around the corner any minute.

We ordered some pancakes and coffee; the coffee was free re-fills, and the pancakes came with everything from eggs to syrup and banana and bacon all on the same plate. I couldn't face that amount of food so I just ordered scrambled eggs on toast, it was a nice surprise to see they were of a normal size, but Maisy's was a different story, she ordered the pancakes with cream and banana, and got a stack of five pancakes oozing with cream banana and lashings of syrup smothering the top and dripping down the sides. Tam had just gone for a coffee and muffin. She did help Maisy eat hers.

We finished and got a cab to central park, without stomachs full we were ready to be wowed. The cab dropped us by the opening to hit the park. There are two main ice-skating rinks in Central Park, each with skate and locker rentals. Wollman Rink and Lasker Rink. There was a third, which is free but only available at Conservatory Water when proper ice conditions permit. We chose 'The Wollman Rink' it was by far the most popular and well-known ice - skating rink in Central

Park. It was located on the east side. We enjoyed gliding across the ice with the New York skyline as a back dropped. I just wanted to pinch myself to make sure I wasn't dreaming.

We couldn't hang out there to long as we only had until seven pm to do everything that we wanted before getting back on ship, and it was already eleven am. We dropped off out skates and headed towards the Empire Tate Building situated in the centre of Middletown, Manhattan. I remember seeing that building in King Kong . The eighty sixth floor was our destination, and I was so excited. We entered the foyer to a replica that sat behind glass of the full structure of the building. Telling us about its history. It has since been updated and a new entrance has been put in on thirty fourth street in 2018.

We got into the elevator and braced ourselves for the ascent to the eighty sixth floor. The Observation Deck wraps around the building's spire, providing 360-degree views of New York and beyond. The views were outstanding as we stepped out onto the Deck, we could see Central Park, The Hudson River and East River, The Brooklyn Bridge, Times Square and The Statue of Liberty, to name a few .

I felt as if my head was swirling as I edged closer to the rails. Tam told me to look down, but I thought my knees were going to turn to jelly, when the magnitude of the drop hit me. I discovered from that day that I really didn't have a head for hights. I stepped back to lean against the wall of the inner observation area and felt me way until I reached the door.

"Jo! where are you? Are you ok luv" Maisy shouted out wondering where on earth I had got to?

"It's ok, don't worry about me I'm ok just looking at the view from in here." I tried to keep my voice from wobbling. One of the door porters smiled and in a fantastic New York accent, re - assured me that I wasn't the only one who did that exact same thing. We both laughed as the two girls walked back in.

" What's so funny" Tam asked looking puzzled.

"It's ok I don't seem to have my hight legs" They all laughed at me but I relly couldn't wait to hit the ground level. After a hotdog from one of the street vendors we headed to Greenage Village for some shopping. Often called the 'Village' by the locals and situated on the west side of Manhattan. With Musicians, sunbathers, skateboarders, dog owners and NYU students all hang out around the historic fountain in the shadow of the arch there had been a lot of films and televisions shows made there. The surrounding neighbourhood echoes with beat-poets where Paul Simon, Bob Dylan and Joan Baez began their careers.

Time was getting on and it was dark and very cold. We had managed to do the things we had planned but it was time to head back to the ship. With a last look at the sky line (including the twin towers) I walked up the gang way and headed to the cabin. We grabbed a coffee in the mess before heading back to the cabins. I was done in and just wanted a hot shower and an early night. What a day!

CHAPTER 33 – DID THE EARTH MOVE?

Nothing could top the Visit to New York, I was still in ore at the magnitude of the buildings. We had left New York and were now heading back the way we had come and headed to L.A, another place I was looking forward to going. Karen walked into the salon and asked me to join her in her office. I couldn't help thinking that I was in for some bad news. Everything ran through my mind as I sat down on the chair opposing her. It was quite a small space, with lots of files and a computer sat on the table to one-side. The lighting was pretty bright, and it smelt of massage oil. A beautiful fragrance of frangipani.

"Jo, thanks for coming in , and I would like to start by saying how pleased we are with your sales, targets, you have exceeded our expectations" There was a but coming I could feel it.

"After a lot of agonising between myself and head office we are transferring you to the 'Ecstasy' sister ship to the 'Fantasy', I tried to get you on the world cruise, but unfortunately head office had already promised it to someone else. They did say that if you want another contract that they will consider you" Her face was softer than normal; I think she felt my pain. She informed me that it was Rose and me that would be leaving in L.A and catching flights, for to connect with the Ecstasy and Rose to go on home , she had finished her eight months.

I was so disappointed because after I had hit such an amazing target for New York and that I had continued with my efforts, I was sure I would get it. I was well and truly 'Pissed off' and I could feel myself deflating as I walked back to the salon.

Tam took one look at me and knew in an instant that something was wrong, she checked with the reception if we could go for coffee, grabbed my arm and took me to the lounge to talk. I told her that I have to leave in L.A which was just under a week away. We looked at each other and stayed silent whilst we contemplated the news.

"Well kiddo, we've done it before . so, we can do it again, quick goodbye, we'll see each other again on another ship , I just know it" Tam squeezed my hand. She was always so up-beat, but I was beginning to understand that it was the only way to be living a ship life.

We were due to dock that morning in L.A I had all my stuff together ready for the off. The announcement that followed shook me up a little. 'There had been a substantial earth-quake in L.A at four thirty am, the port was a no-go area for the moment. We will be staying at sea until we get an 'all clear'. The seas were going to be a little rough but nothing to worry about. Any problems contact the pursers desk.'

I went to find Karen, who had a telex from the airport. We had to wait and see what would happen and how safe it was before we could disembark. She would let us both know in due course.

We were on tender hooks, not really knowing if we were coming or going, and if we were going, just how bad would it be?

We went to the lounge bar where there was a TV with the news playing and quite a captive audience had congregated around it, passengers and staff. The devastation that the earthquake had brought was catastrophic. It had measured six point seven on the Richter Scale. The news reader an-nounced I quote.

A huge earthquake has rocked Los Angeles, killing more than 20 people.

The earthquake, which measured 6.6 on the Richter scale and lasted for 40 seconds, struck at
04:31 local time (1231 GMT).
More than 1,000 people have been injured and the death toll is expected to rise as rescuers
continue to pull bodies from collapsed buildings.
Mayor of Los Angeles Richard Riordan has declared a state of emergency and an evening
curfew has been imposed.
The airport has been closed due to a lack of power and doctors are having to perform surgery
in the open air because hospital buildings are severely damaged.
'Stay home, stay calm'

" What are we going to do?" I could feel the panic starting to rise in my voice. I closed my eyes and gave myself a serious talking to, trying to calm my nerves.

" It's fine Jo, we will just have to wait and see what happens, they won't let us off if it's dangerous" Rose had a lovely calming effect on me.

Karen walked through the door and waved us to follow her. We did as she asked. She asked us to sit down in the office.

"Ok girls we have had 'all clear' to dock and even though the airport is closed at the moment it is due to open within the hour. There is a lot of disruption, but we are assured that it is safe for you two to disembark and catch your flight."

We looked at each other with trepidation in our eyes. Reluctantly we made our way to our cabins to collect our bags and head to the pursers desk to collect our passports. The two girls who were picking the ship up were re directed to the next port of call, as their flight was due to land just after the time of the earthquake and had to divert. They were lucky, that could have been disastrous.

The ship was later than they thought docking but watching us cruise in we could see the devastation from up on the top Decks, as could everyone else. The silence was deafening, and the scenes were shocking. The dock had a crack running through the middle, which was a little worrying and I could see a couple of bridges that had collapsed, and a few building had half disappeared.

The captain made an announcement that all was safe, and it would be another half an hour whilst passport control gave us the go ahead. He reassured everyone that there wasn't any damage to the terminal building and wished everybody a safe journey home.

We meet with Tam on our way to the gang way. She joined us as we moved in silence passed passengers who were still watching the news. Some were in tears as their homes and loved ones had been hit. It felt like we were in a real-life disaster movie.

At the gangway we could smell essence of fires burning and rubble. It was all a little earie, not how I had imagined L.A to be. I looked at Tam and our original packed went out the window as we hugged tight.

" Stay safe Jo, try and send a telex from somewhere letting me know you are safe" she whispered in my ear. A tear dropped to my hand as I looked at her. I must say I was very frightened by the whole experience. One I never want to repeat. I let go of her hand and lifted the handle of my case, waiting for Rose to say goodbye. We turned and walked to the crew area of the terminal. I glanced back and saw Tam standing there looking really small wiping tears from her eyes. I put my hand up to wave, but she had turned to get back on the ship..I didn't blame her for not hanging around, I wanted to get to the airport and get in the air more than I have ever wanted anything before.

Rose and I were on the same flights to St Louis which took 4 hours from LAX. As we took off the horror of the Earthquake took hold of me. There were smoke plumes trailing in a spiral merging with the low clouds that had adorned the downtown area. Fire engine lights were flashing on most streets and the buildings looked as though they had melted into the dusty ground. Streetlight were down or knocked sideways and balconies resembled a wave effect. Freeways were missing and the rubble of large stores were widespread. I had never seen such destruction.

I sat back in my seat to take it all in. Rose had zoned out with her headphones buzzing at the volume of the base was turned up to loud. He eyes were closed, and she looked quite peaceful. She certainly had the right idea to block it all out.

St Louis was freezing with a light covering of snow which looked like a spiders web meshed together and thrown over the grass verges. We had to change flights to get to Miami. The plane was due to stop off at Tampa which was where Rose had to get off to catch her flight home. What a nightmare, but that's how the company kept their cost down I suppose. By the time I arrived in Miami I had lost three hours, which when added on to the three- and half-hour flight time from St Louis and the four hours from L.A it was now two am. I ambled to the taxi rank just outside of the terminal in Miami and fumbled with my bags as I gave them to the driver to easy them into his trunk (boot) I was booked back into the Holiday Inn where my rooms seemed to get bigger with every different hotel I stay in.

By the time I got into bed it was three thirty am and I was due to board the Ecstasy at eight am. Thankfully I didn't have that far to go to the terminal later that morning, but it didn't leave a lot of time to sleep. My head hit the pillow and I was out for the count.

CHAPTER 34 – FANTASY
OR ECSTASY?

It was strange being back in the salon, the exact same decor in the exact same place as the Fantasy, yet I was on the Ecstasy. It was bizarre. All around me was the same but all the faces had changed. I had only had time to dump my case in the cabin and change before I had to be in work. Fred my new manager, briefly introduced me to the staff, before I was being bundled down to do a demonstration in the auditorium. Unfortunately for me I had to speak. Not really having done that except on the first two ships I was really nervous. My hands were shaking, and I could feel a rise of bile in the back of my throat threatening to make an appearance at any time. I used my breathing techniques that I had picked up from some of the dancers on the Achille before I did the crew show, basically there wasn't any tequila to hand to that had to do. I took a deep breath and introduce myself and welcomed everyone on board to the Fantasy.

Fred cleared his throat rather loudly and mouthed 'ECSTASY' in very large movements.

"Oh, I do apologies everyone, I was on the Fantasy just before and forgot where I was for a minute" I smiled and carried on like it was nothing. Inside I was mortified and wanted to die a thousand deaths. The audience laughed.

Fred was laughing when we finally finished, I thought he was going to strip me off a peg or too, but to my relief he thought it was hilarious. He had done the exact same this a couple of contracts ago. Fred was late twenties early thirties, very effeminate and fair. He believed in time off and winning time off as incentives as well as cold hard cash. The cruising we were doing was Key West, Cozumel (Mexico), a sea day then back to Miami, then three day was Miami, Nassau overnight, Miami.

My first visit back to Nassau was full of surprises. Not only did I receive a letter from Lucas which had caught up with me via the Statendam, but he was there waiting for me at the gang way when we docked. The letter had announced how sorry he was that he had upset me so much, and that he had realised what an idiot he had been. (I could think of better words to call him) Also that he hoped that we could put it all behind us. I spat my coffee out when I read that bit. Lucy who was sitting next to me at the time moved out the way very quickly before she got covered with it.

"What's the matter with you" she said wiping down her clothes of some splatters that reached her. I explained to her the trauma that I had had with him. She told me it was so common on the ships that she just kept well clear of the men on board. I was beginning to believe he. I couldn't help myself at the same time. I was realising that I was a bit of a push over for some romantic notion I had in my head from when I was a young girl, watching Cinderella at the cinema. I always thought that I would get my happy ever after and that my prince charming would sweep me off my feet. I was on a different planet to the rest of the world.

Lucy was a lovely girl from Essex just up the Road from Stevenage. Small world, and she was the same age as me. It was nice to talk with someone that was familiar with my neck of the woods. We decided to get off together and go to the beach at Paradise Island. My favourite place in Nassau. It was hot that day and the sun was high up in the sky by the time we reach the gang way. I could feel the heat at we emerged from the ship, with the glare bouncing off my sunglasses, making it hard to see. I could make out a silhouette in the standing opposite the ship getting up and walking towards up. I put my hand to my forehead to shade my eyes a little trying to block the sharp rays out. The image came into full view as did the sight of Lucas, smiling as he approached.

"Do you know him" asked Lucy.

"Lucas" I said

"Say no more, I will wait for you in the bar in an hour" she added.

"Thanks Lucy" I watched her walk off jealous that our day was going to be cut short.

"Hey Jo" Lucas's sheepish voice echoed in my ears. I smiled not really sure what I wanted to do. Hit him, run or talk.

He put his hands up in front of his chest, as if he was reading my mind(or my facial expressions)

"Before you say anything Jo, please here me out. I would really like the opportunity to explain, if you will let me".

I wasn't sure how I felt but was intrigued to hear what lame excuses he was going to come up with.

"Well the least you can do is buy me a drink." I said walking off towards the nearest bar.

He followed like a lost puppy, trying to please its new owner. Harsh I hear you cry, but in my defence, I think I had earned the right to be a little stand offish considering what he had put me through.

We got a table in a bar, which looked as though it had been picked up from a beach and placed on the street. Full of authentic beach hut paraphernalia we settled looking out to the docks with the Fantasy and Ecstasy in full view. What a site it was.

Lucas ordered drinks, sitting forward to take my hands in his. I pulled away immediately, making sure he knew that I wasn't taken in that easily.

" Jo, I'm so sorry that I hurt you" 'Sorry you got caught' I thought. He starred at me." Oh, sorry did I say that out loud?" I said.

"Maybe, if I'm honest." Why do men have to be so honest when they know that it will hurt you.

" I hope you got my letter"

"Just this morning"

"Oh, I was hoping you would have had time to digest it" a look of disappointment flooded his eyes as they met min.

"Look Lucas why are you hear, what is it you want from me" My patience was wearing a little thin.

" I was hoping for a second chance, after Tara had told me how upset you were when you left. I had no idea that you felt that way about me and quite honestly until you left, I had no idea how I felt about you, can we just start again? Can we just meet up when we finish in a month and see what happens? Can we just be together again?" he tried to hold my hands for the second time. I took them off the table completely.

" I'm sorry! Is that all you can say? Do you know what I saw you doing? Do you know what that did to me? Obviously, you had no idea, or respect for me. I am no push over Lucas. It's not ok and not alright and no I'm not just going to come running back into your arms, when you ask me too. I thought that we had something special, but I was the only one. If you didn't want to be tied to someone , you only had to tell me, and at least I could have made that choice, to be with you or not."

My heart was racing, and I thought that I would never stop. The emotions of that situation and the previous one with Lucas were coming to a head. Why did men think that they could do that to whomever they wanted without any consequences was quite beyond me?

" Will you at least consider it Jo?" he added hopefully

I stood up and pulled myself together,

" Lucas, if you really wanted to be with me you would never have done that. I understand that you want to be free to do as you please. I have realised that I also want that. I don't think that a relationship between us will ever work. You're on a different ship to me and that's how it will stay. I wish you well Lucas" I walked as calmly as I could out of the door and back into the heat of the sun.

What a relief to finally have a say. I felt as light as a feather and surprisingly not upset at all.

After leaving Lucas at the bar I had caught up with Lucy and spent the rest of the afternoon on the beach. Such a tonic lying in the sun, feeling the tension melting away from my body. The sand cascading through my toes was wonderful. We reluctantly went back to the ship desperate for more time. I was emptying my bag on my bottom bunk, (Finally I had a lower bunk) and Lucy was chilling out on hers before we changed to go to work. I caught my breath as when the door swung open and a man dressed in U.S Navy uniform, shouted for us to on the bed, pointing his finger at us as if it was a gun. At first, I thought it was a joke someone was playing on us, but soon realised he was in fact rather serious about his intensions.

" Get on the bed " He shouted " I will shoot you if you don't do as ii say"

I did as I was told and got on the bed. I caught Lucy's eye and she was motionless. I was so afraid; my head was all over the place.

" Don't make a noise " he put his finger to his lips and shushed us to be quiet.

He was silent for a few minute as if he was listening for something.

" What do you want" I said bravely

"SHUT UP" he bellowed

" No, you SHUT UP AND GET OUT OF OUR CABIN" my god where did that come from. I don't know what got into me.

He looked at me startled by my outburst, twisted the handle and was gone. I looked at Lucy and she hadn't moved. I ran after him, not with the intention of catching him up, but I needed to get to security and fast. Thankfully we were just around the corner, the same as on the Fantasy. I explained the situation to the guards. They left in hot pursuit.

We didn't hear anything until much later when one of the officers came into the salon to take to Fred. He explained that the man was from a U.S Navy ship that was in port with us. He had lost mind and was convinced he was on a mission to blow our ship up. We were the enemy. He had shimmed up the ropes and descended to our Deck and we knew the rest. They had caught him on rope Deck trying to escape. My outburst had brought him back to reality and he was frightened. They now have him back on ship in the medics centre trying to establish his health. They had apologised for the alarm and reassured us it would never happen again.

My second contract had come to an end and the rest of the cruising to Cozumel and Key West were uneventful in comparison. We attended Carlos and Charlies which is world renowned for having a fantastic time dancing on the tables until the early hours. We had such fun there. It was never long enough, we always had to leave before midnight because of the tenders we needed to catch back to the ship.

My flight left Miami at midday to Heathrow London . I wasn't sure who was going to meet me there, but as always, my little Mum stood there silently anticipating my arrival.

It was so good to see her, but the jet lag over the first few days was awful. My body clock was all over the place. I had slept for twenty-four hours, just getting up to use the bathroom. I finally had a chance to talk to Mum on the Sunday, where she cooked the most delicious dinner. The smell was out of this world. We had the works, roast potatoes and beef, gravy, Yorkshire pudding peas and broccoli. I could have died and gone to heaven right there and then and be the happiest person ever. Ok a little extreme I know, but you get the picture.

Mum lit a cigarette and inhaled deeply.

"You want to give them up" I said to her hoping it would make a difference. Forty a day was excessive, but she always said she would rather die young and happy than old and miserable. She never knew how right she was.

She paid no attention to me and asked how things were with Lucas. I told her and also apologised for not writing very much. I was on so many ships it was hard to keep up with the post. Some of the parcels Mum and Dad sent me are still floating around to this day. Someone somewhere has gained some nice undies.

I asked how she was after the bailiffs had come. She said she had been very frightened at the time. So much so she hid in the garden. I couldn't believe it.

"Why had they come Mum?"

"There has been some mix up over some bills we needed to pay. Jacob Al's accountant was supposed to pay them, but they had got missed." I wasn't sure then, but now I know there was a lot more to that story than I or she had realised.

Al was away on business again during my two weeks home. I was quite glad that I had some time for just me and Mum. She had to work a few day that week, but I managed to catch up with Dad and my brother in between. Things had settled down a lot since I left before my first contract. We all seemed to get on much better and I felt we had finally found our peace. Well for a while anyhow.

Mum was drinking much more now; she was hitting at least a bottle a night. I still didn't think it was too much compared with myself on ship. But I was noticing all the same. I thought that it was strange that she didn't talk about Al much whilst I was home, but when I next saw her after my third contract it all became clear.

CHAPTER 35- 'THIRD TIMES A CHARM?'

Two weeks flew by as always, but instead of being dropped at yet another airport, Dad was dropping back at the original house, right where I had started my journey. I had taken the opportunity to do management training at head office before I joined my next trip. So here I was amongst some rookies, who were waiting to join their first ship. They were all so lovely and had so many questions which I enjoyed answering. If only I had, had the opportunity to do that before I had got on.

I joined in with the fun and games getting to head office on the tubes and I was glad of the company. At least we were heading into the spring, so the evenings were lighter, and it wasn't as cold. The last time it was winter and freezing.

The rookies went through one door towards the training academy and I went through to the offices where I was to undertake accounting, management and target setting with my trainer Frances. She was mid-thirties and had been with the company for five years. She had started with them as a beauty therapist and completed one contract before she became manager. She had met her husband onboard ship and settled in the U.K, where she had taken the post as a trainer. It suited her better, as now she had a young family and could travel. She did miss it.

We went through the modules without too much fuss. I had already become efficient in the book keeping from my time on Carnival being head stylist. I was there for just a couple of days before I headed to New York to pick up the QE2.

It was remarkable I couldn't have asked for a better ship. It was due back in Southampton within five days, but they needed me to get familiar with the set and help cover the epic cruise of all. The celebrations of D-Day at Normandy, with Britannia. I was more than excited for that one. I had no time to go home and say my goodbyes to I rang both parents to let them know the details. My Dad was made up, he loved everything about the war. I was very familiar, especially having to sit through film after film on a Sunday afternoons of Bridge over the River Kwai, Dam Buster and the Great Escape to name a few.

I had been a little wary of flying to New York alone. The last time I was there I was with two others. This time it was just me. The plan journey was a little bumpy, but bearable. I stated in the Ramada Inn near the port and picked up the ship the next day without too many problems. I was getting an old hand at it, flying around the globe from one city to another. I had become quite the jet setter.

The QE2 was designed to be a transatlantic cruise ship sailing from Southampton to New York. She was named after RMS Queen Elizabeth and served from 1969, right up until the Queen Mary took over in 2004. She was designed by Cunard in Liverpool and built in Scotland. QE2 was retired from active Cunard service on 27 November 2008 and docked permanently at Dubai's Mina Rashid, she has been lovingly restored to her former glory as a 500-room floating hotel in 2018. She was a beautiful ship and very upper class, no matter which class of cabin you had.

I stepped onto the QE2 in total ore of her. The most famous ship in the world and I was here to do my management training and attend to passengers during the D-day celebrations. How fantastic. The manager at the time was a lovely lady called Charlotte, and she certainly had her work cut out for her, as everyone wanted to get on that ship. That included area managers senior management and CEO's to name a few. She was constantly get visited. But considering it was one of our companies flag ships it had to be perfect.

I was met by charlottes second in command Carol who was assistant manager. She led me up through the many levels of the crew area's and back down round in a maze of cabins working areas and bars to where my cabin was. I shared with just one other which was usual. But rather than putting on my pink uniform I put on a black dress of the same style, it felt good to get out of that horrid colour. I met Charlotte in the office in the salon where she told me that I would be over sea the staff in the salon where I could get plenty of practice for stock control, target setting, cashing up and many more practical aspects of being a working manager. It was going to be all hands to the pump. We only had a couple of cruises before we set of for our D-Day celebration cruise from New York, via U.K and onto France.

Hair and beauty are on Deck one and the spa was on Deck six and the gym was on Deck seven right down the bottom. We were very spread out on there and our manager spent a lot of time in the spa working so it kept us quite fit running up and down in the crew areas. We were not allowed in passengers areas at all on the QE2, unless we were doing a demonstration or with our manager. We did however have a few crew bars to choose from and a massive canteen. We had to do compulsory aerobics at 7.45 three times a week, to help us stay fit and I was able to try out the hydrotherapy bath, so I could recommend it to the passengers. That was amazing. It was like a large bath all to yourself with jets spraying into different muscles to massage the tension away. It was fantastic and I didn't want to go back to work. They certainly looked after us on there. We could go out onto the large rope Deck to get fresh air weather permitting.

It was extremely rough on the five-day sea crossings in between Southampton to New York. The transatlantic crossing was renowned at being rough. Thankfully we were embarking on our last for a while. It was the last pick up from New York and the anticipation of the massive cruise ahead was massive. We had taken on extra stock and we were prep at the passenger list, some of which were very famous, such as Dame Vera Lynn and Bob Hope to name a few. We were all so excited. I hadn't bothered to go out to the crew bar very much on that ship because I didn't want to get involved with the staff too much and I needed to keep my wits about me as I was heading into management and I didn't want to tire myself out for my first ship. I still hadn't heard anything of where and when I was going but I was hopeful that it would not be that long after our epic cruise.

We were docked into Southampton on the third of July and we stayed overnight which was fantastic. However, before I got my hopes up to high to visit home quickly, I was informed that I would be working. 'Typical.' I though as I heaved up some stock at Southampton dockside.

I walked back into the salon with my client list for the afternoon and to my surprise Dame Vera Lynn was one of my clients. I must admit I got a little star struck, but I put my best foot forward and dived right in.

She was wonderful, a true star of stars. So elegant and happy. She put me at ease straight away. She must have known how nervous I would be, but it turns out she was just like any other person. There wasn't any class or prima donna air about her at all. There was however a little hype around our reception desk, with the massage therapists. Apparent Bob Hope had requested a therapist to attend to him in his suit. The girls didn't want to go, understandably, so one of the male therapists offered to take her place. He allergy said he found Mr Hope to be quite demanding, how true that was is anyone's guess.

The atmosphere on the ship when we left Southampton was surreal. I did Dame Vera Lynn's hair a couple of times one of which I believe was before her concert which was out on Deck. Unfortunately, we were unable to see any of it, but we did get out onto rope Deck to watch half an hour of the celebration when we were just off of the beaches of Normandy.

I remember standing out on Deck with hundreds of other crew and staff, all standing witnessing the great Britannia and HMS Edinburgh and HMS Hecla, surround with many small vessels. A Lancaster I believe flew passed and dropped a cloud poppy into the sea. The horns of the vessels blew, and the chills ran down my side as I watched the procession. I could only imagine the sense of dread that the soldiers had who landed at the site fifty years ago. My uncle who I had lost recently was one of those brave men onboard a ship moored off the coast of Normand. I don't believe he stepped foot on the beaches, but he was there all the same. Before the end I had to go back to work as we were so busy ready for the formal night.

I had finally received notice of my first management position onboard the Regent Sun. Ironically we had left New York for the last time at the beginning of June just after the D-day celebrations and was heading back to Southampton when I got the telex to disembark when we docked and fly back to New York to pick up the Regent Sun. It all happened because I had to replace a manager who left for family reasons. What a pain. So, I headed to the airport from Southampton docks by cab and flew back to where I had been five days earlier In New York. My body clock was all over the place.

CHAPTER 36 - THE SUN

Here I was again Deja Vue, standing looking at the glorious white ship sparkling in the midday sun in New York Harbor. What a sight she was. She wasn't as big as the QE2, but she was, as I would class it as a proper ship. After Regency went bankrupt in 1995, she was laid-up for a while until she sank off the coast of South Africa on her way to India to be scrappers in July 2001.

The Regent Sun held eight hundred and fifty-seven passengers. It started its life as the SS Shalom and was a combined ocean liner /cruise ship that was built in 1964 by Chantiers de l'Atlantique, in St Nazaire, France. In 1967, SS Shalom was sold to the German Atlantic Line, becoming their second SS Hanseatic. Subsequently she served as SS Doric for Home Lines, SS Royal Odyssey for Royal Cruise Line and SS Regent Sun for Regency Cruises. The ship was laid up in 1995 following the bankruptcy of Regency Cruises.

It was very strange not being met at the gang way by someone, but the previous manager left before I got there. I headed to the salon which was situated next to the pursers desk. It was a very small salon but very sweet. There were only four stylist two beauty and one fitness instructor. The salon was closed due to being in port, but the previous manager had left the keys at the pursers desk where I also found my cabin keys and a list of my staff members. 'Wow loved the welcoming committee.' I thought.

I had found that the salon doesn't open until five on port days after grabbing a few previous programme. It reminded me of the Achille with those times.

I took advantage of the time I had alone by becoming

acquainted with the salon and beauty salon which was three Decks below before I took refuge in my cabin.

The salon had four chairs a reception desk, where I found a ships computer and lots of paper work. At the top was a letter from the previous manager apologising for not doing a hand over and that she hoped she covered everything I needed to know in the next few pages. She had given me a personal appraisal of the staff also including personality and job descriptions. That was handy. She ran through the salon protocol and a typical day, plus a few note on what to do on cashing up. She said the rest was pretty much the same as most ships. God, I hoped so. It wasn't a lot to go on, but I'm sure I would make it up as I went along. I wanted to be back in the salon an hour before the others so I could be there when they came in.

I headed for the beauty salon which was down a few Deck. It compromised of two beauty rooms plus spa facilities. The gym was adjacent to that. On the way down I had to pass by the dining room which smelt delicious. There was a head waiter on the door, very dark and very tall. He smiled as I went past. I nodded thinking how friendly he was.

Once I had finished in the beauty rooms, I found my cabin at the end of passenger Deck next to the officers' quarters. I had gone up in the world. As I walked in with case in hand, I stood motionless at the door. with my moth wide open I couldn't believe my luck. That was the moment I knew I had done the right thing.

My cabin had carpet for a start and a PORT HOLE. I could see outside for the first time. How amazing! To the right of the front door was another wooded door leading to a bathroom with a shower , sink and toilet. It had a mirror above the basin and a small cupboard under the sink. Ooh the little things were great. I went back into the main room where to the right after the bathroom was a single and half size bed, not a bunk and actual bed, with a bedside cabinet and a phone. At the base to the left was a wardrobe and at the foot of the bed was a desk / dressing table. It was wonderful and it was just for me. No more sharing, my own space. Management was definitely an improvement.

I unpacked and got changed into my black uniform to try and find something to eat as I had missed lunch. It was approaching three pm and I only had an hour before I got back to the salon. I grabbed the papers and set off to Lido Deck. I could usually find something there to eat.

As I was, we were allowed to eat there and drink with the passengers. In fact, as a manager I could go and eat and drink anywhere except for the dining room. But that would also be ok if offered by the Captain.

Talking of the Captain I met him on Lido Deck just as I was walking into the dining area. He was of Greek nationality and quite a slim built man, very lovely. I shook his hand then he left, as quick as that. Very busy I would imagine. I crabbed a cappuccino and a slice of pizza from the food area and sat down to gen up on what and where everything was.

I pulled myself away from the sun-drenched Deck and reluctantly hauled myself down to the salon. I let myself into the salon only to be followed by a very flam buoyant man called Larry who was a purser. He was twenty-nine and wonderful. His blonde hair was cut short and his pale kin was slightly sun kissed on his nose. He stood about five foot seven and had the most amazing smile.

"Hi, let me introduce myself, I'm Lance the accounting purser" His American accent was so familiar now, I loved it.
"hey"

"I thought that you may like some moral support"

"That's so kind, I'm just trying to familiarise myself with the ship"

"Oh, don't worry too much, everyone's really friendly on here" He said throwing his arm up like he was on stage introducing the next act. I guessed he was gay, but you never wanted to presume anything. We became great friends over the next few months. He really had my back as far as the

accounting went, I could never seem to get the numbers to
tally or work the onboard computer.

The girls started to wander in fifteen minutes before we
opened. I sat them all down and waited for Peter the fitness
instructor to arrive. They told me he was always late but
really good. So, I decided to carry on. I introduced myself
and asked if I could meet with them individually at some
point during the rest of the evening, just to get to know
them.

It all seemed to follow very easily, and we were set for a
fantastic cruise, full off travel agents down to the Caribbean.
They were usually uneventful for us, but it gave me a great
chance to find my feet and work out what the salon had been
doing.

The cruise was a great success and we had been really
busy surprisingly, with the agents wanting to try out all of
the ships different facilities. My new buddy Larry was made an
honorary member of our team. He would come in daily trying out different products and getting his hair done regularly.
He was fantastic.

Our first port of call was San Juan, the capital city of
Puerto Rico one of the most popular destinations in the
Caribbean. This was an amazing place, a vibrant culture, and
old-world elegance, so different than the other places I had
been. San Juan was and still is, the busiest cruise port in
the Caribbean , with major cruise lines stopping as par or
the course on a two week cruise, giving cruisers world class
attractions and rich cultural experiences that can easily be
done by simply walking across the piers. I did this many
times, mainly due to banking the cash we had received in the
salon. Not always very safe but a necessity none the less. The
tourist areas spanned over eight miles of the beautiful Atlantic coastline, from historic Old San Juan to the beaches of
Isla Verde in the neighbouring town of Carolina. The capital
city is the cultural centre of Puerto Rico. San Juan is a happy
place all year round and around the clock! Residents from

across the island flock to the capital city to attend cultural events and visit the many points of interest. We however didn't get to taste much of the culture and its wonderful shops ,as it was out embarkation port for a while. We would need to do our welcome on-board demonstration and tours around the salon and spa.

The cruising over the next two weeks were fantastic stopping at some of the most beautiful places in the Caribbean. We stopped at St Maarten on a number of occasions always seemingly falling on a Sunday. This was an opportunity for us to sample a British restaurant we had found on the sea front which did the most amazing English breakfast. Sausage, hash browns, egg, toast, beans and bacon to name a few delicious ingredient they used. We could also get a proper cup of PG tips tea. It was to die for. The lady that run it was from London in the U.K. She always welcomed everyone but had a soft spot for us Brits.

We arrived in St Kitts one Thursday, where we were doing mandatory lifeboat drill, it was a little late in happening on that particular cruise, as it's supposed to run within twenty-four hours of leaving our home port. I was doing my now regular spot of demonstrating how to put on a life jacket and how to operate the light and whistle, when I heard a gentleman trying to get my attention, rather rudely I thought at the time.

"Excuse me miss, could you come outside please"

" I'm sorry sir but I'm in the middle of life drill at the moment, can it wait?" I added feeling a little put out.

"No, I don't believe it can, it's really important" He was getting quite anxious by that time. So, I asked Chris to take over from me. She was one of the other hairdressers, who was rather concerned that I had just dropped her in it.

Shrugging my shoulders at her I apologised and left through the glass double doors, which opened out onto the main Deck at the back of the ship.

"Ok sir, you have my attention" He could tell I was not

impressed, but I was the ever professional and adhered to the passengers are always right and I must meet their needs if I have to.

He motioned for me to come over to the port side of the ship where he told me that there was a dead body floating around the side of the ship. I laughed because I thought that I was in the middle of another initiation to the ship.

" That's a good one sir" I said grinning slightly bemused as to why they thought that it would be a funny joke.

"ok. Ok I will play along" I said and walked reluctantly to look over the side of the ship.

As I glanced at the man's concerned eyes, I had the feeling that he was not actually messing about. The sun was beating down onto the ocean's surface, mirroring the sunlight and sending a Sharpe dazzling light straight back to the rear of my eye sockets. I squinted to push the rays to one side, and as I did, I saw the body of a man face down in the water floating . No movement nothing.

I looked at the passenger, apologised for not believing him and hurried to the phone hanging on the wall beside the doors. I dialled the bridge and asked to speak to the staff captain or captain as a matter of urgency.

The Staff captain came onto the phone. I explained who I was and told him there was a dead body at port aft side of the ship and that the passengers were due to come out to their master stations any minute.

He flew into action and diverted the passengers to the starboard side by the loudspeaker and he and a couple of officers came immediately down the outside staircase to where I was standing in a matter of minutes.

" Where is he Jo" the staff captain leaned over the side and I pointed to the man's body.

"Ah yes, I see him" he muttered something in Greek to the other officers and directed me to pass the word along to keep passengers on the opposite side until they could move the body. " Well done Jo, quick thinking than you" He patted me on the back and left.

I thanked the passenger who had alerted me and asked if he would keep it to himself until we can deal with the situation. We didn't want to cause any undue distress to other passengers. I offered him a free drink at the bar to calm his nerves, but he assured me he was ok and declined politely and moved away as if it was an everyday occurrence. I later found out he was in fact a police officer from New York, so to him it was an everyday occurrence.

I walked over to Chris and told her briefly what had happened and to pass on to the other staff members about keeping the passengers away and telling them there is some maintenance work going on. The staff did as they were asked, and the passengers were none the wiser.

I headed back out to the port side and watched as a boat lifted the man out of the water and headed back towards the docks, where an ambulance was waiting. I thought that it was a little late for that, but you never know I suppose.

When the drill was over, the passengers disembarked for a lovely day in St Kitts, but I headed to the Lido bar for a strong coffee and a sit down. I felt so sorry for the man I had seen and couldn't quite believe what had happened. Larry came bouncing in and slammed down beside me.

" You ok chic" he said putting a comforting arm around my shoulders. "I heard what had happened, well done you though for acting quickly. Everyone's talking about it"

"I bet. Does anyone know what happened"

" Well, yes apparently it was a local, diving for some fish off the side of the jetty. He hit his head on some rocks and knocked himself out. Nobody could reach him in time as the ship was in the way. Unfortunately, he had drowned."

"Gosh, that's terrible" I was staring at Larry with my mouth open.

" Don't worry, you did what you could. Now get that coffee down you, I'm taking you for lunch at this little place I know, where they do the most amazing burgers" I got up not really feeling like eating , but thought it would be good to get off the ship for a time all the same.

I didn't bother to change and kept my blue suit on that I had decided to wear as my daily uniform. I was supposed to wear my black dress, but the suit was for embarkation, and with a white t-shirt or blouse it was much more comfortable.

We headed down to the gangway passing by the dining room, where I noticed a tall dark man dressed in the head waiters uniform standing at the doors which lead into the dining hall. He looked up just as I was walking down the stairs and smiled. he was gorgeous. Bronzed with white teeth and a moustache. That was a first, but very nice all the same. I could feel him following me with his eyes as I descended to the lower floor. I caught up with Larry and asked who he was.

"Oh, that's Arend the head waiter. Stay away from him Jo, he's a bit of a ladies man."

He didn't offer any other information to go with that , so with a smile I put him out of my mind. I should have done that permanently!

CHAPTER 37 – HEAD OVER HEELS.

I was finally making some decent money. Mum was quiet at home, so I presumed things had settled down with her there and life was good on the ship.

We spent most of our evenings in the crew bar as it was the hub of the ship for us where we all congregated after our shifts. The music was Latin, and we would dance and have fun. Once that shut, we would head down to the cabins for a party where that would finish in the early hours, five am most mornings.

One night I was chatting to a few of the other staff one being Valerie a casino girl from Darlington, U.K, when Arend the head waiter came in. I had never seen him in there before, he was usually on duty. He was still in his whites and ordered himself a large whiskey from the bar. He came over and pulled up a chair and sat down next to me, invading my personal space just a little too much.

"Hey Jo, how you are doing" his Dutch accent what very strong.

I'm good thanks" wondering how he knew my name!

" How are you liking the ship?"

" Yeah, I love it, what about you, have you been on here long?"

"No, not really, about a month, I suppose" His English was impeccable.

"Where are you from?" I asked, being very nosey, but it comes with the job, always inquisitive to know more about people.

" I'm from Rotterdam, in Holland" I loved his accent it was very dreamy, and his eyes twinkled the minute he started talking about his home country. He told me all about his family and that Rotterdam was small but very lovely place to live.

We carried on chatting about our cruising experiences, the ships we had been on and our love of watching films, when the opportunity arose. I was telling him about the Achille Lauro where they played the Voyage of Terror on the exact same cruise to Egypt and Israel, when Larry turned up and pulled me away for a dance.

"Jo, you need to stay clear of that man, he is bad news!" I couldn't help wondering why he was so concerned but carried on regardless thinking that Larry just may be a little jealous of the attention I was getting. I never did listen to him and couldn't help but be intrigued by Arend.

I pulled off my uniform and was just about to jump in the shower, when there was a knock on the door.

"Who is it" I shouted. I had learned to lock my door after my interlude with the soldier on the Carnival ship.

"It's Pepe, your cabin steward" Pepe was lovely he was from Guatemala and looked after me, cleaning my room and taking my clothes to the laundry where they came back all ironed even my knickers. I giggled at the thought. I tipped him well, to keep him on side.

"I have something for you" I quickly put my joggers and a t-shirt on and opened the door. I was faced with a T.V coming at me with Pepe's head just peeking over the top.

"What's this Pepe, why ? what's happening. What are you doing?"

"It's O.K Jo. Mister Arend sent me to bring it to you, he said you would enjoy a movie later, after work"

"Oh, how strange, I thought" not wanting to embarrass Pepe, I allowed him to put it down on my dressing table, in case he dropped it. He left with a token of my appreciation and dropped it in his pocket.

I sat on the bed and just looked at it. Wondering what! why! and how! he had found out where my cabin was. Something was a little odd.

I showered and dressed for my evening shift where we were inundated by ladies and gents for formal night.

Looking through the doorway of the salon as I was busy styling a client's hair, I could see the hustle and bustle of the party goers congregating outside the pursers desk. That was a regular occurrence, if there was something , anything to moan about there would always be someone there doing it. You know I heard a rumour once of a passenger complaining to a purser about the noise of a helicopter that was dropping off one of the stylists. The girl had told her the previous day, that, it was how she got to work every day after the passenger had asked if she lived on the ship. The stylist had allegedly replied that they didn't, and a helicopter brought us in every day and dropped us off on the top Deck. I had to laugh, I wouldn't put it past one of the girls to do that, and for a passenger to complain about it. A smile curled up the corners of my lips as the memory flowed through my mind's eye, just as Arend walked into the pursers desk to make his nightly announcement that the dining room was open. He caught me smiling and presumed it was for him and waved at me as he passed.

I could feel my cheeks burning with embarrassment, blushing as he did so and got angry with myself for allowing it to happen. I turned my back on the door to finish the other side of my clients hair. Daniel a tall leggy blonde, smiled as she glided towards the reception desk. I couldn't see who it was that had just walked in and carried on with what I was doing. I could hear her giggling and turned to be faced with Arend grinning from ear to ear at me. I smiled a half smiled and carried on talking to my client. He left and I felt a little sink in my stomach. What was going on with me?

Once I had finished off the marathon of blow dries for formal night, I cashed up and asked Daniel what Arend wanted.

" Oh yeah, I nearly forgot, he said he would see you about midnight, tonight"

"Oh, did he? where?"

"He didn't say" she smiled and flounced off towards the backwash and carried on cleaning.

"Do you know something I don't" She laughed and at that second again great timing, Larry walked in with a drama that had kicked off in the pursers office about some money not tallying and it had taken him all day to find it. He sat down with his hand on his forehead and sunk into the chair.

"You drama queen," I said and grabbed his hand to pull him up and led him down to dinner. Glad of the distraction from Arend talk.

I headed to my cabin after my nightly stint in the crew bar wondering what Arend meant about seeing me later at midnight. I presumed he meant in the crew bar, but when he didn't turn up, I headed back to my cabin a bit deflated and perturbed by his no show.

I turned the corner on Deck five, where my cabin was situated, to be faced with Arend sitting leaning with his head against my door, his knees bent, and his eyes closed.

"Oh flipping 'heck, you frightened me " I said holding my hand to my chest feeling the heat soring to my cheeks again.

He stood up casually and said he had come to watch the movie with me. Talk about invite yourself , I thought. But let him in anyway.

He made himself comfortable on my bed and opened a beer that he brought with him. Offering me one in unison. I went along with the situation curious to what he wanted. When he told me that he thought I might like to watch some movies and knew of someone who was selling their T.V, he thought of me , after our conversation the other nigh about liking movies, he thought that I would like it . I on the other hand didn't realise that meant with Arend, but very touch that he had thought of me.

He seemed to be harmless, as we sat and watched Pelican Brief with Denzel Washington and Julia Roberts. It was a great film, and very long. By the time it finished it was getting on for three in the morning. I assumed that Arend would leave but he opened another bottle and offered me one.

I sat down at the other end of the bed not sure what to do. I was feeling a little insecure and very aware that we were alone on my bed with the door shut. He eyes pierced mine; his thoughtful dark brown eyes were surrounded by long black eye lashes. His lips were deliciously full and protruded beneath his bushy black moustache, at the corners of his mouth , the silky hairs sank into the little folds of skin that produced the cutest dimples. His bronzed skin glistening in the neon light coming from the bathroom through the slit in the door . He broke into a smile of amused friendliness and pleasure which aroused feelings of warmth, and something more inside of me. I blinked as if to snap myself out of my mesmerized state. He laughed and stood up from the bed, breaking the atmosphere that had suddenly got very intense.

I need not have worried about being alone with him, he was a perfect gentleman. He finished his beer and arranged to meet dock side the next day to disembark together for a tour of Grenada. With that he kissed me on the cheek and left.

I shut the door behind him and lent against it for what seemed like hours just wondering what the hell I was doing, going down that path again. But as I sunk into my cool bed sheets, the feelings of despair and memories of past encounters dispersed as I slumbered into a deep sleep.

CHAPTER 38 - GRENADA

I dressed in denim shorts and a in a bright sky- blue vest top. My hair was blow-dried straight, and I skin felt fresh from the cool shower. I had butterflies in my stomach from the anticipation of meeting with Arend. I approached the gangway like a cat creeping towards its prey not wanting to be seen until it was ready. Not that I had any intentions of pouncing but more to the point I didn't want Arend to see me until I had composed myself.

I was half hoping that he wouldn't be there. That way I could just shrug it off as typical and never bother with him again. I looked around the corner and saw the back of his dark hair glowing in the sun light that danced across his hair. It took me a little while to drink in his appearance now he was out of his white uniform and back in civilian clothing. His crisp white shirt hung outside a pair of tanned cargo shorts which enhanced his muscular legs and medium frame and a white pair of trainers with short socks on his feet. A lite grey ruck sack spilled over his shoulders when he turned and caught me just standing admiring the view. Every time it was as if he was reading the exact thing that was running through my mind.

"Hey" I said trying to remain calm and casual

"Hey yourself, you look lovely" I laughed and shrugged it off like I had not given it much thought but knowing dame well I had just taken the best part of an hour agonising over what to wear.

"Shall we go" he pointed to a jeep parked just up from the dockside.

For the first time I looked to see the wonderful scenery

that surrounded us. Grenada consists of the island of Grenada itself plus six smaller islands which lie to the north of the main islands, it is a sovereign state in the West Indies, in the Caribbean Sea . Grenada is also known as the "Island of Spice" due to its production of nutmeg and mace crops. The 'Spice Isle' boasts rainforests, hot springs, tumbling waterfalls, and an abundance of wildlife. Driving on the left from the port located in the town of St. George's. (St. George's is considered by many to be the most picturesque port in the entire Caribbean.) we could see the lush mountainous terrain and interesting colonial architecture that surrounded us. There was even an old fort called "Fort George" which had great views over the city and harbour.

We headed to the right of the port towards Grand Anse Beach, the aroma of spice trees included nutmeg, cloves, ginger and cinnamon were playing games with my senses, bringing them to a high alert and then squashing them into a mild trance. It was thirty- one degrees, scorching hot. The wind danced through my hair in our open top jeep, and the breeze skipped from my checks in a playful manner.

I looked at Arend and asked what our plans were for the day.

"Just wait and see, you're going to love it."

A few mile later we parked up along a Road just set back from the most amazing beach I have seen yet. Two miles of sweeping sandy white beach fronted by turquoise blue water that melted into the hazy horizon. The palm trees swayed from the breeze; the sun sizzled on the hot sand.

The beach was made up of The South Side, The Park Side, and The North Side, each is as lovely as the other but suit different tastes. The South Side as its name suggests was to the south end of the beach where you are sure to see a few couples enjoying the scenery. The further south you go on Grand Anse Beach the more secluded it gets. The Park Side was the middle of the beach this was where you would find the locals with the shopping Mall right across the street. The North Side further up on the North side was mainly hotel guests soaking up the Grenadian sunshine. That's where most of the passengers would head to when the cruise ships are in port. The vendors market was also on the that side of Grand Anse beach. There you could do some shopping for local crafts, spices.

We headed south of course away from the crowds to the more secluded end of the beach. Arend grabbed his ruck sack and laid his towel in a beautiful spot under the shade of a huge palm tree. Someone had hooked up a hammock between two small palms a little further up. With a towel dangling off the side and a pair of sunglasses that had been thrown casually to one side , it looked very much like a staged photo shoot.

I laid my towel next to Arends and headed off into the sea. The turquoise sea was so inviting I couldn't help but indulge in the divine warm waters of the Indian ocean. The water was all encumbering and the tension just flowed straight out of my shoulders. I had almost forgotten that Arend was with me.

I could feel his dark eyes watching my every move. Suddenly feeling very self-conscious I waved him to come in.

" It's lovely and warm" I shouted up the beach very aware that I had just broken the silence of the waves caressing the sandy beach.

He got to his feet and sauntered towards the water. He wore his vibrant red swimming shorts now which must have been under his clothing. His tattooed chest of a tiger stood out from his sun kissed chest . He smiled and joined me in the water. My heart skipped over a few beat as he waded towards me. I could feel his arms wrap around my waist which sent shivers and goose bumps charging over my skin. The sensual touch made me flinch a little, but he pulled me closer. His breath was caressing my top lip as he kissed me very gently and slowly. That was the first moment I knew it was too late to turn back, too late to save my heart from hurt. The moment when the world stood still. From that precise moment in time was when my whole world changed, and my emotions and reactions were no longer my own.

CHAPTER 39 - HEAVY HEART

After our trip to the beach in Grenada, Arend and I spend every moment we could together. He slowly moved into my cabin and our lives intertwined to a point that the other ports we visited rolled into one. Looking back now, I do regret not seeing more of the islands and visiting some of the tourist hotspots would have been far more beneficial than spending most of my time on the beaches. However, in my defence I was starting to burn out, with the long working hours, the lack of sleep and the main fact that I just hadn't given myself enough time to recoup between contracts. It was starting to take its toll.

Our fitness instructor Peter left at our next visit to San Juan and replaced by a lovely girl called Mia from South Yorkshire. She was blonde and full of life. She really lifted the team with her ideas and get up and go thinking. She organised for us to start crew fitness classes. It was the fresh air that we had all needed. I had certainly taken my eye off the ball since Arend had come along.

We organised the demonstrations to become more of a show case with us all showing a small portion of an aerobics class, as well as some of our fitness gear to boot.

One of the last events that the whole crew got involved in was Halloween. Of course, a massive event in America. So, all the crew, shops, casino, entertainers decided to dress up in spooky costumes. Our theme was the Addams family. I was Morticia, Mia was Frankenstein (Hermon) the two girls Chris and Daniel were the twins Wednesday and Eddy, and Donna was 'Cousin IT.'

We looked the part from outfits put together from our

own wardrobes. I shoved a pillow into the shoulders of Mia to make her look large and added some make up to us all to resemble dead or the gloomy. We were a right sight. Our clients thought it was such fun that we were part taking in the celebrations. Us being English and reserved. The evening went without a hitch and the ship had made the night part of their itinerary so that the passengers could join in. Some of the costumes were amazing and really quite realistic. You never knew who you would bump into on your way to different part of the ships. Of course, my handsome head waiter joined in by making his face white and blood protruding from his neck. Somehow though he still looked gorgeous and tanned.

Our relationship was going from strength to strength with plans of spending our holidays together. Arend was finishing a week prior to me, but he had some loose ends to tie up with his employer in Miami before he was due to go back to Rotterdam. Apparently, he had a car waiting for him there and would drive down to meet me in Orlando where the ship was due to dock in a few week, time where I would disembark for annual leave.

We had been planning to fly back to London, where we would get spend a few week with my family before heading to Rotterdam where I would meet his mother. His parents were separated, and his Dad lived in Indonesia. His father originated from there and left for Holland back in the late sixties where he had meet Arends's mother and settle to have a family.

Arends parents were together until he was six when he decided he could no longer be away from his beloved country and left. He and his two sisters had regular contact with him over the years but only got to see him when he went to holland on visits once a year. I could imagine how that must have felt for them. Arend told me that his father had actually had a string of affairs whilst he was in Rotterdam and also a family of his own in Indonesia. What a terrible time. But as I have said before everyone on the ships at that time was always running from something or searching for something. I think Arend was doing both. He had joined the ships in his early twenties as a waiter and worked his way up to head waiter quite quickly. He had worked for a few cruise lines, one of which was Royal Caribbean cruise lines and now regency. He loved the life and at twenty -eight he was very good at what he did. He told me that some of the women passengers would put their cabin keys in his pocket, this was a way to invite him for some extra curriculum activities, if you get my meaning. He said that a few of the guys would take them up on it and they would earn some good money in the process. It did spark a little fear into me thinking if he would do such a thing, but he re-assured me that he did not.

Larry our inherited member of staff had backed away from me over the months that I was with Arend, maintaining that he would break my heart. I never knew then just how substantially right he would be.

The dreaded day had arrived when I had to say my goodbyes to Arend. I thought my heart would break in two. He told me that it was only a few day and we would be back together again. I couldn't wait. He held me so tightly I assumed he felt the same. A tear in his eyes reinforced that point. He took my head between his hands and gave me a long lingering kiss to seal our fate of being together. His eyes penetrated my soul, and I knew then he had my heart forever.

I watched him descend the gangway from my vantage point on the rope Deck, as I couldn't let him see me crying. The tears flooded from me like a water fall cascading down a mountain side. The hole in my heart was ripping me in two. I felt so lost I could hardly breath.

Larry approached with caution from behind trying not to scare me as he put his arm over my shoulders and pulled me close.

"Hey Chica, don't worry it won't be long, the next few days will fly by." It was good to see him. I felt so awful, I was losing the love of my life and gaining the guilt of not spending time with Larry, it really hit hard.

I turned a crumbled into Larry's chest, sobbing like a baby uttering how sorry I was for not listening to him.

"Don't worry Jo, I probably wouldn't of listened either, and I could see how happy he has been making you" My sobs subsided as I straightened myself out to deal with the final embarkation day and what was left of my time on the Regent Sun.

CHAPTER 40 – HEART BREAKING.

Orlando was a beautiful sight, as we approached the dock the anticipation of the day was written all over my face. Larry described me as being in a constant state of surprise. My eyebrows were up and my eyes wide open. My smile never left my face as I was watching us for the last time draw into Port Canaveral, Orlando Florida.

I couldn't wait to disembark and meet Arend; I ran down to the lounge waiting for the customs to give us clearance to disembark. As always it takes a lot longer when your waiting for it. I was sitting with my feet dangling over the arm of a chair in lounge of the passenger areas of the ship, with a dozen other staff and crew that were also waiting. There was an excited atmosphere as we couldn't wait to see loved ones again. Some of the crew had been away from home for more than a year. Pepe my cabin steward being one of them. I handed him an envelope with fifty dollars inside as a thank you for looking after me. I knew he needed all the money he could get to look after his wife and six children, all under ten back home. He gave me a hug and walked off when it was announced that we could disembark.

I saw Larry ambling towards me with something in his hand.

" Hi Larry, it's finally here" I said jumping up and down like a kangaroo on steroids.

I could see the girls from the salon closing in around us, wondering what was going on, one by one they said their farewells and wished me all the luck in the world and thanked me for being a great manager a swore to stay in touch. Usually only a small number do. Mia and I are still in touch some twenty-five years on.

As the last girl left Larry indicated me to sit down.

" What's up Lar" I said thinking he was really upset about me going.

"Jo, you need to read this, I have a weird feeling about it, a courier handed it to me this morning with important written on the front" I looked at him as my mood changed rapidly. This looked serious. Larry's face reflected that with his eyebrows clenched tight and an upturned mouth.

" I don't want to open it Larry, If I don't read it, everything will be the same"

"I know darling, I'm here for you"

I had sunk into the armchair beside me and with trembling fingers I opened the envelope and took out a small piece of writing paper.

The envelope was address to me as manager of the salon on the regent sun. With 'IMPORTANT' written in large red letters.

I unfolded the paper and saw it was from Arend. I was suddenly awash with nausea. I read:

"My Dearest Jo,

It breaks my heart to write you this letter, but I cannot let you leave the ship without telling you that I cannot meet with you as promised. My father has been taken ill and I have to go to Indonesia.

By the time you get this I will be by his side. I hope you can forgive me Jo. I will be in touch with you once you are home in the UK.

All my love always yours Arend xxx"

I read it and re read it, the tears springing to the corners of my eyes. I wiped them away and looked up at Larry. I passed him the letter to read,

" Oh, Jo I'm so sorry, but it's better than I thought. His father is ill, this doesn't mean anything. I expect you will hear from him when you get home" Larry, seemed to be really upbeat about it. That was unusual for him, especially about Arend.

I wiped my tears and stood up; Larry followed my lead.

" Your right, he will get in touch when I'm home" I wasn't sure at that time who I was kidding. I'm not sure if I was actually kidding anyone, not even myself.

I gave Larry a big hug and squeezed the life out of him, trying to get rid of some pent-up energy, I think. Larry returned the hug and we laughed. It was like leaving Tamsin all over again. I was so confused with the torrent of feelings I had to get out of there. We swapped addresses and with that I was gone.

In the taxi to the airport I couldn't believe I was alone. I had been so looking forward to seeing Arends's face waiting by the docks for me , just like he did in Grenada. It wasn't meant to be. I just wanted to get home to Mum where I could wait for him to be in touch.

It was the middle of November when I touched down at Heathrow airport. I had written to both Mum and Dad telling them about my new boyfriend and how both of us were coming home.

Mum was standing at the arrivals gate waiting for me to head through. I had called her from Orlando airport to tell he it was just me coming in and I would explain when I got home.

She knew I would be upset, so she arranged for my brother to take her there. She hated driving in busy places. My brother David was waiting outside at the drop off zone hoping I would arrive on time, so he didn't have to pay for parking.

The moment I saw my Mum the tears rushed to my eyes and ran down my cheeks. I had been waiting for that moment all the way home. The last five or so hours on the plan felt like eternity as I couldn't sleep and was not really concentrating on the film. I had a bad feeling about all of what had just happened with Arend and it poured out of me as Mum encased me with her hug.

"It's ok darling , Mum's here" the familiar smell of her was all encompassing and was like a blanket of goodness surrounding my being. I needed her so much at that point. Not knowing that she needed me just as much.

I jumped in the back seat of David's car throwing my bags in next to me, rather than waiting for him to put them in the boot. He smiled through the rear-view mirror at me,

" Alright, how was the flight" His voice was a familiar sound of our mild London accent. It was lovely to be back

" Yeah good thanks" I kept it short and sweet and didn't really say much else all the way home, well back to my Mum's. David dropped us off with my bags and said he would be back later to catch up properly. He had some work to catch up on before that.

I watched the car turn the corner of the cul-de-sac onto the main Road. I looked around and pulled my jacket in closer to me, the coldness in the air was really started to dive deep into my bones. The day was dark and dreary and mimicked how I felt inside. Good old blighty always guaranteed to be a miserable day.

Mum had the kettle on already when I walked in the door. She shouted that I would be in the back room again, which overlooked the garden and a maze of fences and roof tops. There I was again looking out to a similar view that I had done as a child all those years ago. This time with the memory of far exotic places and Arend still very fresh in my mind. I sighed at the thought of never seeing him again . What would I do now? I thought to myself. I have no home to call my own, only a suitcase full of my worldly possessions and no transport. As if Mum had been reading my thoughts, she shouted that a cuppa was on the table.

" Come down, let's have a chat, I want to ask you something" Not too sure what was coming, I couldn't take any more bad news.

I relaxed into the sofa and looked at Mum who was sat opposite me.

" So , how are you doing and what happened to Arend" she didn't hesitate or glide into the questioning slowly like before. I filled her in crying in between when the realisation sunk in that things may not work out how I had hoped. Mum said it sounded like a wonderful holiday romance that may stay just like that. I needed her to know for me it was much more than that, but because I had been here before I didn't think she would believe me and think it would most probably fade away without too much hardship. It never did!

I asked her about Al and her, but she side-tracked a few time before I could pin her down over the next few days to exactly what was happening.

Al was working over the first week I was home, so it enabled me to spend some much-needed quality time with her, shopping and having coffee out in BHS. Which had always been my favourite place to go with her, it reminded me of being a kid. Not the poshest of places but a familiar one all the same.

"That was what I needed to feel like I belonged," I said to Mum over a cuppa in BHS restaurant.

"Yeah I know that feeling. I don't feel like I belong here, in Stevenage"

" why, what's happening Mum?" she looked at me as if for the first time. She looked down to her coffee cup and said

"he's been having affairs."

"Who, what Al has" I stared at her in disbelief.

" Yeah about five years now, with one person or another. I'm at the end of my tether with its Jo. The last one I found about turned up on our doorstep demanding to see him, as if he were hiding from her behind me. Who did she think I was the cleaner? "

"Oh my god Mum, why didn't you say?"

"I didn't want to worry you darling. You were so far away, and I knew you would want to come home. But there would be nothing you can do. Don't worry I soon told her who I was and she left with her tail between her legs" I did give a little snigger because if there is one thing I can say about my Mum, you do not want to be on the wrong side of her because her bite was so much worse than her bark.

She told me that they were going to go their separate ways, but he assured her that he had no intentions of doing it again and that she had nowhere to go, so they decided to give things another go. I could tell that it was taking its toll on Mum, she looked so much older than when I left. She was only in her late forties.

I could never look at Al in the same light and it took me all my restraint not to confront him about it all. I had promised Mum not to and also not to say a word to David my brother. He already hated Al from him taking her away from my Dad. That would have been the proverbial icing on the cake.

It had been just over a week since I got back from the Regent Sun and I had heard nothing from Arend. I was losing hope by the day. I had tried to call him a couple of time on the number he had given to me. Which was his home number, but his Mum said that he was still in the states. I explained who I was and what had happened but although her English was good, it was hard going talking to her. After the third conversation and decided to forget it. I was so upset and at a loss at what to do. Mum had done her best to cheer me up, but she was struggling herself.

The weekend came and when without much drama. I had seen Dad, but he was busy with Trisha's son's and David my brother was busy with his world. He had his own dramas of women problems. Self-induced but still a pain in his side.

Mum had gone back to work on the Monday, and I wondered around her house not knowing what to do with myself, feeling very lost and alone. The sky was grey and faint marbles of rain were working their way down the window looking out onto the street. I decided to give head office a call to see when I could go back out.

Brenda picked up the call and was glad to hear from me so soon. I could get them out of a very difficult situation if I could join the Regent Star at the weekend. I hesitated for a moment thinking that Arend may call at any time, but suddenly found myself saying yes and to send the details straight away.

By Tuesday I had the letter of confirmation in my hands. I warned Mum the night before what my plans were and passed on the details to Dad later that day. Mum was upset, she thought that I would be home for Christmas. But I just couldn't hang around doing nothing.

I was due to fly out on Saturday 9th December to Miami and catch a connecting flight to San Juan. It was going to be a long journey without a stopover, but I was ready to go.

As I sat in Heathrow airport at departures, I took stock of everything that had happened within the last month. I was definitely living a jet set lifestyle, but it was starting to have an impact on me. I felt at a loss wherever I was, not quite belonging anywhere. At first being on the ships felt like home, as time went on it felt more like a steppingstone to something better, I just didn't know what that was.

On the aircraft I could smell the familiar odour of jet fuel combined with whatever the humble delights of dinner maybe for our flight. I was sitting alone and looked at all the people surrounding me. Holiday makers and businesspeople. You could tell the difference. Those who were on holiday were smiling full of the excitement of their holidays, but those that were unlucky enough like me not to be flying business class, but who were on business , it was more of a sedate manner.

The roar of the engines set my heart alight. I hated that bit, when the plane left the ground. We took off just like I had done many times before. Up we went. The feeling of someone pushing down on my head trying to defy gravity was very apparent. I looked out of the window watching the clouds flash by as we ascended into the air. Fluffy cotton wall, I could hear my Mum saying when we took off to go on holiday to Spain when we were kids. I watch the cars turn into toys and the ground was swallowed up by the think dark grey sky.

I was just relaxing into the flight when the aircraft bumped and jolted around. Turbulence I thought. With that my arms and hair and drink flew into the air as the plane plummeted down. I thought I was going to be sick. My heart was in my head and screams descended into my ears from around the cabin. People were crying I was crying the fear of god had come down on me hard. The plan stopped after what seemed like forever. I took a breath and felt the crushing feeling on my head again as we climbed back up. The aircraft was still experiencing major turbulence. I caught hold of my knees as it did the exact same thing. The free-falling effect was not pleasant as the plane dropped again. The screams were louder this time. The man beside me had his head in the crash position and another was yelling to his wife that he loved her. I thought that was our lot. I waited endlessly for the plane to hit the ground. But it had stopped, and I felt the climb and roar of the engines once more.

I was frightened to the core and didn't look up until the plane had straightened out. I still had hold of my legs when a stewardess came around and asked if I was ok. The passenger next to me had called her when I hadn't moved for more than half an hour.

I looked up with a tear stained face and beads of sweat that had formed on my forehead.

"Oh, Yes, umm, sorry, yes I'm fine thank you." She offered me a glass of water just as the captain came over the speaker apologising for the bumpy take off.

I heard the women behind me say to her husband in a very loud voice.

"BUMPY, that wasn't BUMPY that was falling out of the bloody sky" the air stewardess asked her to keep her voice down as she was scaring the children. She was scaring me not just the children. Unfortunately, I have never liked flying since that episode and take off and turbulence frightens me to this day. In fact, I would go as far to say that I would rather avoid flying altogether now a days.

We finally landed in Miami without any other hitches. I was certainly glad to get off. But I had to get a move on to a connecting flight to San Juan. I found the departure lounge and there I saw who definitely another girl with Sanctuaries was written all over her. I approached her and asked.

"Hey, excuse me but you aren't by any chance from Sanctuaries, are you?" she laughed and nodded.

"How did you know?" she asked. I told her that we all seemed perfectly done. Meaning that there was a look of fear and togetherness with hair and makeup.

"Is this your first contract"

" Yeah I'm joining the Regent Star. A bit scared to meet the manager"

"Oh, you will be fine I hear she's really nice" I giggled and did finally admit that it was me who she was meeting. The relief on her face was great to see. I was obviously not too much of a witch. Well maybe not then.

Unfortunately, we were sat at opposite ends of the plan for the next leg. She had also just got off the flight from England and it scared the hell out of her too.

I looked out of the window at the propellers that were to take us to San Juan, praying that it wouldn't be a repeat of the last flight. We landed without a hitch and very smooth it was. I on the other hand must have held my breath through the whole journey until we landed. I just couldn't relax. Every bump and tremor I were agitated.

I had arranged to meet Dawn at the baggage area. We had landed to torrential rain in San Juan. We scurried outside to the cabs and asked to go to the Regent Star at the port. It wasn't far and to my surprise was confronted with a ship that looked similar to the regent Sun. Deja Vue.

CHAPTER 41- MY SHINING STAR!

The Regent Star shone like a white diamond against the grey sky, she entered service in 1957 as Holland America Line's SS STATENDAM, which I found funny as I had been on the Statendam in a previous contract. She became an instant hit on North Atlantic crossings from Rotterdam to New York and in seasonal cruising. STATENDAM was mainly a tourist class vessel, but one of the keys to her success was the quality of her accommodation, which aspired to first class standards. She became the Regent Star in 1986 until later in 1995 went out of service when Regency cruise lines dissolved through financial difficulties.

Everything look the same inside, so for me it wasn't too much of a transition from the Sun to Star. I finally met the previous manager who was disembarking that day. She filled me in on the staff of three soon to be five and handed over notes of demonstration times etc.

It was like riding a bike. Our cruising was about to change, and we were heading off to Canada after Christmas. That I was looking forward to . For the remainder of the Caribbean cruising we were heading to Montego bay and Ocho Rios. I wanted to visit Dunn's River Falls. I was determined to enjoy the ship and had a few thing to look forward to. Arend was still very much on my mind, but I felt better to be busy rather than moping around.

The crew and girls were lovely except one. This time I had Dawn who was beauty who I met at the airport she was twenty-one and from Cardiff. Very funny girl and such joy to be around. Penny was a hairy (hairdresser) from Plymouth, slightly quieter that I was used to but nice and pleasant all the same. Sid was from the states he was twenty-seven from Miami. Very full on fitness guru and planned to have us all kicked into shape. Then there was Suzi the other beauty therapist, she on the other hand, had an attitude problem. She didn't want to work or join in. The fact was she thought that she was there for a holiday. That was the impression she gave me.

I was constantly running up and down from the hair salon to the beauty salon chasing her to greet her clients and to check in and do some work. She kept turning clients away saying that she was too busy. But she was not, her column was empty, and she was not even down in the salon according to Dawn. This carried on for a few week until I call her in for a chat.

I took her for a coffee on Lido Deck, where I confronted her with the facts and evidence that she had not been pulling her weight in the salon, which showed in her figures, she was 75% below everyone else. That was a lot.

"So, why do you think that is and are you settling in Ok" I was concerned that she may be homesick.

" I don't know do I" she barked at me with a stern, Sharpe edge in her voice.

" well tell me how you feel about the ship and your work. It sounds to me that your unhappy?" I was trying to keep things positive, but the conversation turned into a disaster. She told me in no uncertain terms that she was not here to work just have a good time. I couldn't believe what I was hearing and had never come across that attitude from any staff. I hadn't even heard of anyone before who felt that way.

I made it clear to her that she had signed a contract of employment and that she was here predominantly to work and that if she continued to have the same outlook then she would leave me no choice but to take things further. I got her to sign a verbal warning and ask to meet with her in a couple of days to re visit the action plan.

I couldn't understand it. The last manager hadn't said anything to me about Suzi and how she had felt. I presumed it was me she was taking offense with until I spoke with Penny and Sid later that day. They had called me to meet for coffee before we went to dinner .

According to them Suzi had been giving Laura a hard time since she had got her two weeks ago, but Laura the previous manager had a lot of issues going on at home and couldn't deal with that as well. I decided to dig a little deeper and asked if this was her first contract and if there was a boyfriend etc, but nothing. She was a bit of a loner and didn't mix with the other girls.

Over the course of the next few days I watched as she turned away client after client, twice she was a no show to work and when I confronted her about it, she told me to go do one. By the time we got to Montego bay I had had enough.

I disembarked early that morning to call head office. I had filled them in on the last few days and said I had gone through all of the warning procedures with her. I had also told her that she would be sent home if she continued. Her response was I would like to see you try. There was no reasoning with her.

I was told to disembark her immediately and we would get another member of staff at Ochi Rios. I was authorised to pick up a plane ticket from the local port agent who escorted me to buy the tickets at the travel agency, where Sanctuaries had authorised it. I headed back to the ship nervous of the response. I passed by the pursers desk to get her passport, where they sent a security guard with me to escort Suzi off the ship. I found her a sleep in her cabin, which made things easier as she was supposed to be at work.

I informed her that she had half an hour to wash and pack and that she would be leaving for London in three hours from the airport . I waited with the guard outside the cabin and escorted her to the gang way. Nothing was said between any of us. I stopped her as she was leaving and said ,

" Suzi, never threaten people and challenge them to do

anything, as it will always backfire on you. You could have turned this around , but I do wish you well and hope you have a good journey"

"I didn't think you would do it " she said hanging her head down flushed in her cheeks as she was escorted to the port agent, who would take her to the airport to make sure she left on the right plan to London direct.

I walked back to the salon where the others had obviously heard through the jungle drums what had happened. I calmed them and said I didn't want to talk about it and that a new member of staff would join us at our next port.

What a week that had been. I was looking forward to our excursion to Dunn's River Falls in Ocho Rios. I leant over the side on top Deck trying to catch the breeze on my face. The toll had mounted up all week and the release of tension from my shoulders was amazing. I looked into the sun to allow the heat to penetrate my skin. It felt good. My thought turned to Arend and all his promises. What a bloody nightmare I thought. You just can't trust anyone , what with Al and Arend and now Suzi, I could almost give up on people, until I remembered Larry and Tamsin my good friends from previous ships. A smile formed at the corners of my mouth. I opened my eyes a looked down at the docks, just as a familiar head of black hair disappeared inside the ship at the crew gangway.

It couldn't be, my stomach lurched into my mouth and I froze to the spot, I literally couldn't move. The sweat was now pouring from me. I had to get out of the sun, I was seeing things. It was probably someone who looked like him. I was thinking about him at that moment. I put it out of my head. Stupid me !

The day had been a long one and we were finishing off in the salon. The team seemed calmer after the earlier events and normality was restored. I felt I had a great bunch now and whoever was to join us would feel part of a great gang.

I cashed up and the girls left to get some dinner, when the

announcement for evening dinning came over the speakers. The familiar Dutch accent seeped into my ears. It stopped me in my tracks. Goose pimples ran down my spine and the hairs stood to attention on the back of my neck. I was frightened to look up as I could feel the eyes pinned to the crown of my head.

"Hey Jo" the trickle of excitement ran cold through me as I looked up to be Faced with Arend

I was speechless, I must have stood with my mouth opened, just looking in sheer surprise, that the love of my life was in front of me. I had to stop myself from running into his arms and jumping for joy. Play it calm I said to myself.

"What are you doing here?"

"What can I say , I needed to come back to the ships"

"What... " I stopped myself

"Well you are a surprise I will give you that." I really didn't know what to say to him.

"Can we meet later in the crew bar? I feel like I ow you an explanation"

I agreed curious to know what had gone so wrong. I can't remember the next three hours as I waited for him to arrive in the bar. Every time the door opened; I was expecting him to walk in. I had given up once midnight had come and gone. So, I sat having a great time with the French guys that I had befriended. Sacha, Maurice and Claude. They were funny and spoke great English. They laughed at my schoolgirl French and teased me to say some more words all naughty mind you.

We fell about and they really cheered me up. They were from different parts of France Sacha and Maurice from the South and Claude from the North. They all seemed to get along ok and became great friends to each other and me. We arranged to meet the next day for our tour to Dunn's River Falls, as my new staff member wasn't arriving until just before we sailed so I had plenty of time.

Just as they were ribbing me even more, Arend walked in

and stopped at the doorway, looking for me.

"Sorry guys I need to dash" with that I got up and left.

"Come with me" Arend said.

I followed him to the top Deck by the funnels where it was quiet. He took a couple of beers with him and handed one to me, just like our first meeting in my cabin. Thankfully we were on neutral ground.

"I'm sorry Jo" he said trying to grab my hand. I pulled back. I knew if he touched me, I would melt in his arms all over again.

"What the hell Arend" I almost spat it at him.

"Jo , my father was so ill, I didn't have your number with me. In all the confusion I must have left it in my cabin when I left the Sun" he was reeling out excuses so fast my head was spinning.

"I called your house and spoke to your mother. I left me number every time."

" my mother and I are not talking to well at the moment. She didn't want me to go to my father, for obvious reasons. So, I have not been in touch with her"

How could I not forgive him, it's not like he did it on purpose. I couldn't help feeling sorry for him as he seemed so distressed.

"Kasper, so you would have never got in touch with me if you hadn't turned up on here" I couldn't help it, I was so mixed up. He told me that he had contacted my head office to look for me and requested the ship. I looked at him in disbelief, but he swore it was true. I wasn't so sure, but the thought was nice.

CHAPTER 42- LIFE GOES ON.

I met up with my new friend at the gang way to go to Dunn's River Falls, in Ocho Rios. The girls and I hopped onto a local bus with Sacha, Maurice and Claude, the French waiters, with a dozen other crew from the Star. Unfortunately, Arend had to work, but I was glad of the distraction. I hadn't slept much the previous night; we had talked until the early hours of the morning as Arend was trying to make up for lost time and calm the situation down between us. I had forgiven him, but I was still in protection mode.

The hot sun was out in all its glory and the temperature was hitting above thirty degrees in the shade. Dunn's River Falls is one of Jamaica's national treasures. The Arawak name "Xayamaca" - land of rivers and springs. The Spaniards called the area "Las Chorreras", the waterfalls or springs and it is truly one of the most beautiful spots on the island and a Stone's throw from Ocho Rios. Dunn's River Falls has a fascinating history, it is said to be the location of the Battle of "Chorreras" which was fought in 1667 near the Falls. The fight was between the English and the Spanish Expeditionary Forces from Cuba trying to get ownership of the island. The English won that battle. The name "Las Chorreras" has short-ened over the years to "Ocho Rios" (meaning eight rivers), although there are actually only four rivers in the area - Cave River, Roaring River, Turtle River and Dunns River. The "Chor-reras" are characterized by clarity, unending flow and swift descent, punctuated by rapid cascades and waterfalls which pour directly into the Caribbean Sea.

We stood at the bottom of the falls looking up to one hundred and eight food high ascent to the top. It was sure going to be almost impossible to do. Yet many people had climbed before and I'm sure many have climbed since. We formed a human chain to aid our ascent and falling and laughing the whole time. It was so scary trying to keep your balance whilst the water cascaded fast around your legs. The flow of water was quite forceful in some places. We stopped at an area known as 'massage parlour' and experience of a jet that really did massage your body just like our man-made hydrotherapy pools. It was sensational, sitting watching the water flow down to the beach. I could see the golden sands being lapped by the aquamarine waters of the Caribbean Sea, it was a totally natural experience and all of the structures, crevices, and natural pools of water were made by the actual flow of the water's current

What a day to remember and such fun, now that's a place I would love to go back to, but like everything now perhaps tourism has spoilt it. It was busy enough then and that was around twenty-five years ago.

The return to the ship was a little de-flatted although I did feel like my skin had had a thorough clean.

Time progressed on and so did my relationship with Arend, we had been back together for a few of months, Christmas had come and gone, the crew dinner at a secluded hotel up above the beach in Montego bay was to die for. The pool and the atmosphere were lovely, not Christmassy at all but beautiful all the same. It was very hard to make any Christmas feel the typical Christmas in thirty to forty-degree heat. But any excuse to have a party was the motto on the ship.

I was approaching my twenty sixth birthday as we sailed up to Canada from the Caribbean. Now another place on my all-time favourites. So clean and fresh. We had gone to Bar harbour in Maine, Portland where Arend took me to the most amazing chowder restaurant and then to Quebec and Montreal. It was a lot different to the Caribbean, for one thing it was colder. I did have to take a second look at Arend when we stopped at our first port in the colder climate, he was wearing a tanned suede jacket with tassels down the arms, all the rage apparently on Holland at the time, according to him. I wasn't so sure, by that point I was completely head over heels in love with the guy, so I would have believed anything. Which I did until I didn't anymore and that was it!!!

Things had started to change; Arend had talked about us getting engaged and as you can imagine I was over the moon with excitement. We had been spending more time in the cabin as I was burning out quickly from parties and. No sleep exploring the places we stopped at. It was never ending. The salon was so busy I didn't know up from down . The girls had out done themselves with promoting the products and services and our new beauty therapist Clara was brilliant, a complete change from Suzi, a breath of fresh air.

So, to say I took my eye off the ball was an understatement. It started to dawn on me that Arend was getting back to the cabin later and later, but I passed it off as being so busy as were we.

It had been a long cruise when we hit our home port of Montreal, I had been off a few time visiting different places but this time I decided not to bother. Arend left as he usually did in his smart trousers and white shirt, but he had left his jacket over the chair. I darted out of bed and grabbed it , hoping to see him in the corridor. It was too late. I had missed him. I changed into my joggers for speed, but as I looked out of my port hole, I could just see him disappear into the crew kiosk where we made calls.

'that's funny 'I thought, he had not said anything about having the morning off. I threw his jacket on the bed to balance myself as I pulled on my trousers and noticed that a passenger cabin key fell out of his pocket. I picked it up thinking it was his keys to his cabin , but the numbers did match.

I sat down on the bed and stared into space, not really knowing what to make of it, when a comment he had made about passengers putting their cabin keys in some of the waiters pockets sprung to mind. Nausea threatened the back of my throat.

'Nah' I said out loud 'He wouldn't' I passed it off as a coincidence and put it back where it was, just as Arend came rushing in a grabbing it from the bed.

" I was just about to find you as I see you had left it"

" Thanks " he said digging in the exact pocket of where the keys were sitting , checking and letting them stay snuggly undetected. Or so he thought.

As he left, he blew a kiss and was gone.

Twenty minutes had lapsed before I moved, something was amiss. Or was I just paranoid? Maybe a bit of both, but I thought it was time to do a little research. My detective head was well and truly on my shoulders and I was on a mission. Not really expecting to find much.

CHAPTER 43- MISDIRECTION

Things kept cropping up that were out of place. A tie of Arends was handed to me by the purser that was left in the cinema. His shirts were smelling of perfume and he was disappearing at the oddest times. But on each occasion, he seemed to have a plausible answer. A passenger had hugged him to say thank you, he lent a tie to another to enable then to enter the dining area on formal night and that he was just really busy.

I always gave him the benefit of the doubt, but something inside of me was screaming that he was lying.

I also had been in contact with Mum and she was telling me that Al was up to his old tricks again. So that didn't help me on the trust side, and I felt complete out of control of what was happening at home. My Mum needed me, but I couldn't get to her. I could hear it in her voice the strain of the last few months was taking its toll. She did tell me that she was ok, but you just know when someone is paying you lip service .

I could no longer concentrate, everything was spinning in my head, my Mum, Arend the job, how tied I was , I was not thinking straight. I felt nauseous all the time. I stopped going to dinner on occasion, and when I did, I couldn't keep anything down, the worry was completely taking over.

I decided to do something radical!

Arend was in the dining room as usual, when I locked up the salon, but instead of heading to dinner I took off down a long corridor, descended some stairwells in the crew area and found myself outside of Arends cabin. I had only visited it once before, but I managed to remember where it was.

Now what! I thought.

The cabin Steward was outside getting ready to clean the area. I don't know what came over me , I found myself asking if he would let me in, as I had left my purse inside. He gave me a puzzled look and said that he shouldn't really do it. He looked at me a few time and obviously decided that I was harmless enough and opened the door.

I knew I had to be quick. How long does it take to find a purse? Thankfully everything was in its place and I went straight to the draws. The cabin was an inside one and he never shared with anyone, so I was fee to look everywhere. As I opened the top draw of his desk a folded letter fell on the floor. I retrieved it and opened it out.

'My darling Arend,

It was so good to speak with you on Thursday, I have missed you so much. Tango does to, she had been pining for you scrapping her little paws at the closed bedroom door, meowing so loudly.

I can't stop thinking about our trip to Paris on your last vacation. It was so romantic. I know I have hesitated, but as I said, when you are away, I find it so hard to be here alone whilst you are working on the ships. My imagination runs wild, but I know you will always be true to me and I can't wait to be with you forever.

I'm looking forward to the day you pull into Orlando and I hope it won't be too long. I am glad you have made friends and that your time in Canada doesn't drag too much. It was good you tried the chowder, but next time perhaps ask one of the other waiters to go with you. You must get so lonely doing all those things on your own.

I will sign off for now but be sure that my heart is for you.

Miss you ,Love you always

Diana xxxx'

I checked the date on the letter and sure enough it was written since he turned up on here. That meant, he was not with his father.

The tears fell from my eyes like huge raindrops falling from the sky. I couldn't breathe, I had to get out of there and fast. I re-folded the paper and put it back in the draw, just allowing enough time to count the number of letters from her. Ten in all. I couldn't believe it. I got to the door in time for the cabin steward to be checking on me. I flashed him my cashing up purse that I used in the salon adding,

"found it" as I rushed past him up the stairs back to the safety of my cabin.

Collapsing on the bed my head was racing and my heart was breaking all over again. What to do, what to do I couldn't stand it. I burst into tears.

I lay there for hours blankly looking at the celling, I had thrown up a couple of times since I got back, but I managed to calm myself down. This couldn't be happening, again. All the times he was with me, promising me that we would be together forever and visiting these glorious places, he was telling her what we had done, minus me.

I knew things had been odd, but I never imagined it to be as bad as that. I had to find out more, exactly what was going on , before I told him that I had found out, I needed to be absolutely sure what type of man he was. I was hurting so much; I knew he could come up with an excuse to explain what was happening. He was good at that.

I tidied myself up and approached the pursers desk with trepidation. Not quite sure what I would say or ask. One of the pursers approached me.

"Just the person , I was coming to find you. Have you got a minute?

"Yes sure," I could ask her after about Arend.

I followed her to the lounge where we grabbed a coffee. Sofia was lovely. Small, dark and very beautiful. She was extremely clever and as head of the pursers desk I could understand why. They were always so full on with passenger complaints and problems. I took my hat off to them for that.

"Jo, I'm not sure how to tell you this, but I know if I was in your situation I would want someone to tell me" I couldn't

JO HAMLIN

help but feel there was something really bad coming my way.

" I know you have been seeing Arend for a while now and it devastates me to say this to you. But " There it was 'but', always but, you knew then that what was to follow was sure enough going to be horrible,

" But, Arend has been taking passenger keys to take passengers back to for the night. He thinks that we don't know, and I shouldn't be telling you this, but we have known for a while. I can't sit here anymore and watch you fall further and further for him." She looked and held her breath waiting for my reaction.

I smiled graciously and thanked her for telling me and that I was glad that I knew what was going on. I was so calm. She held onto my hand a few minute to make sure I was ok.

I gave her a small hug. Half smiling

"It's Ok Sophia, please don't tell him that I know" and with that I walked away knowing exactly what I needed to do.

I packed my bags the next morning after Arend had left for work. I had to make sure that he knew nothing about my next move. He would convince me to do what he wanted otherwise. After I left Sophia, I had gone to the radio room a telexed head office for an immediate transfer to another ship. I had said that I felt I could not offer the salon anything else and needed a new challenge.

Within minutes I received a response to disembark in New York and catch a flight to Orlando where I would pick up the Starship Atlantic. I couldn't believe what I had just done but knew deep inside that I needed to do it.

I was in the middle of putting my last item in my case when the door opened and Arend walked in.

"What's going on Jo? Why are you packing"

"You really have no idea?" I said with such venom in my voice.

"No, I don't" His tone suddenly changed as the realisation dawned on him that I knew. But how much I knew he couldn't be sure.

"how could you Arend, you promised me that you saw your father, all the excuses you made to me about different things, now I find out that you have been lying"

"What do you mean, lying about what exactly" the hurt in his voice made me question me actions.

"The fact that you have been sleeping with passengers behind my back" I decided to keep back the knowledge that I knew about his girlfriend in Orlando.

"I can explain, there's no need for you to leave"

"It's too late Arend I leave today, my flights booked and I'm picking up the Starship Atlantic in Orlando". I wanted him to know that I would be in Orlando to try and prompt him to admit everything. But he didn't.

"But I love you Jo" he looked to the floor and tears rolled from his cheeks hitting the floor one by one.

"I'm sorry Arend but I have to go, if you love me you will do what's right and let me go"

"I can't " he went to grab me, but I moved

"Don't Arend, don't make it harder than it already is" You know where I will be the rest is up to you.

I left with my heart at my feet, feeling so destroyed at what I had done. Was I overreacting or had I done the right thing?

CHAPTER 44- DETERMINE

Leaving the Star was one of the hardest things I had ever done, but I had to get away and far away from Arend. I had boarded the Starship Atlantic in a daze. Normally I would find out all about the ship and its history, but this was different, I was different . My heart just wasn't in it. I had gone through the motion of meeting the staff but who they were and the time I spent with them I didn't care or want to find out. The salon was running pretty smoothly without any input from me.

I spent every evening after finishing work in my cabin listening to the CNN news channel as it was the only thing, I could get on my T.V. Every night dead on five I could hear the child carers marching passed my door with their little warriors following, singing M.I.C.K.E.Y.M.O.U.S.E, then singing the Mickey Mouse theme tune over and over again until they faded away. I was on a Disney ship. Bumping into Disney characters all over the ship. Ordinarily I would have loved it , but I felt miserable.

My head would not stop turning, I was confused and alone and I needed to go home. Mum was not great; I wasn't coping, and I was stuck.

I turned to not eating which in turn switch to becoming bulimic, not that I knew what that was then, but now I realise it was a way of controlling my situation. I would show my face in the crew mess then come back and throw up . Mostly due to the feeling nausea but also because I could.

I spend most of my time alone in my cabin counting down the days until I could go home . It was the end of April and I had ages to go until I could leave. July was such a long time away.

I saw Mabel the nurse on the way to the salon.

" Jo, the doctor would like to see you, lovely" she was from the West country and so kind and caring. I followed her to the onboard Doctor, Zac

" Great, Hi Jo ,please sit down" I did as I was asked not really paying too much attention to what was going on.

" Jo, we have noticed that you have lost a lot of weight, since joining us, is everything ok with you" I looked up between Zac and Mabel.

"Oh, yes everything is fine, thanks for your concern"

"It's just we are worried about you; you seem lost and unwell"

" No, really I'm fine honestly, I've been trying to drop some weight, so it must be working." I laughed and stood to leave.

As I went to walk through the door Mabel grabbed my hand.

" Jo if you need to talk, I'm here for you. She added sympathetically.

"Thank you" I left and went straight back to my cabin.

I looked in the full-length mirror for the first time since I had arrived and noticed that I had lost a lot. My skirt was falling off of me and my face was looking gaunt. God, I looked awful.

A note was pushed under my door.

'Jo'

Was written on the front. I opened it and it was a telex from the Regent Star. Arend

'Jo, I miss you so much. Meet me in Orlando the next time the ship is in. Arend X'

I stood there blinking, reading and re – reading, wishing a clue would jump out at me, my protection mode was on high alert, yet I was desperate for him to choose me. I couldn't understand what was happening. I need to get out of here, the ship wasn't due in for three more days, I couldn't stand it anymore. I couldn't do anything, whilst trapped on here.

We were due to dock in Nassau the next day, so I found

myself adapting an old telex from head office. Changing the dates and times. I photocopied it in the pursers office so it would look authentic. I wasn't even thinking about what I was about to do I just did it. The focus was to get off. I had to find out the truth and I had to get to Mum, I had a gut feeling everything was not good with her.

I gave the telex to the purser, so she knew I was disembarking in Nassau.

The telex had stated that I needed to pick up the plane tickets from Nassau's travel agent and a manager would replace me in Orlando. This gave me time to get away from the ship.

I didn't sleep a wink all night. I didn't really have any idea exactly how I was going to do it, but I knew I was desperate.

We docked early and I was off packed ready to go. I left my luggage on the ship whilst I went to the local travel agents to purchase a ticket back into the states.

I handed it to the purser to examine and she handed me my passport.

"Well Jo , Short but sweet, I hope you have a great journey".

"Thank you" I tried not to snatch the passport and run instead I gentle put it in my bag and walked off the ship calmly. I didn't say goodbye to the girls in the salon, I didn't want to raise the alarm and answer too many questions, I could lie to their faces and I would not involve them, I said nothing to no one. I just left and never looked back.

'What was I doing?'

It was like I was in a trance, going through the motions. I think that was how I blagged my way through the passport control to get back to the states without an ongoing ticket to the U.K. I gave some 'cock and ball' story about my parents waiting for me in Orlando with my ticket home. It would never happen today, but I think the guy felt sorry for me. I must have looked terrible.

It had been a month since I had seen Arend last, but I was determined to find out what had happened before I went home.

I met the Star at the Docks, trying to blend with the rest of the passengers not allowing anyone to recognise me.

As it was, I bumped into Sacha the waiter I was friends with.

"Jo, what the F*** are you doing here?"

" I can't explain , it will take too long, but I'm here to meet Arend"

" Jesus Jo, didn't anyone tell you he got the sack and left the ship a week ago, for playing around with passengers"

The blood drained from my face I had no idea that he would have had to pay for what he did. I knew the Star would be in that day after it's Canada cruising , but I assumed Arend would be on it.

I gave Sacha a hug and left. I knew where he would be!

I hailed a cab and gave him the address I had copied down from the letters I found in Arends cabin. It was about half an hour away, but I didn't care. It was time to face the music.

We pulled up outside a typical American one-story house. The houses were set out with large spaces set between them; the lawns cascaded down a small bank onto the Road. The house I was looking for was very pretty and really large. No gates at the outside just open lawn.

I asked the cabby to wait, just in case I needed him. He did as I asked. I approached the door carefully not wanting to give away my arrival. The door was bright red with a bell set to one side. Yellow flowers were in full bloom in a pot set to one side of the enormous door. I rang it.

I had a lump in my throat and terrible anxiety in my stomach. I could see the outline of a figure coming to the door. I couldn't make out if it was male or female. As the shadow got closer the realisation, that it was Arend hit me like a tidal wave. I stumbled back as he opened the door.

"JO" the horror on his face was preposterous.

" I knew you would be here, I just had to check, and hope I was wrong"

"How on earth...." His words petered off. " You can't be here"

"Why, will Diana be home?" the sarcasm was spat out of my mouth like daggers, thrown aiming for his heart.

"Well yes .... But how did you know?"

" I found your letters. I've knew when I left the Star, that's why I left, not just because of the passengers, that I could have forgiven, but this, I could not"

"I was going to meet you in a few day, to explain. I'm leaving Diana to be with you"

" Really then I have saved you the bother, we can tell her together."

"No... not like this"

" Really why, it's more than I got"

" I can't hurt her like that , she has done nothing."

" Neither had I Arend, it's been all you."

We stared at each other, neither one of us knowing who would break the silence first. As it was the cabby beep his horn.

"look I have to go, if you are serious, meet me dockside, with a suitcase ready to head home. Then I will know that you are serious with what you say"

I ran to the cab and jumped in indicating to the driver to take me back to the nearest hotel at the port. I glanced out of the window, just catching a woman, dark like me, about the same age, slim with curly hair, walking up the path to the house smiling at Arend. That had to be her, I knew it.

CHAPTER 44 - CATA-
STROPHIC DEMISE

I was up looking out over the water's edge from my balcony at a motel I stayed in. The cabby had been wonderful, realising I had had some bad news he took me to the nicest inexpensive place that he knew on the beach not far from the docks.

I had arranged for him to pick me up that morning at ten to take me back to the docks.

There would be no cruise ships in, and we would be free to talk properly. It was the days before mobiles so I could only hope that he would be there. I had no way to contact him and no way for him to contact me.

I couldn't help wondering what had happened to my dreams and the excitement had definitely left me for a life on the ships. I knew it would be my last contract, especially after Sanctuaries found out that I had jumped ship.

I couldn't think about that then I just needed to get to Arend and then get home to Mum. God only knows what she was going through.

I stood in the carpark of the terminal waiting for Arend. Not sure what would happen, but I knew it would be the last time I would wait for him.

Over an hour I was there before his car appeared . He pulled up next to me.

"Get in" I did as he said. We were silent on the journey to the airport.

As we pulled up it struck me that we were not in a hire car. The airport was in full view and I had a sinking feeling that penetrated my whole being. He wasn't coming with me.......

He parked the car and we headed into the airport; he still hadn't said two words to me. He took my cases out and took my hand. He led me to the bar situated just by the check in.

He ordered to Whisky's and cokes and handed one to me. God this was going to be bad, midday and we were on the heavy stuff all ready.

We sat for a few second and I could feel the tension building, .

" Jo, I Love you, you know that. But I cannot come with you. I have to be honest; it's gone too far, and you don't deserve how I've treated you and I never expected to feel how I do about you. But that's why I have to let you go."

" So why did you contact me, why didn't you just leave me?"

" One of the head waiters who I know on the Atlantic contacted me when he found out who you were. He told me you were in a bad way. That you had lost so much weight and that the doctors were concerned. I needed to make sure you were ok, but I see he was right" He gesture to my ill-fitting clothes that was hanging off.

" I had to tell you. I cannot leave Diane, she is not well, I'm mean seriously unwell. Hence the reason I lied about my father before, it was her not him, but I couldn't tell you that at the time. I know if I leave her, she will go downhill really quickly."

"What about me Arend, don't I count?"

"Yes you do a lot more than you will ever know, but you are strong, or at least I thought you were, until I heard what you were going through, I'm so sorry I Jo" he handed me a an envelope" I want you to take this, it's the least I can do"

I opened the seal and pulled out a ticket for a single passenger back to London.

" I can't take this" I looked at him tears cascading down my cheeks and dripping from my chin to the table.

" I don't want to hear another word. You take it Jo . "

He dismissed me instantly. I took the ticket and put it in

my bag.

" I'm not going to delay things any further, it's hard enough for both of us. Good bye Jo, it has been a privilege to know you" I thought my heart was going to crack in two.

He stood, kissed me on the cheek. I gave a sharp intake of breath as I watch him leave through the same doors we had just come through. I just stared. I was heartbroken.

How I managed to get myself through customs and onto the plane was beyond me. I must have just gone on auto pilot. My teared stained face was raw, where I had wiped the tears away over the last couple of hours in departures waiting for my flight to be called. I cried all the way back to England. I never knew pain like it. It finished me completely.

I woke up with a feeling of falling, the decent for Heathrow had begun. I had managed to sleep for the last couple of hours. People was looking at me.

" Are you ok " Said the lady to my left.

"Yes, thank you" I looked at her inquisitively.

" You shouted out in your sleep, something about Arend." I was embarrassed, thank you for your concern I am fine .

As we departed the plane, I hung my head low trying not to entice any other cause for concern. When I got in the terminal, I headed straight for the toilets to wash my face. I peered into the mirror to find a horror story looking back at me. My eye had black circles under them, my skin was blotchy from crying and, but eyeballs were bloodshot. I looked a right state. I couldn't let Mum see me like this. I retrieved my bags and stepped into the showers at the airport. I freshened up and dressed in clean clothes from my case. I re -applied my make-up and did my hair which was now past my shoulder blades where it had grown so much. I put it a simple plait.

I stepped into the sunshine, which was very odd for our great country but the relief to be home was overwhelming. I had to try not to cry again as my mind kept leaping back to Arend and our last conversation. I had never felt so alone in the world as I did at that point. It was probably one of the worst times of my life. I hadn't eaten for two days and was just living off alcohol and water.

I stepped out to the taxi rank and asked how much it would be to take me back to Stevenage. It was the first time there was no one to pick me up. At least I had come back to Heathrow and not Gatwick which was right around the other side of the M25.

It took a couple of hours to get to Mum's as traffic was horrendous. I pulled up outside of Mum's paid the Taxi and rang the bell. Her car was in the drive, so I knew she was home thankfully.

She opened the door and her mouth dropped; she cried the moment she realised it was me. Her arms flung around me, and she pulled me in.

"Oh, my goodness Jo, I thought we had lost you, Where the bloody hell have you been," the anger took over the relief that I was home safe and sound.

She ushered me in and sat me on the sofa. I burst out crying and told her the whole horrid story before I had even taken my coat off. It just came flooding out.

She helped me off with my coat and cried again when she saw how thin I was. She gasped but covered her mouth with her hand to hide her surprise.

"I need to call your Dad; he has been frantic"

I could hear them on the phone arguing as he wanted to come over and give me what for. Apparently head office had been on the phone concerned for my where abouts. Of course, no one knew. By the time I got home it had been a week since I left the ship. They were not impressed to say the least.

When Mum had come back, she had a bottle in her hand, filling her glass as she sat down.

"You want some" she handed me one. We didn't really talk much as I just wanted to go to bed and sleep. I was worn out.

It was mid-afternoon before I rose, Al was in the garden

cutting the lawn and Mum was in the kitchen. It was very quiet, I could hear Mum sniffing and passed it off as a summer cold.

She walked past me rather hastily, enough to make me look up.

" You alright Mum"

"Yeah I won't be a minute" She disappeared upstairs. Half an hour had passed as I sat just looking at the T.V but not really looking at it. I heard the tinkle of the receiver being placed back on its handles upstairs. The next thing I know the phone was ringing. Mum didn't pick up.

" That's odd " I said out loud. " Do you want me to get that Mum?" There was no reply. I picked it up as whoever it was, did not give up easily.

"Hello"

"It's Roger" My uncle said at the other end.

"Oh Hello"

" no time for pleasantries Jo, you need to get upstairs, it's your Mum she's taken some pills"

"What, what do you mean pills"

"Jo just do it, don't ask questions , just go up I'm ringing an ambulance from here, they should be with you shortly, get her up off the bed and walk her around, keep her awake" with that he hung up. I ran upstairs, my hands shaking at the news I was just told. I headed for Mums room. She was lying on the bed unconscious, with an empty bottle of wine and pills all over the bedroom floor. I was crying but I just when into another zone I never knew I had.

"Mum wake up, can you hear me Mum" I slapped her face trying to get a response" Oh Mum please no, I can't lose you too, don't do this, you silly woman" I couldn't take it in. The doorbell rang and it was David my brother. Roger must have called him too. Boy he got there fast.

David picked my Mum up and lifted her downstairs,

"No time to wait for an ambulance it will be faster if we take her, go tell Al, where is he anyway?"

Al was still in the garden; he had no idea. He had just shut off the mower when I shouted to him to get his arse in quick . He came running to find us pilling Mum into the car. I explained quickly what she had done as we were leaving. We left him standing at the door staring and watching us.

Mum was fading in and out of consciousness. We got her to A&E department just in time. The nurses took over and wheeled her off to resus.

I stood in disbelief. My brother and I were motionless until Al came running in. How my brother restrained himself from flooring Al I will never know.

I told him to leave and that we would inform him on what was happening later. Of course, he did not go.

The nurse came out after an hour and told us that Mum was ok, she had not taken enough pills to kill herself but enough to make her incredible sick. She was going to be fine but will feel pretty lousy.

They had to follow protocol of an attempted suicide and have the mental health department assess her to make sure she was no longer a danger to herself. They will also want to talk to us.

Attempted suicide, the words hung in the air. What the hell had been going on. I knew about the women but there must have been more to this than she was letting on.

I told David what I knew, and he filled me in on the rest.

The company Mum had been made secretary of, had been caught for tax evasion. Which meant Mum was in a lot of trouble, but it was Al and his accountant that had falsified her signatures and Mum was trying to prove that it wasn't her and failed, gaining a CCJ (county court judgement) against her name. It must have been that and all the comings and goings of different women, was too much for her. Then I added to that by disappearing.

"I knew Mum was bad that's why I needed to get home, the last call I had from her was very distressing, but I had no idea she would do this" I put my head in my hands. I had

been so wrapped up with Arend that I had missed the signs.
David put his arm around me
"It's not your fault Jo, we have all been distracted and taken our eye off the ball"
Al was very quiet in the corner, I sat beside him and told him that Mum would not be coming back. I will be in touch about her stuff.
The nurse came and told us we could see her.
I walked into the cubicle and smiled.
"Oh Mum, where were you going?" I said smiling.
"To see my Mum and Dad" That was my nan and granddad she was talking about, who had been dead for ten years.
"Well there is no need to do that, I'm here for you now and I will look after you, I'm not going anywhere"

CHAPTER 45 – NEW BEGININGS

The last few months had been a struggle. Sanctuaries was going to take me to court for jumping ship, but when my Dad told them about Mum, they checked with the hospital and the doctor Zac on the Starship Atlantic they decided to drop the case. Understanding that I was under a huge amount of pressure. They never knew about Arend.

Mum and I spent some time together at her house, after Al had moved out to allow her to re coup. The doctors had deemed her ok to go home as long as I was with her. She had also been put on HRT to help with her menopause symptoms. It was a cross between her time of life, the problems with Al and the company issues that took its toll.

I had weight seven stone by the time I got home. It took a good few month to gradually increase my food intake back to normal. I hadn't eaten properly since I left the Star.

I never did hear from Arend again. Properly a good thing, I realised that I could never let myself get so caught up with one person so quick again. Ship life always did intensify everything. I had to learn to except the things I couldn't change, as much as I wanted it to be different. Over time my heart healed, and I became stronger. For that moment I had to learn to love myself and who I was.

My Dad had apologised to my Mum for getting at her about me disappearing and they had a good chat about the future.

By the time Christmas arrived we had moved to Weston super mare near my Uncle. Mum and I shared a flat just down the Road from him and it felt like I was finally part of a family again. Her house was sold whilst things got sorted out. It took another five years for that to happen. My Mum got better for a while, but the drinking didn't subside, in fact it became a massive issue. She died of ovarian cancer in 2004, which had only been diagnosed post-mortem. Initially the doctors thought the cirrhosis of the liver was caused by the drinking. Either way she lost her fight five weeks after diagnosis. She did however clear her name and Al and his accountant got found guilty and served a prison sentence. Many years later I found out that Al had also died of what I will never know. Dad relationship with me went from strength to strength and I can honestly say he is one of my best friends now. He has really been there for me in my later life. And was with myself and my brother when my Mum passed.

I had grown so much over the time I spent on the ships and realised how resiliant I was as a person, dealing with death, relationships, good time and bad. The fun and laughter it had really been a blast and an experience I have never forgotten, even though some memories are a little sketchy now.

Looking out of the window of our flat in Weston, I imagined the world beyond the roof tops. Do I, should I, could I............

I picked up a hairdressers journal and turned to the back where the jobs were advertised.

WANTED - HONG KONG
HAIRDRESSING MANAGER REQUIRED!!!!

Printed in Poland
by Amazon Fulfillment
Poland Sp. z o.o., Wrocław